Undoing the Cli: n

American University Studies

Series VIII
Psychology
Vol. 21

GESTALT INSTITUTE
OF CLEVELAND

Gestalt Institute of Cleveland Press
1588 Hazel Drive   Cleveland OH 44106

COMMUNITY & CONFLUENCE

Undoing the Clinch of Oppression

Philip Lichtenberg

A GestaltPress Book
Cambridge, Massachusetts

Copyright © 1990 by Philip Lichtenberg

A GestaltPress Book
66 Orchard Street, Cambridge MA 02140
gestaltpress@aol.com

Distributed by: **THE ANALYTIC PRESS**
101 West Street
Hillsdale, NJ 07642

All rights reserved. No part of this publication may be reproduced, stored in a retrieval system, or transmitted, in any form or by any means, electronic, mechanical, photocopying, recording, or otherwise, without the prior written permission of the publisher.

Excerpts from *John L. Lewis: An Unauthorized Biography* by Saul D. Alinsky. Copyright © 1949/1970 by Saul D. Alinsky. Reprinted with permission of Vintage Books, a Division of Random House, Inc.

Excerpts from *Gestalt Therapy: Excitement and Growth in the Human Personality* by Frederick Perls, Ralph F. Hefferline, Paul Goodman. Reprinted by permission of The Julian Press, Inc.

Excerpts from *The Selected Papers of Sandor Ferenczi: Problems and Methods of Psychoanalysis, Volume III* by Sandor Ferenczi. Reprinted with permission of Basic Books, Inc.

Library of Congress Cataloging-in-Publishing Data

Lichtenberg, Philip.
    Community & Confluence: Undoing the Clinch of Oppression / Philip Lictenberg.
    Includes bibliographical references and index.
    ISBN 0-88163-251-1

Cover design by Diana Puppin.

Contents

1. A Beginning 1

2. Identification With the Aggressor:
   A Clinical Formulation 9

3. Projection Upon a Primed Vulnerable Other:
   A Clinical Formulation 19

4. Empowering and Disempowering Reciprocally 33

5. Some Qualities When People Fuse 51

6. Self as Agent, Self as Agency: A General Statement ... 61

7. Cautions on Taking Psychological Ideas Into
   a Social Action Arena 65

8. The Angry Weak and the Angry Powerful 69

9. Intense Social Emotions are Key 79

10. The Quick-Circuiting Process and the
    Delusion of Fusion 109

11. Working with the Full Delusion of Fusion 113

12. Noticing and Changing Faulty Identifications 121

13. Discovering and Undoing Projections 141

14. Recovering and Reorganizing Anger 157

15. On Anxiously Acting Assertively 181

16. Who Wants Social Change, Who Starts It,
    Who Supports It? 191

17. Is All This Practical? 199

    Notes 207

    Index 221

dedication

For Elinor, Nicholas, Drew, Jenny, and Emily

And a future in which they can more readily be agents.

Acknowledgments

This work has been supported in many ways during its development. Without that support it would surely not have been completed, so I am happy to acknowledge my gratitude.

Early on, Evelyn Harzinski provided research assistance in locating literature on identification with the aggressor — a remarkably broad literature spilling into many streams of knowledge. Also in the early days, Susan Levine was a research assistant who helped articulate the main themes, co-authored a paper on the material, and shared another paper that was presented to a professional audience. The Reverend David Gracie read an early version of the first half of the book and offered important critical suggestions. His enthusiastic understanding of the work and positive requests for a different emphasis were very helpful to me. Charles Menzel, also, read the first half and had many useful comments to make. Mary Martin, who taught a course with me in which we used the material, was both very challenging and encouraging.

Two groups of doctoral students at the Bryn Mawr College Graduate School of Social Work and Social Research responded to the ideas and offered examples, interest, criticism, and support. I am very indebted to Risa C. Atterman, Betsy C. Blades, Nancy S. Buck, Christine M. Carducci, Nikki K. Castle, Betty Lee Davis, Susan E. Dawson, Kai Heng Fong, Catherine Hertzel, Joseph A. Mason, Carolyn M. Morell, and Donald D. Tomlinson for their contribution early on, and importantly to Beth Barol, Nancy Bauer-Manley, Isabel Cox-Johnson, Jill Jones, and Lynn Long in the later stages of the work.

Two sets of colleagues, also, have been personally bolstering in the days of decision about continuing with the project. From the Gestalt Therapy Institute of Philadelphia I've received help and support from David Henrich, Joyce Lewis, Mary Lou Schack, as well as from Jacqueline Cohen and Virginia McIntosh Scranton. From a consultation group, I've received important support, and my appreciation to Daniel H. Gottlieb, Sylvia Elias, Myrna Kahn Marcus, Joyce Lewis, and Linda Welch is deep.

Three critical readers of the completed manuscript, each of whom gave significant advice and ideas, were David G. Gil, Grendon Haines, and Harold Lewis. They have influenced the development of the work importantly and I am thankful for their assistance.

Isadore From offered rich reassurance and inspiration at several critical times for me. Carol Roman has been a collaborator, source of examples and ideas, co-author, and shepherding friend throughout the enterprise. Without her contribution the work would have been stillborn.

My wife, Elsa Russell Lichtenberg, has been patient and fortifying, as ever she has been, and I once more thank her for it all.

Finally, Hunt Cole spent many months working with me on the editing of the manuscript. He was everything I could want in an editor. He was demanding, attended to detail, checked for consistency, kept it clear, sought punch when it was needed, extracted illustrations and instances when they were required, encouraged me when that was necessary, understood the project and sympathized with its purpose, and made the manuscript his as well as kept it mine. In short, he was a wonderful editor, and I am pleased to acknowledge his contribution.

I am grateful to Random House, Inc. Alfred A. Knopf, Inc. for permission to quote from *Gestalt Therapy*, by Frederick Perls, Ralph F. Hefferline, and Paul Goodman. Copyright © 1951, 1979 by Frederick Perls, Ralph Hefferline, and Paul Goodman. Reprinted by permission of The Julian Press, Inc. I am also indebted to them for permission to quote from *John L. Lewis: An Unauthorized Biography*, by Saul D. Alinsky. Copyright 1940 by Saul D. Alinsky. Copyright © 1970 by Saul D. Alinsky. Reprinted by permission of Random House, Inc.

Acknowledgments

Basic Books, Inc. has permitted me to quote from *The Selected Papers of Sandor Ferenczi: Problems And Methods Of Psychoanalysis, Volume III*, by Sandor Ferenczi, Michael Balint, Editor. Copyright © 1955 by Basic Books, Inc.

Introduction

As social historians have long noted, at least in American political life periods of reform seem to come around generationally, about once every thirty years or so. Thus the turn of the century gave us trust-busting, the rise of unionism, the beginnings of labor and environmental law, and in general the first restraints on robber baron capitalism, which as always was threatening to destroy the social fabric on which it depends. The 1930's gave us a new surge of union rights and civil liberties, and the beginnings of the "social safety net," recognizing a limited claim by every citizen for some minimal standard of social support. Then came the 60's with the burgeoning of the civil rights and peace movements, a new awakening of the movement for women's rights, and a new concern for social support on a wide variety of issues.

Philip Lichtenberg believes we may be in for another such period of social action and community progress in the last decade of this century -- and none too soon, given the desperate state of community life in the wealthiest nations of the world. Only this time, Lichtenberg argues, there is a significant difference in the social field, which is that over the past generation the insights and methods of psychology and psychotherapy have begun for the first time to percolate through the professional and popular culture. When you stop to think too that psychologists and other change agents now in their forties, fifties, and sixties came to their various professions in large numbers out of the various social action movements of a generation ago (including importantly the feminist movement), than you begin to see the outlines of an intriguing, even exciting line of thought. Haven't we learned some things, professionally, about individual and social dynamics in general -- and the dynamics of power and oppression in particular -- that would stand all of us in good stead when the day comes again, as come it must, for social activism and political change? Lichtenberg answers this question with an emphatic yes, and provides us with this beautiful book-length essay to back up his answer.

Central to his argument is Lichtenberg's analysis of the dynamics of oppressor-oppressed relations. Why is it, Lichtenberg asks, that the oppressed so often support the regimes of their abusers? Plainly the dispossessed are far more numerous than the dominant; why then do they not rise up more often, and more effectively? Even in nations with a fairly safe and stable democratic process, a minimum standard of social justice is seldom met. Why? This is a question pondered by social analysts of the left and right alike at least since the time of Marx, and the answer is by no means obvious. Certainly fear plays a part, at least in many cases; but Lichtenberg argues that fear -- or at any rate real, present external fear -- cannot explain the phenomenon. Rather, as in the case of abusive families, a part of the loyalty of the victims to their abusers must lie in the dynamics we generally lump together under the general heading "identification with the aggressor." That is, the weak, to contain and manage unsupported feelings of their own (rage, shame, anxiety), identify with the strong, and in the process project or "give" even such strength as they do have to those who are stronger already. Likewise the oppressors themselves project broadly onto the oppressed, and thereby disown *their* own feelings of weakness, anxiety, and oftentimes "dark" passions of a variety of sorts.

Undoing projective dynamics of this kind is a tricky business, as Lichtenberg explains, because the undoing involves the resurfacing of all the painful and even overwhelming feelings that the projection itself was created to manage and contain. In other words -- and here the special clarifying power of the Gestalt model shows to good effect -- the projection/identification itself was a *creative adjustment* , to a challenge which the person or community involved did not have enough *support* at the time to resolve in a different way. Thus the support available in general -- and *the support for bearing difficult feelings in community in particular* -- become crucial for breaking the projective fusion between victim and oppressor, which in turn is critical for serious change.

Identification with the aggressor is a term which has been around for a long time; but -- as is often the case with powerful insights from psychoanalysis -- even the few brief strokes given above show how illuminating the Gestalt model can be, in clarifying the process dynamics at the intra/interpersonal boundary, and in designing and supporting experiments and other interventions for change. To continue with Lichtenberg's insightful analysis, what about the social and internal dynamics of oppressors? To put it bluntly, are oppressors happy? Are they satisfied? Are they even "autonomous," in any meaningful sense of the term? And if not, why not? -- don't they "have it all?" Lichtenberg answers no, to all of these questions -- and here we turn to the most controversial part of his argument: namely, his insistence that oppressors too are caught up in unhealthy and unsatisfying projective dynamics, outside their own awareness. And thus *they too need support* , if these dynamics are to be de-structured and allowed to reconfigure in some healthier way, for them and their victims alike.

Support for oppressors? for Reagan-era fat cats, slurping (as my old father used to say) at the public trough? for wife-batterers? child-abusers? even (why not pitch the argument at its most extreme) Nazis? To-gether with Cynthia O. Harris of the Gestalt Institute of Cleveland, I recently completed translation of a book of German essays on psychotherapy with children of the Nazi era (*The Collective Silence* , Jossey-Bass Inc., 1993). And even before publication we grew accustomed to the response we sometimes have gotten to this project, which is the quite understandable one which goes, "Why try to understand such people, why dignify monsters by treating them as if they deserved understanding?" And these were just the *children* of the actual oppressors! (significantly, we have not gotten this reaction from children of *victims*, who seem to understand instinctively the importance of the bridge in the second and third generations). Behind this lurks the fear, "to understand all is to forgive all." Lichtenberg himself well understands this fear, and well knows how to make the discrimination between support for the *abuse* , on the one hand, and support for the abuser's *experience* , on the other -- without which meaningful change may well be impossible. I cannot reproduce the centered and deeply sagacious voice with which he kindly and firmly refuses -- without patronizing the rest of us mortals -- to demonize anybody. For that experience, I can only refer you to the book ahead.

There are many other riches in the books as well -- and many of them further examples of how the Gestalt model serves to clarify dynamics, internal and social and (most crucially) at the boundary of these two domains, that remain obscure in other models (and thus remain impossible, or nearly so, to correct). To give one more case in point, what is it that happens when you *resist* a projection? Under the Gestalt model, Lichtenberg points out, we understand how and why it is that resisting the projections of others only strengthens those projections. What to do? -- *move to the phenomenology of the field*, the projector/abuser's own experience, to uncover the unsupported and (thus) unbearable feelings that led to the creative projective resolution in the first place.

This brilliantly simple reminder serves to clarify political dynamics everywhere -- escalations and de-escalations alike. Take the example of *satyagraha* -- the practice of non-violent resistance used so effectively by Gandhi in India, and Martin Luther King in the American South. Why does it work? Surely the answer lies at least in part in the way it supports/enables the oppressors to begin undoing projections about the oppressed (commonly that they are weak, inferior, irrational, childish, perhaps bestial and uncontrollable). I am reminded here of a business colleague of my father's in the 1960's, an unreconstructed American Southern racist of the old school (the colleague, certainly not my father, who was a classic exemplar of the tradition of Southern liberal dissent, with all the virtues and contradictions of that school of thought). This particular projector sent a thousand dollars -- quite a hefty sum in those days -- to the fund for the great Black March on Washington in 1963, in the Machiavellian conviction that as soon as you put thousands of African Americans together like that, they would surely run riot, and then the Civil Rights movement, which he of course feared and opposed, would be over.

In the event, as we know, the March was characterized by enormous dignity, restraint, and emotional intensity (which is not to imply that the oppressed are obliged to be saintly, but merely to remark on the transformational power of nonviolence, under certain circumstances). The importance of that signal event in the undoing of longstanding White cultural projections, examined and unexamined, has not been completely appreciated and understood -- partly for lack of a well-articulated model for making sense of process phenomena at this level, ranging fluidly from the intrapsychic to the mass social and back again. Until the Gestalt model, or some other model capable of the same range, is put out more fully in writing, in works like this one addressed to the wider community of clinical and organizational (and political) agents for change, then all of our efforts for social reform -- and Lichtenberg's dream of a new kind of social reform *process* -- will remain to a degree handicapped for lack of the practical conceptual tools necessary to frame and direct the work.

Confluence and Community is a model contribution to that larger project, which is the articulation of a model for addressing the interface between politics and psychology, the experience of the individual and the dynamics of the group. That he cannot possibly complete the project he begins here is not a flaw in the book, which is as nearly flawless as a work of this kind can be. A generation and more ago Paul Goodman wrote, in *Little Prayers and Finite Experience*, that just as there is psychotherapy, which addresses rigid and archaic disturbances of creative adjustment in the individual, so there is a therapy for abnormal and oppressive social institutions: *"it is politics."* For most of the past century these two domains have tended to be sundered into separate terms, "public" and "private," in a telling example of those splits which Goodman taught us to see as characteristic of neurotic process. Now Lichtenberg redirects us on a path of wholeness. This is an essential text for the 90's and the opening of the century to come, a book that will renew your commitment to your professional identity, to social action, and to the Gestalt model. May many more follow from this example.

Gordon Wheeler
Cambridge MA, 1994

Preface to the Second Edition

This essay is meant to be a contribution to liberation psychology, a psychology whose purpose is more than the description of oppression and more than an explanation of how oppressive institutions are created and maintained by all members of any system that is based on domination and submission. While it is indeed intended to be a description of some of the psychological mechanisms of oppression, and it carries an analysis of the means by which members of an exploitative community establish and support devastating forms of domination and submission, it is clearly meant to be more than a thoughtful appraisal. The central goal I have had in pursuing this essay is that of offering support that is useful to all members of such communities in their efforts to undo oppression. I want that persons shall have available to them at those times when they are acting with a commitment to the fundamental alteration of oppressive systems, the wisdom that has come from clinical work in psychotherapy. Thoughtful and informed struggle needs not only the contributions from history of political and social thought; it needs, desperately I believe, everything that we have learned in the clinical setting working with people who are trying to deal with the inevitable effects of living in competitive and abusive social institutions. Any effort devoted to fundamental social change that does not incorporate this psychological wisdom will self-destruct in its unfolding, as so many revolutions have done in the past. Liberation psychology is a necessity for the next steps in world social advancement.

Basic to the liberation psychology that I am endorsing is the notion that all members of a society are determined by the oppressiveness of a given system, and equally that all members of a society are determiners of the nature of that society. I reject the postion that the oppressed are determined (powerless, nothing but victims), while the oppressors are free to implement whatever they wish (are simply powerful, freely acting, able to choose in an uninhibited way). We are all both influenced and influential. Of course there are social classes, and members of these classes are differently placed within exploitative systems. But the simplistic view that the upper classes are free and the lower classes powerless does not hold up under scrutiny; and it is one of the purposes of this essay to demonstrate the ways in which this view misses the psychological underpinnings for the installation and maintenance of oppression.

Similarly, it is a central belief underlying this work that *all* members of a society at some times, in some ways, are acting to change the system that is oppressive. Revolutionaries are not privileged as the only citizens aiming to change our social order. At most they give voice or expression to tendencies which we all act out and express in our daily lives. Some of us are more of the time engaged in actions aimed at changing the system, and some of us are more effective at it, but we are all doing it. Similarly, every one of us is conservative: we are each acting to keep the status quo in place. We have painstakingly found a way to manage our lives, and we are adjusted to, and sad to say, committed to the oppressive systems in which we live. When we polarize individuals and groups into those who are only agents of change and those who solely resist change, we are disguising to ourselves and to each other what we give to one another. Thus if we adopt the conservative position and rail against radicals, we nonetheless carry radical ideas and interests, but place them in the personage of those we are attacking. We know this reality only too well in the therapy groups we run (in which polarization around a scapegoat appears, for example), but we have not insisted that the larger world come to terms with our insight.

The liberation psychology contained here bears a kinship to liberation theology, while at the same time it is importantly different from that theology. Both liberation psychology and liberation theology identify the major social issue of our time as the struggle to change in a fundamental way the exploitation that characterizes the social and exonomic systems throughout the world. What is innocuously called the "market economy" has spread to nearly every corner of the globe, and it is basic to that way of organizing the production, distribution, and consumption of the necessities and luxuries of life that human relations too readily involve domination and subordination. Similarly, both the psychology and the theology that ally themselves with the goal of "liberation" emphasize that ideas must be in the service of action, that informed effort is more central than knowledge for its own sake. Indeed, psychological theory, like religious dogma, that merely tries to explain what is, invariably promotes powerlessness rather than the liveliness that inheres in liberation endeavors.

But liberation psychology, at least in the variant proposed in this work, differs from liberation theology in two very fundamental dimensions: it does not call for sacrifice on the part of any activist engaged in the liberation struggle, and it does not privilege the poor. Sacrifice is, after all, the subduing of self, the limiting of one's full engagement, the putting away of essential desires and ambitions that motivate daily existence. Sacrifice also places one in a lesser position with respect to others who are to benefit from the self-negation. What has been learned in psychology over the past century, especially in the psychology of Freud and Adler, and after them the psychology of Gestalt Therapy, is that sacrifice is inevitably paired with aggrandizement: she who sacrifices now, will aggrandize later; he who sacrifices for the other places the other in a posture of aggrandizement. To meet as equals in the contact of dialogue is the essence of a liberation psychology. It is the movement away from the call for sacrifice on the part of anyone in the exploitative system that differentiates a liberation psychology from a liberation theology, that animates the secular version of the commitment and actions that are aimed at transforming systems of exploitation into systems of cooperation among equals.

Because each of us is oriented both to change and resistance to change, we are all available at one time or another for efforts to alter exploitative systems. Rather than privileging the poor as change agents, as in liberation theology, a liberation psychology privileges whoever is acting to change the system at the time they are now promoting that change. The focus of attention is upon actions that facilitate the dialogue of equals, whatever the source. Thus, revolutions are often led or supported by persons coming from the presumably "well-off" classes or groupings. Change depends upon support of all who embrace it in whatever degree that is embraced.

I am pleased and grateful that this work now appears in a new edition, and one more accessible to many people. We live in turbulent times, with the rumblings of more trouble to come, much more than was obvious when this essay was first written. I hope that the thoughts herein contribute in some small way to actions aimed at creating a better human community.

Philip Lichtenberg, 1994

Chapter 1

A Beginning

This is an essay on becoming a subject of the realm in contemporary society. In the same way that the realm is no longer a kingdom in most places in the world today, so becoming a subject is no longer to be conceived as binding oneself to a superior by obliging oneself to pay allegiance, as putting oneself under the dominion of another or in the control of the other. To be a subject, in modern terms, is to be an aware agent, an architect of one's individual life and a conscious maker of social life. To be a subject is to be a citizen, one who impressively lives in his or her time. Becoming a subject of the realm in the most developed sense is becoming a participant in shaping strong democratic practices in all the groups and social systems in which one's life is played out. I shall be discussing what is involved in fostering conditions in which many people can and will become subjects in the contemporary sense.

That I plan to address the notion of *becoming* a subject of the realm means I have the idea that by and large most of us do not yet function as fully aware and confident citizens, that we are more like the old notion of subject of the realm, ready to hand over our responsibilities and choices to others. While I would not go so far as to describe most of us operating in modern society as serfs or servants, my work as a psychotherapist, a teacher, and a consultant to schools and social service agencies leads me to believe that we are most of us far from aware and effective citizens.

Our readiness to live as diminished individuals derives from a universal conflict: we all want things to stay the same while we also want things to change for the better. If things stay the same, they are at least predictable, and we have learned how to manage from what has gone on before. We generally find it easier to live from memory, to follow established habits or programs, than to create new ways in the here and now, to take our assessments of the present, our current perceptions, and set out to make more of what is presently before us. Yet the universal conflict is alive and well; although we seem to prefer to repeat the past, we find ourselves doing the novel despite ourselves.

Alice Miller[1] has presented the idea that we are not fully aware citizens in another form. She has argued, quite persuasively I believe, that child abuse is the norm of experience in the modern world and that we have all been victims of it. At the center of child rearing has been the enterprise of breaking the will of the child so that he or she will become socialized. Children are commonly viewed as egocentric and willful, and the force of parental teaching, sometimes violent, sometimes merely controlling, is seen as necessary so that children can be tamed and brought into the community of civilized human beings. Politicians are wont to pontificate that we must instill values in children, as if they were not naturally inclined toward cooperative bonding with their parents. This willbreaking activity is purely and simply child abuse when looked at closely and with a clinician's eye. Such tyrannical behavior is accepted by the community because parents, having themselves been victims, have in that very event been prepared to be victimizers and see nothing abnormal in it. Parents, who have loved their own parents and identified with them, have learned how to be dominant as well as submissive in victimizing relationships and, sometimes to their own surprise, find themselves acting like their mothers and fathers did.

Because we were all to some degree abused as children — think back to the discipline in your own life, remember the punishments, the threats, the fear — we have all experienced oppression. Whether we were forcibly toilet trained, kept from playing outside in the evening, punished for being lively in school, forced to do our homework when we didn't want to, ignored when we felt helpless, unexpectedly screamed at by our favorite aunt, or isolated by our parents' marital problems, we have all been hurt by oppression. As a consequence, we have accustomed ourselves to relationships of unequal power and have become oppressors in some circumstances and oppressed in others. The obedient worker is the dominating parent, the dutiful teacher takes fluff from the administration and passes it along to students in the classroom. The kid in the neighborhood who resentfully submits to very controlling adults is the same youngster who lords it over his peers. Both in growing up and within the institutions where we now work and play, we have learned the lessons of domination and have made our individual accommodations to the facts of oppression.

If this judgment seems unduly harsh, it is because we are numbed to our own pain and seldom acknowledge it. We are protective of our parents who abused us, which itself is a mark of the abused, as I will show in the pages that follow. We want to be loved by our parents, all the more when they have mistreated us, an irony of the human species, so we overlook our anger with them and protect them from our hatred of them as abusers. So too with the institutional leaders we encounter. We do not identify ourselves as oppressed and our leaders as oppressors, because to do so would cause us to become aware of our pain and would also motivate us more clearly to change the systems in which we live, a scary proposition at best. Over the years we have frequently become disappointed with our leaders, as Lloyd deMause[2] has shown, but we find it difficult to hold on to our awareness of their indifference and cruelty toward us.

I will refer to child abuse often in the following discussion for the simple reason that it is a marvelous exemplar of the general problem of oppression. There is clear disparity of power between adult abuser and child abused, the psychological processes of both victim and victimizer parallel what is seen in general social oppression, and much of child abuse, as much of oppression at large, has a sexual component to it. The dynamics of the abused and the abuser will be key to the argument of this essay.

If the bad news is that we have all been victimized and have adapted to that experience and made believe that it is the normal human condition, the good news is that the great majority of us live our daily lives in a relatively adequate manner. Many of us may be drug-addicted, others depressed, others bewildered, and some may be lying and cheating in many domains of their lives, yet we carry on as best we can and we appear to do all right while carrying on. It is the rare mother who murders her young child, though if we allow ourselves, we can remember our temptations to do comparable deeds. We are friendly with our neighbors most of the time, and we work in a rather adjusted fashion. Victims we are, and we are *also* more than that, *also* somewhat healthy in our social and emotional activities, *also* attuned closely to reality and successful in mastering the tasks of ordinary life.

But it is important to attend to the bad as well as the good news because the processes of transformation of individuals and society rely upon awareness of both the unhealthy and the healthy ways of functioning as individuals, and similarly, upon recognition of social practices that promote deadly as well as enlivening group experiences. To bring about the transformations I am referring to involves undoing negative personal and social habits and routines sometimes and simply fostering or enabling positive ones at other times.

I have come to believe that too often persons and social movements intending to change the existing systems have acted as if individuals were already subjects of the realm in the modern sense, as if they functioned only maturely, as if a call to reason or a presentation of reasonable argument could mobilize citizens in the service of overturning a social order built mostly on forms of domination. In the past, agents of social change have acted as if a system of exploitation were merely clothing on the body politic such that our psyches were unaffected, as if domination had not distorted our personalities, as if we could shed at a moment's notice the outer garments, or personas, we have adopted to fend off the worst aspects of the oppression we have known. Such persons and movements have not spoken to us as whole individuals, as being both healthy and unhealthy, committed to being exploited as well as opposed to it, but only to those parts of us that were reasonable and rational. And that approach has not been enough.

I am mindful of Andras Angyal's[3] "theory of universal ambiguity" here. Angyal, a holistically oriented psychiatrist, noted, as did Alice Miller, that every child has experienced both healthy and traumatic environmental conditions, and that as a consequence, every child's personality forms two distinct patterns. One of these patterns, obviously derived from the child's traumatic experiences, is founded on isolation, with accompanying feelings of helplessness, unlovableness, and doubt. The other pattern comes with a confidence that one's basic strivings are likely to be realized directly and fruitfully. Accordingly, says Angyal, we all live in two worlds, the world with the unhealthy principle as guiding factor, and the world with the healthy principle in command of our being. These general ways of being, which he calls the Gestalt of health and the Gestalt of neurosis, control our experience, and we shift back and forth from one to the other principle as most in command of our lives at any given time. The aim of psychotherapy, as of social change, is to enhance the degree to which the healthy Gestalt is in the driver's seat.

Angyal has asserted further that the dual organization of human life which he articulates promotes ambiguity: every item of human behavior and experience has two meanings, one set by the feeling of isolation and the other by the overarching feeling of confidence. The sense of dependence, for example, which is major among oppressed peoples, can become intolerable in the context of the neurotic Gestalt of helplessness; it can be a feared feeling, as in the neediness of the person feeling alone and unsupported, or in the profoundly experienced dread of weakness. But the sense of dependence can also arise in a healthy framework and be a positive force in community formation, a welcomed feeling, as in reliance upon a trusted friend or a judicious leader. The meaning of dependence is a function of whichever of the two Gestalts guides the individual at the time.

Agents of social change who have attended only to the healthy functioning of individuals — who, for example, have assumed only the rationality of all potential partners — have denied the full experience of those of us they have hoped to mobilize, and sooner or later, one way or another, they have forfeited the allegiance they have worked so hard to create. We human beings need to be seen as we are, accepted in our best behavior but also in our worst, supported in our complexity, recognized in our ambiguity, encouraged in our efforts to become complete. Unsuccessful social reformers and revolutionaries are typically purists. While those who move more satisfactorily toward achieving their goals demonstrate the patience necessary for dealing with the unhealthy parts of human functioning in an oppressive world. For us to become contemporary subjects of the realm, we need both support in our limitations and challenge of our strengths.

In this essay, which centers upon psychological insights relevant to processes of social change, I describe both the unhealthy and the healthy psychological phenomena. The early descriptions of the workings of the psyche look closely at the negative side, the installation of those personal styles and practices that are associated with the establishment and maintenance of oppressive social relations. These unhealthy psychological factors described in the early chapters of the essay are best seen as emergency safeguards, appropriate to the scene in which they were initiated but maintained beyond that situation, institutionalized, and ultimately limiting rather than protective devices for the individual. Recovery from these structuralized emergency measures leads back to the spontaneity of behavior characteristic of well-functioning persons. In subsequent chapters I look at the personal practices that are more healthy. Wherever I attend to a negative factor, I have committed myself to rendering what the healthy version is likely to be.

This essay is predicated upon the belief that psychological issues and concerns are important to the process of social change. This is hardly a new idea. The names of Wilhelm Reich, Otto Fenichel, Alfred Adler, Thorstein Veblen, John Dewey, Harold Lasswell, Kenneth Burke, Herbert Marcuse, Paul Goodman, and Frantz Fanon come readily to mind as persons who have directed attention to the psychological in social struggle, and such entities as the Society for the Psychological Study of Social Issues, the International Society of Political Psychology, and the Association for Psychohistory, Inc., exist with this perspective in the forefront of their purposes. Acknowledging this heritage, I want also to indicate the niche this present essay fits in, as follows: As consciousness is to action, so the psychological is to social and political activity. Human beings are primarily actors, and consciousness is a secondary, guiding function in the service of making actions more satisfying and more effective. "I do" is prior to "I think," as John Macmurray[4] has told us so well, and thinking is oriented toward regulating the doing of which it is a part. Psychological insights are most useful to social and political movements, therefore, when seen as accompaniments to effort, as supportive measures, sometimes to the fore but more often *also present* and available for use. Too much attention to the psychological detracts from the thrust of social or political action, while too little leaves out the vital subjective side of creating subjects of the realm who are capable of social struggle.

Central here is the following insight from psychotherapy. Its truth is well known in self-help groups such as Alcoholics Anonymous, and is demonstrated over and over again in psychotherapy, especially therapy with a holistic perspective. *We cannot in fact make other people change.* Agents of social transformation who try too hard to change the people they work with or those they hope to mobilize invariably alienate them. Trying to change others brings resistance. Alternatively, agents of change can try to foster the awarenesses that enable others to choose to change themselves. In their social-change efforts as elsewhere, persons need to take responsibility for themselves in relations with others, and need respectfully to allow others to be responsible for themselves, even when they wish to avoid it and to place themselves in the hands of leaders, authorities, experts, or anyone else who will take them on. Agents of change can join with others, share themselves, and offer to others insights that may be helpful to them as they go about making their lives, but the agents of change must also recognize that it is the others who make their own lives and who choose how they will do that. As I hope to show, this willingness not to insist that others change is especially relevant in the context of oppression, because basic adaptations to relations of dominance, on the side of the oppressor as well as the oppressed, are active avoidances of responsibility. In any application of the ideas in this essay, accordingly, my emphasis is upon increasing awareness and then letting go, permitting the other to become aware of what was unawares and use it as he or she sees fit. I know that this noncontrolling form of relationship is hard to implement when one is engaged in tense and difficult struggle, but this is the only way to proceed that stands a chance of working in the long run.

Keeping to the position that one cannot take responsibility for the choices others make is especially exacting in relations of dominance because those who are on the oppressed side of the relationship seem to plead for others to assume responsibility, while those on the dominating side try to appear responsible without standing fully behind that decisive appearance. In relations of dominance, I will argue, we come upon the fusion of part-persons, whereas in democratically grounded interactions we find cooperation between autonomous individuals. There is a great difference between these types of interdependences. The very nature of the psychology of oppressive relationships limits the ways in which agents of change can operate, and this reality makes contributions from the psychotherapeutic world necessary to the world of social and political change. In this work I have taken from the clinical arena ideas that connect with social activity. I start with ideas on the very commonly recognized phenomenon identification with the aggressor, a pattern of functioning found in children who have been abused and in oppressed people generally. After discussing its development and laying out what I consider to be the other processes for the installation and maintenance of relations of dominance, I turn to some general characteristics of such relations. I then direct attention to ideas established in psychotherapeutic work that may stimulate the undoing of these intrinsically harmful and unhealthful patterns of functioning.

First, then, is identification with the aggressor.

Chapter 2

Identification with the Aggressor: A Clinical Formulation

The psychoanalytic concept of identification with the aggressor describes a predictable response to extreme stress in interpersonal relationships, a response well known to clinicians and somewhat known to sophisticated lay intellectuals, but strange and cause for wonder to most citizens and social activists. The idea as presented below was formulated first by Sandor Ferenczi, a major figure in the early years of psychoanalysis, indeed one of Freud's earliest and closest collaborators. His conception appeared in print in the early 1930s, the same period that saw the rise of Hitler and Nazism. While Ferenczi developed the concept in respect to children who were sexually abused by adults, later observers, having the experiences of concentration camps available to them and knowing how common identification with an aggressor could be in the world at large, have applied the concept quite broadly and have tied it to the description of various oppressed and subjugated peoples (e.g., Buss,[1] Fanon,[2] Lasswell,[3] and Memmi[4]). It is now a basic concept in the psychotherapeutic lexicon.

Because nothing can provide a better beginning acquaintance with the concept of identification with the aggressor than Ferenczi's original statement, I want here to reproduce an abridged version of it. He is writing about the sexual molestation of children:

"I obtained above all new corroborative evidence for my supposition that the trauma, especially the sexual trauma, as the pathogenic factor cannot be valued highly enough. Even children of very respectable, sincerely puritanical families, fall victim to real violence or rape much more often than one had dared to suppose. Either it is the parents who try to find a substitute gratification in this pathological way for their frustration, or it is people thought to be trustworthy such as relatives (uncles, aunts, grandparents), governesses or servants, who misuse the ignorance and the innocence of the child. The immediate explanation — that these are only sexual fantasies of the child, a kind of hysterical lying — is unfortunately made invalid by the number of such confessions, e.g., of assaults upon children, committed by patients actually in analysis . . . .

"A typical way in which incestuous seductions may occur is this: an adult and a child love each other, the child nursing the playful fantasy of taking the role of mother to the adult. This play may assume erotic forms but remains, nevertheless, on the level of tenderness. It is not so, however, with the pathological adults. . . . They mistake the play of children for the desires of a sexually mature person or even allow themselves — irrespective of any consequences — to be carried away. The real rape of girls who have hardly grown out of the age of infants, similar sexual acts of mature women with boys, and also enforced homosexual acts, are more frequent occurrences than have hitherto been assumed.

"It is difficult to imagine the behavior and the emotions of children after such violence. One would expect the first impulse to be that of reaction, hatred, disgust, energetic refusal, 'No, no, I do not want it, it is much too violent for me, it hurts, leave me alone.' This or something similar would be the immediate reaction if [the child] had not been paralyzed by enormous anxiety. These children feel physically and morally helpless . . . for the overpowering force and authority of the adult makes them dumb and can rob them of their senses. *The same anxiety, however, if it reaches a certain maximum, compels them to subordinate themselves like automata to the will of the aggressor, to divine each one of his desires and to gratify these; completely oblivious of themselves they identify themselves with the aggressor.* Through the identification, or let us say, introjection of the aggressor, he disappears as part of the external reality, and becomes intra- instead of extra-psychic . . . .

"The most important change, produced in the mind of the child by the anxiety-fear-ridden identification with the adult partner, is *the introjection of the guilt feelings of the adult* which makes hitherto harmless play appear as a punishable offense.

"When the child recovers from such an attack, he feels enormously confused, in fact, split, — innocent and culpable at the same time — and his confidence in the testimony of his own sense is broken. Moreover, the harsh behavior of the adult partner tormented and made angry by his remorse renders the child still more ashamed. . . .

"The misused child changes into a mechanical, obedient automaton or becomes defiant, but is unable to account for the reasons for his defiance. . . . Only with the help of this hypothesis [identification with the aggressor] can I understand why my patients refused so obstinately to follow my advice to react to unjust or unkind treatment with pain or with hatred and defense."[5]

From Ferenczi's description of identification with the aggressor as a response to excessive demand from a trusted authority can be taken or inferred several salient ideas applicable to broader contexts than Ferenczi was dealing with:

1. The child, or subordinate, or weaker person, experiences enormous anxiety. Identification with the aggressor is a response whose purpose is to get rid of the anxiety.

2. The abused person becomes subordinate actively — puts the desires of the stronger person in the primary position and becomes oblivious of himself or herself.

3. The abused person, through introjection, feels the guilt feelings of the stronger person, and beyond this feels ashamed in the face of the stronger person's harsh behavior.

4. The weak individual feels confused, innocent and culpable at the same time.

5. The abused individual becomes an obedient automaton or defiant, in either case bound to the authority by the identification process.

6. The weak and misused person actively refuses to hate the dominating, exploiting individual.

From this description of identification with the aggressor, I have formed two schemes. One derives directly from Ferenczi's argument; the other is an elaboration based on interpretation of his assessment. Each scheme describes a succession of phases. They apply not only to strong adults versus weak children but also to stronger adults versus weaker ones and situations where sexual activity is not the central subject, because domination and the response of identification with the aggressor can happen anywhere.

In the opening, healthy phase of the first scheme, the weaker person is acting spontaneously and naturally, reaching out toward the stronger person with expectations of happy and mutually beneficial encounters. This is the phase of *natural spontaneity*, seen by Ferenczi in the adult-child context as a time when

"an adult and a child love each other, the child nursing the playful fantasy of taking the role of mother to the adult."

The relationship is assumed to be safe, and the weaker person is psychologically open and unguarded, prepared only to find satisfaction in a mutually supportive way with a trusted, more powerful other person. This is the way children normally are preprogrammed to be from birth on — friendly, positively oriented toward others, confident, and spontaneous. (As I have suggested, children are early on disabused of this orientation.)

In the second phase, the weaker person has been presented with demands and actions from the other that are discordant with what was anticipated. The powerful person wants more from the relationship than the weaker person can manage successfully. In the case of sexual abuse of a child as discussed by Ferenczi, the child's play "may assume erotic forms but remains, nevertheless, on the level of tenderness," while the adult's actions are lustful and sexually beyond the child's natural capacities for sustaining excitement. The consequence of the disparity of need and demand between the weaker and the stronger, in this and other kinds of pairings, is the experience of massive anxiety on the part of the weaker person, and this phase may appropriately be called the phase of *profound, experienced anxiety*. The weaker person feels unable to master the situation and helpless in an unsafe circumstance. At bottom the weaker person fears that he or she will be destroyed, overcome by the massive stimulation and excitation that are felt. When a worker on the assembly line who has happily maintained a precarious balance between speed and accuracy, for instance, is now asked to step up production or face the threat of replacement, the worker is likely to experience such anxiety. Similarly, when a manufacturing plant or department store is taken over by a large corporation and the possibility is raised of closing it down unless profits are increased, the situation is sufficiently unsafe to produce great agitation among employees, especially among those senior workers who have been loyal to the company for a long time and have built their lives around working at their jobs.

The anxiety in this phase may be called traumatic anxiety because the amount that is felt is at the upper limit of what can be held in awareness and managed by the experiencing person. Anxiety represents an emotional message to the individual experiencing it that there is danger to his or her integrity and existence. Some anxiety — the healthy variant, which I will describe later in this essay — is vital to productive functioning, but the anxiety we are seeing in this second phase of the process of identification with the aggressor is destructive of healthy functioning.

The third phase in this scheme based on Ferenczi's discussion is replacement of the anxiety by the symptom of *identification with the aggressor*. As he explains:

> "The same anxiety, however, if it reaches a certain maximum, compels them to subordinate themselves like automata to the will of the aggressor, to divine each one of his desires and to gratify these; completely oblivious of themselves they identify themselves with the aggressor.

Various components of identification with the aggressor — self-subordination, introjection of guilt, confusion and automaton behavior or defiance, refusal to hate the aggressor — exist in the final phase as described by Ferenczi.

The outline of this first scheme is thus:

Scheme 1

Natural spontaneity → Profound, experienced anxiety → Identification with the aggressor

This is the scheme that was most used by clinicians and social theorists in the early years of reference to the concept of identification with the aggressor, and I have no quarrel with its essential correctness. It does not, however, capture many of the complex issues that arise out of Ferenczi's discussion; and more recent thinkers have made an attempt to articulate further the unfolding process. Two additions to Scheme 1 seem especially productive in organizing the several components that make up identification with the aggressor: 1) interpolation of a phase of angry feeling toward the abuser between the experience of anxiety and the appearance of the identification; and 2) the merging of the abused person's own wishes with those of the abuser.

Ferenczi, like those of us working with victims of molestation after him, was puzzled that his abused patients did not experience and share with him anger and disgust directed against their abusers:

> "One would expect the first impulse to be that of reaction, hatred, disgust, energetic refusal . . . . This or something similar would be the immediate reaction if [the child] had not been paralyzed by enormous anxiety. These children feel physically and morally helpless . . . ."

Here Ferenczi seemed to approach a belief that identification with the aggressor is not simply a transformation of anxiety, not simply a substitute of a symptom for unbearable feelings of tension and doubt aroused by the trauma, but also a redirection of anger, a turning back upon the self of rage that would naturally have been aroused by the abuser and aimed originally at the abuser. I have come to believe that anger is felt, though fleetingly, by the abused person. Here it was not openly expressed because the child felt helpless as well as angry; and Ferenczi did not observe anger because it had already been turned back upon the self when he dealt with children who had identified with their aggressors. I am suggesting, in other words, that *experienced anger* follows anxiety and precedes identification with the aggressor.

Rieker and Carmen seem to bridge Ferenczi's position and mine. First, they comment on anger as a central response to abuse; second, they hold that victims don't generally experience anger directly, but repress it:

". . . it is important to recognize the centrality of anger as a response to abuse. In contrast to feelings aroused in others who hear about the abuse, victims generally do not experience their anger directly; because it is viewed as potentially dangerous and uncontrollable, it is repressed. Consequently, victims are disconnected from their rage and their aggressive impulses; when these feelings do erupt in other contexts, they are often perceived as irrational and inexplicable."[6]

The anger that is generated by the frightening situation, when it is turned back upon the self, is felt as guilt. I am reminded of Freud's provocative insight in *The Ego and the Id*:

"It is remarkable that the more a man checks his aggressive tendencies towards others the more tyrannical, that is, aggressive, he becomes in his ego-ideal. . . . It is like a displacement, a turning round upon the self."[7]

And in *Civilization and Its Discontents* he argued:

". . . every piece of aggression whose satisfaction the subject gives up is taken over by the super-ego and increases the latter's aggressiveness (against the ego)."[8]

The guilt felt by the abused person is a mixture. Surely a big part of it comes from the withholding and redirecting inward of anger felt toward the unjust authority; another part is, as Ferenczi noted for the child-abuse situation, guilt registered by the distressed and remorseful abuser which the abused person has introjected. The guilt may be strongly felt, or it may barely emerge as a feeling bad about oneself. Either way, the abused person is not aware of the former anger or of the introjection of guilt, and so will feel confused about why he or she should feel this way. There will tend to be less of the feeling of confusion when the desires activated in the abused person by the event are not altogether comfortable — as, for example, with aggressive or sexual wishes that someone has previously criticized, giving the abused person a relatively grounded sense of not being entirely innocent in the matter.

There is, then, a fundamental confounding within the abused person of feelings of guilt. And with this confusing mixture — in the superego, the realm of conscience, of self-control by way of moral judgments and strictness — a merger of self with abuser takes place, and identification with the aggressor begins. This phase that follows anger I call *confusing guilt and self-hatred.* Beyond the merger of self and other in the superego is one further phase of identification with the aggressor. Not only are the inner forces of self-control, self-judgment, and self-punishment infused with the demands and other pressures of a dominating other; also affected in the attempts to master extreme stress are the very desires of the abused individual. Ferenczi spoke of children as subordinating themselves like automata to the will of adults, divining their desires and gratifying them completely oblivious of themselves. But no one can be completely oblivious of self as far as desires are concerned. At most one can act as if the desires of another were one's own and permit oneself the experience of only those desires of one's own which meet the demands of another, forsaking any unique, self-actualizing expression in the interest of placating that dominating other person. These things are done in the final phase of identification with the aggressor that succeeds guilt and self hatred, a phase that I call *fusion of own and aggressor's desires.*

The two parts of identification with the aggressor that I have isolated — confusing guilt and self-hatred and fusion of own and aggressor's desires — actually represent two degrees of merging self with other. In the first instance, the person takes the demands and other pressures from the aggressor, interiorizes them, and mixes them together with his or her own self-regulating activities so that the self-control that is exerted is ambiguous as to its origins and whether it is in the service of self or other. In the second instance, not only is self-judgment altered, but the very desires that are being regulated and organized become ambiguous as to whether they are the person's own or the aggressor's desires. The ultimate in such unhealthy identification is reached when the weaker person lives out the projected (unacceptable) wishes of the aggressor, becomes only a tool in the hands of the aggressor, without volition or choice. In Hellmuth Kaiser's discussion of what he calls the submissive mode there is "obedience without decision to obey . . . The imagined relationship between two people is such that the separateness of the individual appears diminished. Though in all other respects they might be considered two persons, they have only *one* power of decision between them. Or, in other words, one of them appears only as an extension or an organ of the other."[9]

An important sign of the merger of the victim with the abuser is the intense loyalty shown by the victim. Cynthia Solin illustrates this in her discussion of "displacement of affect in families following incest disclosure." She is writing here of incest between a father and child:

"Censure of the offender almost invariably elicits pronounced anger in the mother and children. Their wrath is grounded in family loyalty and fueled by perceptions that the offender himself is being victimized by uncaring and insensitive institutions. Incest victims tend to have a highly developed sensitivity to the feelings of others; a sense of their father's mistreatment mobilizes them to assume a very protective stance."[10]

Perls et al. note the merger and the satisfaction that is derived from joining an oppressive authority:

". . . the self now gets an enormous *positive* satisfaction from its identification with the strong authority. As a whole the self has been defeated, for its conflict has not been allowed to mature and become some new positive thing; but the identifying self can now say 'I am the victor.' This powerful satisfaction is arrogance. What are the elements?

"First, added to the relief of the cessation of suffering the conflict, is the expansive relief from the pressures of threatened defeat, shame, humiliation; by assuming another role, arrogance is expansive, brash, confident. Second, there is the blushing satisfaction of gloating, a species of vanity; in Freudian terms the super-ego is smiling on the ego. Third, the proud self arrogates to itself the fancied virtues of the authorities, strength, rights, wisdom, guilelessness. Last and most important, and by no means an illusion, the arrogant self can now wield its aggression and *continually prove* that it is a conqueror, for the victim is always available for domination . . . . Unfortunately the chief victim of the aggression is just oneself, always available to be beaten, squelched, bitten, and so forth."[11]

The second scheme that incorporates these added phases of experienced anger and two degrees of identification with the aggressor is as shown below:

Scheme 2

Natural spontaneity → Profound, experienced anxiety → Experienced anger → Confusing guilt and self-hatred (identification with the aggressor, first degree) → Fusion of own and aggressor's desires (identification with the aggressor, second degree)

But what of the aggressor himself or herself? To this other side of the story I now turn.

Chapter 3

Projection Upon a Primed Vulnerable Other: A Clinical Formulation

Although the ideas in the concept of identification with the aggressor are impressively descriptive, I have come to realize that a major omission of complementary ideas must be corrected before the theory can be made useful to social action. The omission is of lesser importance in therapeutic work, which may explain why it has been accepted lightly for so long; but the use of the concept of identification with the aggressor in the larger scene, where not only the weak or abused person is to be changed, requires that I attend to that which has been slighted.

I have set forth the response of the weaker person to stress created in the interaction with the more powerful person, and I have traced the steps by which the abused person becomes merged with — or fused with, or confluent with — the abuser. To this point, however, I have left unexamined and undeveloped the social and psychic functioning of the person who is powerful in the relationship. Ferenczi clearly implied that abusers have personal problems comparable to those experienced by the abused — indeed his discovery of identification with the aggressor partly stemmed from psychoanalytic work with adult molesters. He noted that the adult misinterpreted and misused the playful fantasies of the child when rape or molesting took place, and he also referred to the guilt of the adult which the abused child introjected. We most of the time assume something is wrong with rapists, brutal concentration camp guards, wife batterers, and other such aggressors, and their victims often identify with them. Nonetheless, systematic exploration of the psyche of the aggressor has not been included in the analysis of identification with the aggressor — by Ferenczi, who was treating molesters, or by later thinkers. Overlooked has been the possibility that the aggressor merges with the victim fully as much as the weak one merges with the powerful one.

Let me say this again, in different words, to underscore the critical point. The strength of the concept of identification with the aggressor lies in its description of an unexpected and perplexing phenomenon: those brutalized by aggressive practices not only accept their domination but also help to carry out these practices which hurt them, and even come to admire, defend, serve, and promote the interests of those who oppress them. The limitation of the concept is that "identification with the aggressor" implies a one-way influence, from oppressor to oppressed. It would seem to the innocent eye that those who are oppressed merge with their oppressors, take on their practices and values, but those who oppress others are free from the influence of those they dominate. A formula to express this (distorted) view would be: The oppressor is agent, the oppressed is agency.

Agents are persons who act from their own needs, who know they are subjects in relating to objects, who stand behind their actions and acknowledge responsibility for their choices, and who are rightly recognized as the cause of their own behavior. Persons acting as agency are persons who are instruments for another person or for an overriding system, who have a diminished sense of subjecthood, who shift responsibility for their choices to others and who are recognized less as the cause of their own behavior than as persons who carry out predetermined actions. An agent would say, "It is I who am doing this thing," where an agency would aver, "I am doing what I am required to do."

Two factors are hidden in the formula that holds the dominator as agent and the oppressed as agency: 1) underestimation of the responsibility of the weak participant in the transactions, and 2) exaggeration of the responsibility and psychological health of the powerful participant. We cannot understand adequately both the *guilt* of the abused and the *desperate insistence* of the powerful unless we discard the formula and these in fact widely encountered distortions. C. G. Jung is among those who have seen the problem and called for such rectification in his discussion of prestige, which is very much related to the hierarchical situation of oppression:

> ". . .the building up of prestige is always a product of collective compromise; not only must there be one who wants prestige, there must also be a public seeking somebody on whom to confer prestige. That being so, it would be incorrect to say that a man creates prestige for himself out of his individual will to power; it is on the contrary an entirely collective affair. Since society as a whole needs the magically effective figure, it uses the needful will to power in the individual, and the will to submit in the mass, as a vehicle, and thus brings about the creation of personal prestige."[1]

Recognition of the limitation of the concept of identification with the aggressor means that I must take into consideration the transactions between aggressor and victim and attend to the psyche of the aggressor. The schemes that I have thus far put forth must be enriched by incorporating what is happening to the aggressor while the victim is identifying.

Identification with the aggressor is a special case of the general process of identification; it is that pathological form of identification which is activated during interactions with an exploitative or aggressive stronger person. It is pathological in that the weak person becomes *confused by adopting self-evaluative standards that are dictated and enforced by the aggressor and subsequently by confounding his or her own desires with the aggressor's wishes.* That is, the identification process is effected at the expense of the weak person's own needs and values as these would be independently achieved were the aggressor a cooperative rather than exploitative partner in the relationship. Identification with the aggressor, we must always remember, does not appear when the stronger person is democratic, equalitarian, and cooperative in the relationship.

But at the same time that identification with the aggressor is pathological in its ramifications for the individual, it is also adaptive and self-preserving. It happens when the weak person is relating to oppressive or abusing circumstances and enables the person to survive what seems unbearable as well as to refrain from fighting back and making things worse. It has the further consequence of keeping the relationship going. While such relationships with an aggressor are abusive, they are also relationships that the weaker person relies upon out of necessity. The child needs its parent, the prisoner will suffer more by antagonizing the guard, the woman believes she will sink into poverty if she leaves her battering husband, the worker can fear joblessness if he rages against that abusive superior. Identification with the aggressor can limit one's life possibilities, to be sure, but it can also be life-saving.

I assume in what follows that adults who abuse children, husbands who batter wives, concentration camp guards who torment prisoners, and business people who abuse lower-echelon workers are all persons who have failed in their own psychological development. Identification with the aggressor is a two-party event in which the aggressor's personality limitations are heavily implicated. If the weak persons who identify with the aggressor fulfill Kaiser's criteria for the "submissive mode" in their "obedience without decision to obey," it is similarly true that the abusers meet his sense of the "tyrannical personality":

> "The tyrant wants the people he tyrannizes to obey; but obedience in itself is not enough to satisfy him. They should not obey by any rational reason, because they share his goals or are motivated by rewards promised or punishment threatened. They should obey blindly like robots without any volition of their own. He is interested in making demands which are arbitrary and unreasonable, or at least must appear as such to his subjects, in order to make sure that their obedience is not attributable to their agreement with his goals."[2]

In Kaiser's view, the tyrant wants of the people whom he tyrannizes that their role as agent, as persons following their own wants and choices, be suppressed; they must become agency.

Kaiser next indicated that both the submissive and the tyrannical efforts of people are in the service of creating for each individual a "delusional fusion relationship" in which the delusion involved seems to soften the strict boundaries which separate one individual from another. That is, people try to obscure their own boundaries, their separate responsibilities as agents in the creation of social relations, by entering either submissive or tyrannical endeavors, in which they imagine they are merged with others. They choose to be submissive or tyrannical depending upon their established power relation with an other to whom they relate — their spouse, their boss, their child, their friend. Kaiser believed that the delusion of fusion is basic to all psychopathology.

Following Kaiser, I am led to propose that a mutual striving for fusion takes place between aggressor and abused, a striving engaged in by all those connected in an oppressor-oppressed way. While an aggressor may seem to be endowed with unconstrained power and with the apparent ability to arbitrarily impose his or her will, this very aggressor must be understood as also deprived of true autonomy and separateness and as in fact seeking fusion with, and thus becoming controlled by, his or her identified victim or victims. Oppressors can best be viewed as *also* victims.

Furthermore, the pace of the fusion process is exactly the same for the aggressor and the victim. The unfolding of identification with the aggressor as outlined in Scheme 2 is paralleled by a process that step by step brings the aggressor to become fused with the victim. The two paths to intended fusion are intertwined. A new formula would express this view: The extent to which the abused (submissive) is agency rather than agent is matched precisely with the degree to which the aggressor (tyrannical) is agency (pseudo-agent or mock-agent) rather than agent. The retreat from self as agent, or responsible one, to self as agency, or instrument, is a reciprocal process between aggressor and victim. The complete fusion of the weak with the aggressor, if achieved in its delusional form, is also the complete fusion of the aggressor with the weak.

When I talk about violence, rage, mechanical obedience, tyranny, and exploitation, I am obviously talking about power, and more particularly, I am depicting forced and unjust uses of power by the stronger against the weaker. When I speak of the fusion of one person with another, however, and I note that in this merging both parties diminish or lose their capacities as agents and take on the character of instruments, I am referring to the development of a form of powerlessness.

From the point of view of those who fill the role of victims in the social relations characterized by aggressive manifestations of power, there is consistency in the experience of power here. There is powerlessness in respect to the realization of one's purpose, as with the girl who wishes to play mother to the adult male and is raped instead; and there is powerlessness in the psychic sense of selfhood when the victim identifies with the aggressor and loses control over the definition of values and needs that guide behavior.

From the point of view of those who are the identified aggressors, however, the assertion of strength and control in the exploitative mode represents powerfulness, while the fusion with the victim represents profound powerlessness (thus the idea of pseudo-agent or mock-agent). In the situation of unjust power relations, the expression of power by the stronger is associated with an increased powerlessness: the oppressor becomes more powerful and more powerless at one and the same time. This paradox stands in need of clarification.

We can see through to the resolution of the paradox by tracing the *compelled dependence* which characterizes the aggressor's functioning as tyrant. In the first place, the aggressor is dependent upon a certain narrow type of social relation for the resolution of personal desires: the self-regulation of the aggressor, his or her mastery of these desires, depends upon control of an other. The social relation that empowers the aggressor is not just casual or convenient; the aggressor *requires* that an other be available to be of help in the management of unruly desires.

The aggressor may be dependent upon the social relation because the desires are so strong that inner resources are feared to be inadequate to their control or because his or her inner executive powers are so weak that hardly any strong set of needs can be effectively organized. In either case, when the balance of desire and self-regulation is threatened, the relation to an other who empowers the aggressor is vital to the aggressor's internal psychic economy. Peter Marris suggests how this all works, including the consequences for the weaker person, in his assessment of transfer of risk:

> "The powerful, in managing relationships so as to secure for themselves the most highly predictable environment they can, inevitably make that environment less predictable for the weaker. Power is, above all, the ability to transfer the burden of risk to others."[3]

In addition, not simply any other person will satisfy the aggressor; the other person, or persons, in the social relation must possess a special characteristic. *The other must be vulnerable*, that is, predisposed to give up responsibility and decision-making power in the social relation as a way of handling *his or her own* desires. Vulnerability is just this readiness to let an other take over one's responsibility, as in "obedience without decision to obey." This is readily seen in the molested children who drew Ferenczi's attention. These children were abused by parents, other relatives, or closely connected friends whom the children trusted. The abusers were figures who the children could reasonably assume would act in a responsible fashion and so could be counted upon to make decisions for them. The children were predisposed to allocate authority to their abusers. This is a general trait associated with the aggressor-abused relationship, and it means that the aggressor is dependent upon a *vulnerable* other, not an other functioning as agent.

Yet another dependence of the aggressor is this: the aggressor must have the *appearance of control*, of decision-making power in the social relation, without the personal accountability to self and others that is necessary for the development and maintenance of cooperative efforts engaged in by separate, self-directed individuals. This is the essence of Kaiser's remark that obedience itself is not enough for the tyrant:

> "He is interested in making demands which are arbitrary and unreasonable. . . in order to make sure that [his subjects'] obedience is not attributable to their agreement with his goals."

Were others to obey the aggressor in the service of their own goals, they would be denying the special power of the aggressor, and they would be showing themselves as agents rather than as instruments available for the aggressor's purposes. The dominator's intolerance of the autonomy of others is neither idle nor freely chosen; it is a function of dependence on the vulnerable others for the definition of his or her own power.

A final dependence of the aggressor which indicates powerlessness in the social relation is a parasitical relation to the needs of the vulnerable other person that becomes prominent as the relation unfolds. Whether these needs are appropriated by the aggressor or their denunciation and rejection become focal in the relation, the aggressor leans upon the vulnerable one's needs. All aggressors fuse the needs of the vulnerable other with their own needs in the way that the adult molester fastens on the innocent sexual play of the child to live out his or her sexual needs. Here we come upon the complete counterpart to identification with the aggressor: the aggressor expresses own needs by what may properly be called *projection upon a primed vulnerable other.*

The scheme I have formed to describe the unfolding of projection upon a primed vulnerable other is based upon the scheme for identification with the aggressor. The same steps appear because the two processes are reciprocals. The disempowerment that takes place through identification with the aggressor is reciprocal with the controlled empowerment that takes place through projection upon a primed vulnerable other.

At each step a reciprocal process takes place such that while the weaker participant is moving in the direction of identification — a taking on, or substituting in the self, of what belongs to the other, in the sense of values, needs, and desires — the stronger participant is increasingly under the influence of projection, whereby he or she shifts what is unwanted onto the weaker participant, while keeping for himself or herself what is desirable or manageable.

In the opening phase, the stronger person is acting spontaneously and naturally, reaching out in a non-power-oriented way toward the weaker person with expectations of happy and mutually beneficial encounters. This is the phase of *natural spontaneity*. Again, the relationship is assumed to be safe, and the stronger person, like the weaker, is psychologically open and unguarded, prepared only to find satisfaction in a mutually supportive way with another person.

Something goes wrong with natural spontaneity, and the second phase of *profound, experienced anxiety* ensues. The stronger person may have risked more than intended in the relationship, and may feel threatened by exposure to a wider audience; or deep, feared impulses may have surfaced and challenged his or her executive controls; or the stronger person, wanting more from the situation than the weaker person wants, as in the case of the child molester, may have provoked great anxiety and desperation in the weaker person, which in turn has threatened the stronger person. In short, a safe situation has become unsafe, dangerous not only to the victim but to the maker of the excessive demand. The stronger person feels unable to fully master the situation and feels threatened in an unsafe circumstance.

The power differential first appears in the phase of profound, experienced anxiety, wherein the stronger person addresses his or her own anxiety by focusing upon the anxiety of the weaker person. Attempts are made to mollify the anxiety of the weaker one, via assurances that the situation is not dangerous and need not be feared; or efforts are made to control the weaker person so that he or she will not dangerously live out anxiety in public. The molested child, for example, may be told that things are all right, that nothing wrong has happened and nothing is to be feared; or the child may be warned not to reveal what has taken place, since other folks might not understand. In either case, the stronger person acts to manage the aroused anxiety through attending to the weaker person, as well as through implementation of internal self-control measures. It is as if the stronger person were to say, "The excess of my anxiety can be resolved through the handling of your anxiety." It is easy to see this in the adult-child relation, since the adult can mask his or her own anxiety by taking care of the child, who expects to be taken care of, but the same process happens among peers as a control-dependence bonding begins to develop and as the fusion process takes hold.

The third phase in projection upon a primed vulnerable other, as in identification with the aggressor, is the phase of *experienced anger*. Both those who project and those who identify are angry and are aware at some time of their feeling; and both aim their anger at the other who makes them anxious. I postulate here that anger is a crucial part of a person's intensified exertions that are aimed toward influencing others in a threatening situation. Great anxiety mobilizes anger as a means for alleviating the anxious-making circumstance.

Although the stronger and weaker individuals are comparable in being angry outward, focusing their anger on the other in the relationship, they differ in how they are angry. The experienced anger of the weaker person flares into forms that lead toward disempowerment in the relationship (such as exasperated, helpless rage), while the stronger one shapes angry actions that facilitate self-empowerment (such as using power allocated by a larger system in which the two are both embedded to threaten the weaker person). The management of the social emotion of anger in dealings between weaker and stronger involves each person's regulating his or her own feelings and, at the same time, handling the other's angry endeavors. It is quite challenging and difficult to pay this simultaneous attention to self and to other fully with awareness, which is why it can happen unawares that one attends to self *or* to other and power distribution follows. If both the weaker and the stronger person focus attention on the rage of the weaker, for example, the limitations of the stronger are hidden and the unequal power alignment is developed. In this case, the weak individual attends to himself or herself, the stronger focuses on the other, and together they diminish the weaker through underscoring the helplessness in this person's rage.

Projection upon a primed vulnerable other is promoted when the stronger person both develops controlled rage inside and fosters the evolution of helpless rage in the weaker person. On the one hand, the stronger person attends to self-control in the mastery of felt anger; on the other hand, the stronger person encourages helplessness in the weaker person as that person struggles with angry emotions. Both the self-control and the helplessness help the stronger manipulate the weaker more fiercely. The strategies of self-control and rendering the other's rage helpless are thus key components of the process that empowers the stronger person and makes for a tyranny in the relationship. And the strategies can be carried out alternatively: it is not necessary that both be activated at the same time.

The stronger person is seldom free in magnifying the helplessness of the weaker's rage. Rather, control of the weaker is vital to the maintenance of internal integrity and is, therefore, a necessary and compelled effort for the stronger person. That portion of the experienced anger which the stronger person can manage through internal regulating devices appears to the observer as self-controlled anger — and can be seen in a tense face, a stiff body, erect posture, a tight voice — but that is not the whole of the anger that wells up inside the stronger person. The remainder of the anger, which threatens to overwhelm the person and tear him or her apart, is projected upon the weaker person, and control activities are shifted outward toward management of this primed vulnerable other's rage. The powerful one gets distracted from his or her own anger by focusing on the other's.

Incidentally, most powerful people can't admit to being disturbed by their anger, since that would show them as weak. Their inability to admit this is part of the projection process — a way of projecting weakness outside of themselves. I am reminded of President Nixon, under fire from reporters during the Watergate hearings, on television angrily denying that he was angry. He was avoiding experiencing his own rage and attempting to divert television viewers from it by centering on the reporters and their questions — but he did behaviorally what he was denying in his words.

The fourth phase in the development of projection upon a primed vulnerable other, again paralleling identification with the aggressor, is *confusing guilt and self-hatred*. When the rage in the transactions between the tyrannical and submissive persons becomes intolerable and projection of anger and induction of helplessness and its concomitant control fail to solve the problems in making the relationship work, there is a remarkable disappearance of the experienced anger. In its place arise guilt and self-hatred, and these follow the same pattern as the experienced anger; some is internalized and some projected. The rage that was being dealt with by inner control is turned back upon the self and leads to the same sort of guilt and self-hatred experienced by those who identify with the aggressor. The rage that was managed through projection upon a primed vulnerable other is transformed into preoccupation with the guiltiness and hatefulness of that weaker other.

Projected guilt and self-hatred do not look like what we ordinarily call guilt and self-hatred at all. To be guilty is to be focused upon oneself and to blame oneself. Similarly, self-hatred involves hatred either of one's own desires or of one's control over desires, one's aggressiveness against oneself. Self-contempt, self-denigration, self-abasement typify self-hatred. Projected guilt, however, is manifested as hypersensitivity to moral indiscretions by the other. In projected guilt attention is pointed toward the other rather than toward the self, and specifically to the moral foibles of the other that are very like one's own. Similarly, in projected self-hatred, the hate is of the other, not of the self; the subject matter of the hatred, furthermore, is composed of desires and internal controls that are unacceptable to the self, that are part of what Jungians call the "shadow." For example, men who stereotype women as emotional rather than rational are often repressing their own emotionality and projecting it upon women, where they then act to reject it a second time. They are obsessed with emotionality, disallow it in themselves, see it or provoke it in women, and then punish it.

The final phase of projection upon a primed vulnerable other is called *fusion of own and vulnerable other's desires.* When guilt and self-hatred are projected, the stronger is riding upon the guilt and self-hatred of the weaker. In this final phase, beyond guilt and self-hatred, the stronger person merges self with other in the very desires expressed. The stronger person lives out his or her unacceptable wishes through the weaker person. Being pressed within by strong desires and unable for whatever reason to satisfy them directly, stronger persons look elsewhere to deal with them. It is important for them that they find comparable desires in weaker others and that they live through these others, either by encouraging the weaker persons to express the desires they themselves cannot express or by deploring behavior of these others that is based on such desires. Attending closely to unacceptable desires but seeing them only in others constitutes the means by which stronger persons project. The weaker are either to do something or to stop doing something in accord with the demands of the stronger, and those demands are a function of the desires stronger persons cannot take responsibility for in themselves. We here once again come upon the tyrannical mode as described by Kaiser, in which there is insistence upon being obeyed without any decision to be obedient by the weaker. The projector and the identifier have only one power of decision between them; one is the extension or organ of the other; they are merged, or fused.

Projection is the great unrecognized factor in the establishment and continuation of tyranny. And unhealthy projection is a dramatic limitation on human growth and fulfillment. The strong in relations of domination are not self-actualizing in those relationships.

A summary of the phases of projection upon a primed vulnerable other is contained in

Scheme 3

Natural spontaneity → Profound, experienced anxiety → Experienced anger → Confusing guilt and self hatred (projection upon a primed vulnerable other, first degree) → Fusion of own and vulnerable other's desires (projection upon a primed vulnerable other, second degree)

Having laid out complementary schemes of identification with the aggressor and projection upon a primed vulnerable other, I turn to elaboration of the mutual processes of pathological empowerment and disempowerment that characterize oppression.

Chapter 4

Empowering and Disempowering Reciprocally

The processes of identification with the aggressor and projection upon a primed vulnerable other entail efforts to achieve fusion among persons. Such psychological fusion cannot happen without the participation and acquiescence of the other or others in the relationship with whom a person fuses. I have already suggested that the aggressor fuses with the victim as much as the weak one fuses with the powerful one; now I am going to expand upon the idea that the unfolding of the identification and the projection involved is mutually created and proceeds in lock step. Whether the shift from anxiety to anger, for example, begins with one or the other partner in the collaborative relationship, the consolidation into any condition such that experienced anger is the dominant social emotion in the interaction is a result of the combined efforts of the participants.

The shift to a more fused level of functioning — from anxiety to anger, from anger to guilt and self-hatred, and from guilt and self-hatred to the fusion of desires, in short each step on the path from individuals operating as agents to individuals becoming agencies — takes place when the relationship is perceived to be threatened with destruction. The anger of the persons who are interacting, for instance, may mount into rage, and the rageful confrontations may be read as murderous or suicidal. The actors in this drama will believe that they cannot reduce the danger implied by the depth of their angry feelings except by halting the angry encounter. When this threshold is reached and when the participants find that they cannot flee from the relationship, the anger disappears and is no longer the figural social-emotional characteristic of the relationship. In its place appear manifestations of confusing guilt and self-hatred as these are experienced in their differing ways by the weak and the strong. Each shift, accordingly, is like the emergence of a new symptom.

The interplay of identification with the aggressor and projection upon a primed vulnerable other centrally involves complexes of the social emotions I have described: these complexes are the locus of the simultaneous unfolding of the senses of powerlessness and powerfulness in the participants.[1] Power is relational, contributed and developed by all actors in a relationship, and negotiations around power take place through each person's handling of the social-emotional complex that comes to be figural in the relationship. Thus, there are methods for managing each social-emotional complex that maintain or promote equal power, inhibiting faulty identifications and projections, but there are also methods that foster a sense of powerlessness or a sense of powerfulness. Angry feelings, for example, can be addressed to a partner in ways that affirm self without diminishing or negating the other. These ways promote equal power, whereas anger that is meant to frighten, intimidate, or overwhelm a partner aims at creating a power differential. I want now to elaborate on this theme.

When uncertainty about some central aspects of their common efforts spreads among the members of a group, anxiety becomes a pronounced and shared social-emotional factor. People may become insecure about whether the group can reach its objectives, whether the members will be treated with respect, whether their needs will be met, or whether too much will be asked of them. Something entirety unrelated to the group may even bring anxiety to the forefront, as when a member comes into the scene anxious about other parts of his or her life and by means of contagion or resonance that anxiety spreads to others in the group. By any of a number of means anxiety may appear in a group and take hold as the dominant social emotion to be contended with, that is, negotiated, by persons in the situation.

The differing ways these participants grapple with their anxiety may lead to productive management of the anxiety and equal empowerment of all, or they may lead toward the empowerment of some and the disempowerment of others. Angyal's idea of universal ambiguity is applicable here: anxiety may be seen to have two meanings, and these meanings are opposed to each other, since one is based on confidence (the anxiety of anticipation and excitement that we all know before a lively event is to take place) and the other is based on isolation (the anxiety of dread and fear, as in phobias).

The handling of anxiety is not only a private affair for each member of a group; whether the anxiety that dominates the group is managed in the positive or disabling mode is partly determined by the usual methods each individual is accustomed to using and partly by the group process. A group may urge its members to rid themselves of this uncomfortable social emotion, or it may enable them to experience anxiety without fear and retreat. Indeed, one group function is to enable individuals to experience and master difficult emotional effects, a function it may succeed or fail in performing. Whichever way the group moves in this regard, the nature of the group process is one critical element in the distribution of power.

For example, it can be functional for the participants to elevate to leadership in an anxious period persons who are familiar with their own anxiety, and can experience it, tolerate it, contain it, and use it productively to mobilize themselves and others. We know this positive expression of anxiety as alert apprehension, an apprehension that undergirds concerted, challenging, and effective effort. Conversely, it is disruptive for the group members to lean upon those who are paralyzed by anxiety, who must repress it when others are ready to be openly anxious, or who otherwise cannot manage their experienced anxiety in a socially fruitful manner. These functional and dysfunctional qualities may lead to a rational division of influence within the group.

Yet what is realistic in the short run may become distorted over time. If one person is always the leader of the group when anxiety is prominent, then the others in the group may gradually lose whatever capacities for dealing with anxiety they had. This will come to happen if they come to rely on that leader whenever they feel anxious. Instead of acquiring from that leader techniques for increasing their tolerance of anxiety and procedures for making their anxiety serve them rather than disable them — that is, instead of enlarging themselves through the relationship — the participants may routinely diminish their social-emotional executive powers. Little by little they may lose their sense of responsibility for mastery of anxiety and acquire a sense of powerlessness at the merest signal of anxious feelings. Part of the self is given over, and first steps on the path to fusion are taken.

Leadership choices and the expression of leadership styles are not the only group processes that facilitate or undermine the productive management of anxiety. Among the many other group facts which influence how it is managed is the group's norm for emotionality among its members, the standard level of affect encouraged and tolerated by leaders and members of the group. Intolerance of intense affect as the norm of a group ensures that self-controlled persons will rise to leadership and others will be less capable of mature handling of their emotions because they lack the necessary support. Not surprisingly, authoritarian groups strictly regulate emotional life, usually discouraging awareness and sharing of such unpleasant affects as anxiety, or channeling them toward perceived outgroups and not allowing them to influence ingroup interactions. Enveloped by these antiemotional norms, members are ill-prepared to deal with the risky, scary, challenging tasks of life and increasingly lean upon authority in a fusion process when the simplest flicker of anxiety appears.

Another, more nasty strategy for dividing power unequally in the presence of an anxious group climate is to focus attention and concern upon one person who is experiencing and contending with personal anxiety. By turning that person inward and by centering upon him or her in an isolating way, others, including those moving toward self-empowerment, can hide their own anxiety or pretend that it is less than is in fact the case. The highlighted anxious person may be subjected to competing communications: "We care for you in your distress"; "Your anxiety is extraordinary and reflects some kind of inadequacy"; "We will attend to you later"; "You are interfering with our normal process." Bringing some individuals to be self-reflective in a group while others are not is a method for controlling, containing, or diminishing those individuals while simultaneously empowering the non-self-reflective participants.

These illustrations of the uses of anxiety management for empowering and disempowering purposes embody another relevant matter, namely, the fact that the distribution of power is a *collaborative* activity. While it is true that some individuals act to empower themselves by one or another process, it is also true that some act to disempower themselves, as when group participants allow the leader to handle all matters involving anxiety. Some persons do not initiate or direct their efforts toward self-empowerment but do allow themselves to be empowered; and similarly, some are less assertive in disempowering themselves than they are tolerant of being disempowered. Power, it must be remembered over and over, is not an attribute of an individual, but rather is a characteristic of a social relationship, created and maintained by all participants in the relationship. Thus, disempowerment and empowerment may be sought, may be tolerated, or may simply happen without anyone's awareness that they are taking place.

In describing the anger found in persons who are projecting upon vulnerable others, I noted that controlled rage in the stronger persons is paired with helpless rage in the weaker. Some variants in this combination can be sketched to further illustrate the main idea. In one of the simplest, the stronger person may occupy a higher position in a hierarchical setting than one or more weaker persons. In such a situation, the anger of the stronger person may be embedded in the system's privileges, so that his or her personal irritations can hide behind authority to enforce the rules of the system. For example, a military officer rants about neatness and tidiness on the base when disgruntled about something gone wrong at home, and the social-emotional complex of the transaction between the officer and enlisted soldiers becomes one of angry feelings. The "self-control" of his rage amounts to a collapsing of personal animosity into the regulations of the military system. The officer can be quite arbitrary and offensive and still expect the system's support in the expression of rage. His or her confidence in this support is basic to the empowerment phenomenon, as well as to the sense of helplessness and powerlessness felt by those subjected to the abuse.

Because there is a real power differential between officers and plain soldiers, a differential embodied in rules and regulations acknowledged by all, it might be asked where simple, appropriate, task-related anger ends and projection upon a primed vulnerable other begins. One answer to such a question is that a certain neatness is necessary and functional to military life, and the push toward that degree of neatness even in a tone of annoyance and irritation reflects efforts to accomplish good work. Most husbands and wives negotiate around cleanliness in their homes for the similar purpose of being able to work comfortably and easily on the things they choose to do. Beyond insistence on a certain level of neatness, however, commands, whether from military officer or husband or wife, are intended to institute obedience without decision to obey, the automatic obedience Kaiser described in defining tyranny.[2] Excessive anger around tidiness is tyranny whether the weaker person is soldier, spouse, or, as most of us may remember, a child whose parents are appalled at the state of his or her bedroom or play area.

A different kind of answer surfaces upon scrutiny of the responses of soldiers to the officer, or spouse or child to the demanding other. When an officer is angry, the soldiers may be accommodating and accepting of the authority's anger, even though they may be discomfited by it. But they may find triggered in them a crescendo of their own resentment and rage; indeed, they may feel overwhelmed by wishes to be defiant, fantasies of aggression against the officer, anger so profound that it frightens them as they experience it. That deep anger, often accompanied by a sense of futility, is likely to be their carrying of the officer's projected rage. The officer has elicited helpless resentment as part of externalizing his or her own perhaps overwhelming and frightening anger. In effect, the officer has arranged to "experience" his or her own anger in the form of a perception of someone else's rage. In projecting anger, the officer may hope to control it by relying upon the authority of the system guiding all participants in the encounter. The military hierarchy demands submission as part of its system principle, and the officer relies on adherence to that principle. Insofar as the officer does place reliance upon obedience to the system, it can be noted, he or she is thereby becoming an instrument of that system in the sense of being agency rather than agent. Such officers are known as "bureaucratic" military persons, and by this reference is recognized their agency status. Many Nazi war criminals relied for their defense after World War II on being such functionaries — that is, not being personally responsible.

Another example is those teachers, bosses, or parents who are seldom overtly angry but who regularly evoke rage in their students, subordinates, or children. It may be that at the first inkling of angry feeling of their own penetrating to their awareness such individuals squash their feeling and promote it in others; or it may be that as authorities they are hypersensitive to nuances of rage in the weaker persons and foment and exploit those feelings. Either of these kinds of projection is especially effective with rebellious students, subordinates, or children, that is, with others who are vulnerable according to their status and who are primed by their own near-the-surface anger.

An authority's self-control of anger may set in motion a transactional process that elevates anger among the participants and distributes power unevenly in his or her favor. A leader who is always and obviously holding in anger may intimidate those who are subjected to his or her leadership. Subordinates, observing the tightly reined anger, may act as if they were walking on eggs, fearful of breaking a shell and receiving a blast of the anger being controlled. Their fearfulness may stimulate their own anger, which they must now keep under control. The leader, sensing rage in the subordinates, perceives a possible power struggle and becomes more threatening, uses more self control, leans more on the system for authority, and increases his or her power.

Subordinates' anger-management practices may lead to disempowerment. When a subordinate loses control over his or her anger, goes into a tirade, and is ineffective in moving authority or mobilizing support or otherwise accomplishing the aims associated with the anger, disempowerment occurs. The person may feel foolish, self-critical, impotent, or resigned after the flash-flooding of the rage. Confusion about the origins of the anger and its appropriateness may enter awareness. Temper tantrums may be contributors to disempowerment as well as signs of felt weakness. Harriet Lerner refers to such ineffective kinds of anger in the following observation:

> "Fighting and blaming is sometimes a way both to protest and to protect the status quo when we are not quite ready to make a move in one direction or another."[3]

Finally, the simplest process in the use of anger to maintain power-dependence relations is for a superior to intimidate a subordinate by his or her fury. Fear of the superior's wrath, especially if one's aspirations are dependent upon favorable relations with the superior, is a basic ingredient of submissiveness, seen not only in the most lowly in a hierarchy but also in those higher up who are made vulnerable by their hopes or ambitions. Colonels, protective of their careers, feared General Westmoreland's rage in the Vietnam War.

It is fairly easy to see mutually created empowerment and disempowerment by means of anger management in social relations; it is more difficult to trace empowerment and disempowerment when guilt and self-hatred are the figural social emotions. There are many reasons why the empowerment issues are obscured when guilt and self-hatred are prominent, but the merging of the stronger and the weaker is the primary factor.

"Confluence" is the word in Gestalt therapy theory for what I have been mostly calling merging or fusion, and Polster and Polster discuss guilt and confluence in terms pertinent to empowerment and disempowerment:

"Two clues to disturbed confluent relationships are frequent feelings of guilt or resentment. When one of the parties to a confluent contract senses he has violated the confluence, he feels obliged tn apologize or to make restitution for his breach of contract. He may not know why, but he feels he has transgressed and believes that atonement, punishment or expiation is in order. He may seek this by asking for or meekly submitting to harsh treatment, scolding or alienation. He may also try to provide this punitive treatment himself by retroflective behavior wherein he deals cruelly with himself by self-degradation, abasement, or feeling worthless and bad. Guilt is one of the paramount signs that confluence has been disrupted.

"The other party, who feels that he has been transgressed against, experiences righteous indignation and resentment. He is hurt and offended. He has been betrayed, wronged, and sinned against; he has something coming from the offender. He demands that the transgressor shall at least feel guilty for what he has done and that strenuous efforts at apology and reparation shall be made."[4]

I can illustrate problems caused by fusion by once again attending to Ferenczi's analysis of identification with the aggressor in the instance of the molested child. Ferenczi believed that the signal event for the child as a consequence of identification with the offending adult partner is *the introjection of the guilt feelings of the adult*, which transforms what had been harmless play into a punishable offense. The child perceives the guilt experienced by the adult and introjects it, that is, becomes guilty from the adult's self-judgment. But this is just one source of the child's guilt; there is a second, possibly more important source as well: the anger felt by the child toward the adult is turned round upon the self by the child, who is feeling helpless. The internalized, self-directed anger, mixed as it is with anxiety from the excessive stimulation, is also experienced as guilt. Accordingly, the child is confounded in the understanding of his or her guilt because that guilt is composed partly of the adult's guilt which has been introjected and partly of the child's self-controlled reflexive rage. This confusion immobilizes the child and further disempowers him or her.

Erich Fromm in *Man for Himself* has described the dependence that accompanies guilt and disempowerment:

> "Guilt feelings have proved to be the most effective means of forming and increasing dependency, and herein lies one of the social functions of authoritarian ethics throughout history. The authority as lawgiver makes its subjects feel guilty for their many and unavoidable transgressions. The guilt of unavoidable transgressions before authority and the need for its forgiveness thus creates an endless chain of offense, guilt feeling, and the need for absolution which keeps the subject in bondage and grateful for forgiveness rather than critical of the authority's demands. It is this interaction between guilt feelings and dependency which makes for the solidity and strength of the authoritarian relationship. The dependence on irrational authority results in a weakening of will in the dependent person and, at the same time, whatever tends to paralyze the will makes for an increase in dependence. Thus a vicious circle is formed."

The self-hatred that appears in the identifier and in the projector is another ground for the empowerment and disempowerment process. There are two sides to the self-hatred, the hatred directed against one's desires that put one into danger situations, which is the hatred of one's spontaneity in response to impulses; and the hatred of one's self-control, of the rage directed inwardly, of the attempt to accommodate to the threatening reality. Internal conflict from these self-hating activities consumes the person's energies, making him or her less able to contend with reality in a responsible way and so contributing to the powerlessness that is felt in the situation.

The first of these self-hating acts is the hatred expressed in the condemnations coming from the superego: "You are contemptible for having such repellent desires; you are bad in your impulses; you should not want what you want." This self-hatred is associated with the first degree of identification with the aggressor or projection upon a primed vulnerable other. The second of these self-hating acts is the last resort of holding on to one's own desires before the second degree of the faulty identification or projection takes hold. This hatred comes from the side of the desires and is aimed at the excessive forces within oneself demanding self-control: "I hate it that I deny myself what I so much want; my self-restriction is ridiculous; I'm a fool to give up striving for what I desire."

As I have said, some of the self-hatred of oppressors is projected onto weaker persons in the form of preoccupation with the hatefulness of these weaker others. This in fact is done often. The profound self-hatred of oppressed peoples is fertile ground for such projections. Prepared for by contrasting styles of managing anxiety and anger, the collusion between the weak inviting contempt and the strong projecting self-hatred is often quickly established. Those who disempower themselves by identification with the aggressor are predisposed to receive and accept almost anything that leads to guilt and self-hatred, and those who empower themselves are ever ready to project their guilt and to hate the weak. Together, they install oppressive relationships.

Perhaps the fused, reciprocal empowering-disempowering transactions can be better indicated by attending to some of the parallel contributions the stronger and the weaker make. While the stronger stirs up anger and ensures that it is made helpless and turned round upon the self by the weaker, the weaker is simultaneously afraid of his or her own anger and afraid of the anger of the stronger. The push by the stronger person toward angry relations that he or she can then constrain is met with efforts by the weak to avoid situations that provoke anger. So the strong and the weak are ever threatened with open rage and on the verge of having to deal with it. For the strong, anger is in the service of requiring obedience without the decision to obey.

Whereas stronger persons, those who are empowering themselves, foster doubt and self-scrutiny of a debilitating nature in the weak, those who are disempowering themselves overestimate the assuredness and togetherness, the rationality and the self-serving effectiveness, of the stronger. The fostering of doubt has its active form, as when a self-empowering person imposes self-criticism upon a weaker one. Women who have been raped may be challenged in court to demonstrate that they did not participate in the rape, either by inviting it or accepting it too readily or because of having a masochistic personality. Planting the seeds of self-doubt may enhance the power of the rapist or his defenders. Students who object to arbitrary actions of their teachers may be required to examine whether they are being objective or merely rebellious, whether they have what are called problems in accepting authority.

The fostering of doubt may also take a reactive form, as when the stronger person pays selective attention and gives excessive amplification to the self-effacing or self-critical endeavors of the weaker person. Those who minister to people when they are vulnerable — physicians who tend the sick, priests who comfort the aggrieved, psychotherapists who serve the neurotic — recognize how easily they are given a sense of being very powerful when listening to the self-hatred of hurt and guilty individuals. In the training of these professionals, considerable demand is made that the trainees learn to control the sense of omnipotence that is thrust upon them. Exploitative persons know how to aggrandize themselves by facilitating self-abasement and self-degradation when it surfaces among the weak.

While those who are stronger foster doubt and self-scrutiny in the weak as part of the empowerment process, those who are weaker do the reverse as they disempower themselves. In doing so actively, the weak attribute security, inner strength, rationality, and personal superiority to the strong. They may envy the strong, or they may demand that the strong solve the difficult problems of collective life for all who are involved. Reactively, the weak seldom test the pretended security of the stronger. As small children do not want to know that their parents are fallible, or adolescents avoid believing their parents are sexual and probably experience the problems and vulnerabilities of sexual relations, subordinates resist perceiving the inner turmoil of their superiors, or they misread as security the intolerance of inner conflict that characterizes oppressors. The weak are helped along in this avoidance process by the strong, who discourage investigation of their psychological functioning.

In authoritarian hierarchies, the subordinates are saddled with accountability, loyalty, duty, and adherence to norms, all of which are invitations to guilt; superiors are expected to show initiative, decisiveness, autonomy, risk-taking aptitude, and freedom from narrow constraints, all of which promote intolerance of inner doubt, hesitation, and guilt.[6] The intolerance leads toward projection upon the primed vulnerable others.

In essence, the weak denigrate self and overestimate the other in living out guilt and self-hatred. Thus, depression is the malady of the oppressed. The strong diminish others and inflate themselves, and the affliction of the exploiter is paranoia. The battered wife is typically depressed; the battering husband is just as typically suspicious and paranoid about his wife. The two of them are the classic clinical examples of fusion. Together they create the fused power-dependence relationship.

In the final phase of identification with the aggressor and projection upon a primed vulnerable other, the disempowerment and empowerment forces operate through the desires motivating the participants. The oppressed and the oppressor become fused in the very desires that are allowed to impel their behavior, and because they are fused, they become confused. Which of their acceptable desires are their own, and which are induced in them or enabled for them by the other in the relationship? This is the basic insecurity felt by the actors, the origin for feelings of emptiness, of lack of a center, of being agency rather than agent. Loss of the sense of the rhythms and uniquenesses of one's desires is the ultimate price of confluence. Deadness is the common feeling, deadness punctuated periodically by agitated, oppositional, fearful encounters.

If the weak and the strong become fused in their desires, then a whole human unit is formed only when they are in a relationship. Part of the empowerment-disempowerment phenomenon, accordingly, is overinvolvement of the participants in each other's lives. Whether we look at the invasions of authoritarian systems into the private lives of their members, or the intolerance of separations from their therapists of disturbed, borderline patients, or the intrusive engagements of overprotective parents with their children, we observe as one indication of power problems an intolerance of those boundaries that ensure autonomy and separateness for individuals. Inundating collectivity which overwhelms the particularities of persons is both a result of fusion and a strategy for introducing and keeping in place power differences.

Heinz Kohut has described this overinvolvement in writing about his work with narcissistic personality-disordered individuals. These persons are characterized by their grandiosity, their lack of empathy, their self-importance, and their exploitativeness, all of which derive from an inability to differentiate themselves from others:

> "The foregoing considerations — specifically the fact that . . . the analysand experiences the analyst narcissistically, i.e., not as a separate and independent individual — explain the strategic role played in the course of analysis not only by the patient's rage, despondency, and regressive retreat when facing extended separations from the analyst (such as the summer vacation) but also by his severe reactions to small signs of coolness from the side of the therapist, or to the analyst's lack of immediate and complete empathic understanding, and, especially, to such apparently trivial external events as minor irregularities in the appointment schedule, weekend separations, and slight tardiness of the therapist. Significantly, and understandingly in view of the narcissistic nature of the relationship, the analysand reacts with rage against the therapist even when irregularities and interruptions occur which are undertaken at the request and for the benefit of the analysand."

The weak pay vigilant attention to the desires of their abusers, as Ferenczi noted in referring to abused children acting like automata. Since no one can actually give up his or her own needs, however, the weak still have their own desires to contend with — that is, to control. There are three features in their efforts to do this. The weak would prefer to have no unique desires so that they could avoid offending the strong, and so the first feature is repression of own desires, becoming a robot or automaton. If one must have desires-and repression usually fails so there is no avoiding them-then it is better that one's desires please the oppressor, so the second feature is self-censorship such that desires acceptable to this powerful one are tolerated but all unacceptable ones are disowned. The third feature is encouragement of all desires that can be geared to the expressed wishes of the powerful. This may take the form of trying to have the same desires or complement the desires of the strong. In all three instances, the weak confuse themselves in respect to clear ownership of their desires. Thus, self-assertion and a sense of identity are made difficult. One way out of such a bind, as Ferenczi also observed, is for the weak to become defiant. But this is merely to do the opposite of what the abuser accepts, which is another way of measuring one's own desires against those put forward by the stronger person.

The powerful reciprocate. They, too, wish to be unburdened of their own desires, especially when relating to the weak. In relationships with the weak they emphasize and glorify their self-control abilities. And what do they control in themselves but their emotions and their desires! Self-domination is a prerequisite for the acquisition of power. Exaggeration of control leads to estrangement from what is controlled, from affects and desires. Furthermore, those desires the powerful do live out must be acceptable in some way to the weak or their legitimacy as superiors will be lost. Elizabeth Janeway[8] has noted the first "power of the weak" resides in their capacity to take away the legitimation of the powerful. If the powerful appear impulsive, unconventionally loose, unable to delay gratification, they cannot maintain the appearance of being in charge of themselves that is vital to their position of power. The free play of desires, if given full scope, would show their human inconsistency and vulnerability and undermine their striving for personal superiority.

When the weak and the strong fuse by accommodating their desires to each other, they rely heavily in their transactions upon guidance by the larger systems, including social institutions, that surround them. A new otherness is required to fill the void — the lack of individual boundaries — left by the fusion. Together, the weak and the strong form but one unit, and they stand in need of an otherness that helps to define their boundaries as that unit.

That otherness is composed of two main social groupings that become prominent in the regulation of the intricate encounters between the weak and the strong: the ingroup of which they are a part, and the outgroup from which they are apart. Both the ingroup and the outgroup are used to install and maintain the power differentials around individual desires. As people become more and more fused with one another, they give over the design of their patterns of behaviors, and therefore of their desires allowed and disallowed, to the groups in which they are embedded. Individuals, whether weak or strong, become defined by their position in the ingroup hierarchy and by their segregation from members of the outgroup. Fused people live by group requirements and see the group as a controlling mechanism rather than as a chosen means for the realization of their individual goals.

The persons in the weaker position are asked to accept and live by whatever norms define the ingroup, or they themselves adopt conventionalism in their desires and behavior such that their desires are structured according to established mores.[9] They try to learn the rules and fill the roles assigned to their position. Signs of self-assertion beyond typical patterns for ingroup behavior, of reliance upon actions not established as characteristic for their position, are condemned as rebellion or deviance. It is an indication of their own identification with the aggressor that they condemn themselves as much as they are chastised by others for acting upon their own motives when these are unconventional. Their hatred of their own desires reaches a peak in this process.

It is also an indication that identification with the aggressor is fully established when the weak project their unacceptable desires upon the outgroup. Even these projections are group-determined because stereotypes of the group's enemies are targeted. While there are multitudes of examples of this process — poor whites hating blacks in the U.S.A., northern Italians hating southern Italians, the Welsh disliking the English, and so forth — the analysis of such projections that is closest to what I here argue is Vamik Volkan's[10] study of the Greeks and the Turks on Cyprus in the twentieth century. He has illustrated in his study how the oppressed project upon outgroups, who themselves are oppressed, precisely those impulses that are activated in the projector's oppression but are unacceptable to own in the context of the ingroup. Thus, cultural habits develop that allow some actions in the ingroup and externalize others to the outgroup. For example, Greek

Cypriots tend to be loud, while Turkish Cypriots tend to be quiet. Impoverished Turks, then, disallow noisy protestations within the community and stereotype all Greek Cypriots with the loudness they do not permit for themselves. So, to, the Greeks tend to respond with active alertness to external dangers, while the Turks tend toward pervasive passivity. Accordingly, the Greeks readily project their own passive acquiescence in their poor conditions upon the Turks. But while the Greek and Turkish Cypriots are importantly opposites of each other in some dimensions, they are very like each other also, as in their rituals for dealing with the dead and their attitudes about dreams.

It is one of the illusions created in the psychological climate of exploitative relations that those in strong positions are able to live out their desires unhindered and with a directness that can only be associated with self-actualization. Because the strong are fused with the weak, however, it is far from true that they can accept, own, and act directly upon their desires. Like the weak, those high in power-oriented hierarchies are exceedingly conventional. They are constrained by or willingly submerge themselves in the customs, rules, and proprieties of the systems that authorize their power. No groups in society are more attentive to social conventions than groups made up of the powerful, as is seen, for example, in country club life, or in high society, or on the boards of directors of large institutions.

The powerful confound their own desires and those of the system in which they operate. They project all desires that violate the system's customs onto the weak or members of the outgroup. And they go one step further: they are preoccupied with so defining the conventions of the ingroup that those desires they can manage well are recognized as legitimate and those they have trouble handling are outlawed. They pull the levers of power in the attempt to regulate their private, inner struggles. We read of the male legislator, for example, who has sponsored bills in the legislature that are hostile to homosexuals, and who has subsequently been arrested by the police for soliciting another man in a public place. He tried to handle his inner conflict by putting in place social controls. He succeeded in obtaining the social legislation, but he failed in controlling himself by means of it.

The tyrant is arbitrary, and therein lies his or her power; but when seen closely, the tyrant is arbitrary *within the constraints of an accepted system.* Without the support of the forces of the system, the tyrant is naked and alone, vulnerable to defeat and destruction. Support for tyranny may come from raw power such as the police, the army, the ability to fire an employee, the parent's physical superiority over the small child, or it may come from collective acquiescence in allocations of power — the conventionalism of the weak. Yet the support must be there, and that means that the arbitrariness of the tyrant is conditional, or contingent. Here again is the powerless side of the tyrannically powerful individual, the side that he or she projects. As the group is used to distribute power unevenly, so too it is used to contain those who administer its forces.

Chapter 5

Some Qualities When People Fuse

In addition to the fact that the exploiter and the exploited are mutually disempowering themselves and together deciding to become agencies rather than agents, some other qualities of the fusion process stand out, and I want to give brief attention to them here. First, because the stronger and weaker fuse, they become like each other, and the natural consequence is that both identification with the aggressor and projection upon a primed vulnerable other appear in each person. The same person sometimes lives out the faulty identification pattern and at other times, when in the dominant position in a relationship, lives out the faulty projection pattern. Second, the fusion process binds together profound destructive tendencies, so that the possibility of rage and violence is ever present. Third, associated with the fusion process is the tendency, well known in the psychological world, to be intolerant of ambiguity, complexity, or ambivalence. Finally, the fusion process is never simply installed, but must be repeated in each new encounter, and it is reinstalled by a process I call quick-circuiting.

To this point, I have dichotomized the weak and the strong, the identifier and the one who projects, the vulnerable person and the aggressor. I have been following common sense in doing this, and I am clearly not all wrong, because some individuals are much more likely to be victims and others more commonly take the role of oppressor. There are abused children and executives of banks. Yet as I indicated in the last chapter, the strong know powerlessness in their fusion with the weak, a fact that reveals complexity in this

weak-strong dimension; and central analyses of authoritarianism
(Fromm,[1] Maslow,[2] and Adorno et al.[3]), in which the same person
is slave to a superior and tyrant to a subordinate, make the
presence of complexity even clearer. Perhaps the finest statement
on this is that of James Mark Baldwin, written in the early part of
this century — finest because it is explicitly concerned with the
"dialectical movement" in the development of personality:

> "The child's sense of himself is . . . one pole of a relation; and which pole it is
> to be, depends on the particular relation which the other pole, over which the
> child has no control, calls on it to be. If the other person involved presents
> uncertain, ominous, dominating, instructive features, then the child is
> 'subject' over against what is 'projective.' . . . His consciousness is in the
> learning attitude; he imitates, he serves, he trembles, he is a slave. But on the
> other hand, there are persons to whom his attitude has a right to be different.
> In the case of these the dialectic has gone further. He has mastered all their
> features, he can do himself what they want to do, he anticipates no new de-
> velopments in his intercourse with them; so he 'ejects' them . . . Now this is
> what the brothers and sisters, notably the younger ones, are to our youthful
> hero. They are his 'ejects'; he knows them by heart, they have no thoughts.
> They do no deeds, which he could not have read into them by anticipation. So
> he despises them, practices his superior activities on them, tramples them
> under foot."[4]

To be weak or strong is to be in a social relation, and one's position in the relation determines which role is predominant for one.
Beyond this, the weak and the strong understand each other, as
they must if their fusion is to have any coordination at all; that is,
each person knows both roles. Accordingly, identification with the
aggressor and projection upon a primed vulnerable other can —
and do — appear in the same person.

There is another way to see that identification with the aggressor
and projection upon a primed vulnerable other exist in the same
person. Identification is a process by which one takes on and expresses through the self what was exhibited by another. When the
weak person identifies with the powerful other, one characteristic
taken on is the powerful person's tendency to project. The identifier becomes a projector through the dynamic of identification! Is
the reverse case true, namely does the person who projects become

identified with the victim? Of course. That which is projected is one's own unassimilable material, and one meets it as coming from the other. Seeing oneself in the other leads on to identification. In coming to this understanding, incidentally, I am simply rediscovering the fact that the weak and the powerful become fused and also confused.

Once the process of fusion extends beyond mutual anxiety, each step in the development of identification with the aggressor and projection upon a primed vulnerable other represents a new binding of disruptive and destructive tendencies. Anger becomes guilt when the persons in the transaction believe that the rage in the social-emotional atmosphere will lead to murder. Guilt and self-hatred are converted into fusion of desires lest they lead to suicide or, in the case of projection, the bringing down upon oneself of destructive outbursts coming from whoever carries the projected guilt and self-hatred. The paranoia of the oppressor is grounded in this projection process. Racists who exaggerate the sexuality and impulsive looseness of oppressed minority members live in fear of the imagined savagery of those they oppress.

Because of this sequence of binding of destructive tendencies, when identification with the aggressor and projection upon a primed vulnerable other are established and in place, considerable tension marks the interactions, tension of an unstable nature.

The instability of the tension in the social relationship has several particular sources. Aggression that is repressed grows in the unconscious and assumes fearful proportions in the minds of those who are repressing. The apparent profundity of this aggression and the feeling that it cannot be handled well cause the bearer to be keenly alert to inner and outer temptations that might tap the aggression. It seems always to lie in wait, like a panther ready to spring forth at the slightest provocation. That is a source of the instability of the tension. Another source is the delusion of fusion: the individual is not acting alone to manage the destructive urge, but is relying upon an other as well. This situation of the other's responsibility in the management of inner pressures requires impeccable coordination with the other. Given the inherent conflict between the identifier and the projector, that coordination is exceedingly difficult, and instability is an inevitable result. Still another source for the instability of the tension between the actors is the confusion that typifies the internal and social lives they lead. When persons do not know if a motivation is their own or a reflection of another's, when they cannot be sure whether self-control comes from the inner voice of conscience or instead from fear of retribution, their confusion is not conducive to the mastery of destructive tendencies.

Instability of the tension in the relationship means that violence is ever a distinct possibility. Given the fusion and the confusion that exist, violence not only is possible but is the most probable form that destructive urges will take when they break through the controls into action. Direct, mutually managed anger has failed to create a satisfactory resolution to the differences between the actors; guilt and self-hatred in their distinct forms have failed also to diminish the conflict; there is little else available to the participants for managing the threatening situation but the explosive eruption of violence — at least in the eyes of those who are locked into identification with the aggressor and projection upon a primed vulnerable other. This is why so many abused children grow up to become violent parents.

We see or would not be surprised to see violence in the most obvious instances of identification-projection interlock — conflict between the colonizer and the colonized (Memmi,[5] Fanon,[6]), black rage (Grier and Cobbs[7]), incest, child abuse, spouse abuse, rapes, concentration camp brutality. Beyond such instances, there are many, many more "normal" social relations that harbor destructive tendencies. Because violence is the probable expression of the pent-up destructiveness, the individuals involved are very resistant to change. While they would be freed to become themselves, to be agents rather than tools, under a different political or life regime, they believe they must cross the mine field of mutually destructive encounters to approach that new life, and they are sure they will not make it across successfully. This is an important reason why, as is known from the history of revolution and social change, it is that the oppressed equal those dominant in oppressive relations in their reluctance to change the social structures that exist. While they may ultimately institute and carry forth social revolutions, they are customarily resistant to social change and move only when they both are desperate and have some reason to hope,

The obverse of the unstable tension in the kind of social relations I am discussing is the rigid and coercive social control that is called upon to contain the destructive tendencies. Whether persons are acting from identification with the aggressor or projection upon a primed vulnerable other, they require strong social forces to match the awesome aggression they believe exists within themselves and in those they fear. So it is that these individuals rely upon raw force, as in repressive police work, death squads, military action, national guard control of daily life, law and order politics and legislation, and strict religious codes. The more fusion exists in the members of a social system, the deeper are the destructive urges that are being controlled; and the deeper these are, in turn, the more frozen the social institution or society. The delusion of fusion is vital to the freezing of the status quo.

This same rigidity is a characteristic of people who think in terms of dichotomies — good versus bad, weak versus strong, men versus women, blacks versus whites, Greeks versus Turks — a characteristic well known in the world of psychological theory. Sometimes this characteristic is referred to as the defense mechanism of "splitting," in which the "good" other is kept distinct from the "bad" other, the "good" self from the "bad" self. Adorno, Frenkel-Brunswik, Levinson, and Sanford have developed theory about this tendency to dichotomize under the umbrella notion of "tolerance of ambiguity." They have noted the inability of persons considered to be authoritarian to

"face 'ambivalence' — which is emotional ambiguity."[8]

To be able to face ambivalence means to have the capacity to hold contradictory ideas toward the same person or group without repressing one side of the contradiction, to be able to hate and love another at one and the same time.

These authors connect intolerance of ambiguity with repressed rage, a central ingredient in the binding of destructive tendencies I have been discussing. Intolerance of ambiguity, with its dichotomizing accompaniment, is in the service of the repression of hostile emotions in the Adorno et al. scheme:

> "The inability of [authoritarians] to face 'ambivalence' . . . has been discussed in connection with their attitude toward parents and toward the other sex; in these and other areas hostile emotions were found to have been repressed and hidden behind a facade of glorification. A rigid, and in most instances, conventionalized set of rules seems thus to determine the conception the [authoritarian] has of his own and of other people's behavior."[9]

The essence of this line of thought is that intolerance of ambiguity and thinking in dichotomies appear among people who feel trapped in social relations that have much unfulfilled destructiveness in them. When they believe they are unable to escape *and* unable to express their rage directly and productively, people identify, project, and develop the intolerance of ambiguity. Doing these things both binds the aggression, preventing its release against members of their ingroup, and prepares for the expression of hostility toward their outgroup. If the ingroup must appear as allgood, then there must be a place to put the not-good that appears in all of life's activities. That place is the outgroup.

For persons who are fused, there is a dialectic to the dichotomizing. The other must be idealized (ingroup) or negated (outgroup), and in either case robbed of individuality; but the other must also be affirmed as existing, as a complement to the incomplete self. The units of existence for the fused person are the good-me-us and the bad-you, or the bad-me-us and good-you, not the good-bad-complex me and the good-bad-complex you who are separate from but in transaction with each other.

I observed earlier that the powerful are dependent upon being connected to the weak for the maintenance of their inner, psychic integrity. In addition, those who regularly dichotomize, both the strong and the weak, are driven by their fused condition to keep themselves bound to those they negate in the outgroup. They must have an outlet for the bad stuff that arises in the ingroup and is not allowed free play, and the outlet is the outgroup. It is not the case that whites who are racist avoid all contact with blacks or other minority persons of color; women who hate all men do not ignore men or stay away from them. Racism and sexism would be less oppressive if connection were indeed limited, but, because of intolerance of ambiguity, which calls for continuing projection of hostility to an outgroup, racists are *overinvolved* or *preoccupied* with those they negate, sexists are hyperattentive to those they detest.

When a person has become identified with an aggressor or has established a projection upon a primed vulnerable other, his or her difficulties in that social relationship are far from being resolved, in a way not yet mentioned. In addition to the unstable tension that marks the transactions that make up the relationship, tension attributable to the destructiveness that is systematically aroused and then bound, there is a further source of trouble. No matter how adept the person has been in fusing his or her desires with those of the other, the natural biological rhythms of the person produce new impulses and desires all the time. These new desires are not necessarily geared to the social relationship when they first appear because they have their own separate origins deep in the interior of the person's body. While we are sometimes sexually aroused by the presence of a loved other person, so that our sexual desires and social relationships are coordinated, we are also sometimes sexually aroused completely independently of attractive and available others, quickened in the sexual sphere by natural bodily processes. Similarly, sometimes we desire to work slowly because we are tired, not because of disliking the work organizers or resenting the demands of the job that we work quickly. In short, because we are biologically grounded as well as socially embedded, we enter every relationship in the first phase of the process that can lead to identification with the aggressor or projection upon a primed vulnerable other — the phase of natural spontaneity.

Persons who are chained to these identification and projection practices are striving to become fused with others, but they are acting under the *delusion* of fusion, not out of the *fact* of fusion. A person's desires are that person's desires, and the personal, private, and special nature of those desires poses for the person the task of socializing himself or herself anew all the time. Accordingly, persons who are acting under the delusion of fusion begin each new transaction not fused, but alarmingly separate and spontaneous. Then, because they are fearful that the destructiveness associated with the relationship may at any time erupt from its bound state if their spontaneity is allowed to exercise itself and they express their true desires, they move quickly toward fusion.

I speculate that no phase of development is omitted, but rather a quick-circuiting of the process is initiated. With the first awareness of separate desires, the person rapidly becomes anxious, then angry, then guilty and self-hating, whether guilt and self-hatred are expressed directly or projected, and finally experiences the delusion of being fused with the other. The spontaneity is only a flicker, the anxiety only a tick of excitement, the anger but a flash, the guilt and self-hatred a suggestive blur, but each of these is touched in the rush to reinstate the final delusion of fusion. The quick circuiting involves the rapid traversing of each phase, not the omission of any. The persons are intolerant of spontaneity, anxiety, anger, and guilt and self-hatred because full expression of these social emotions would result in the release of powerful, threatening destructiveness. People who are under the influence of the delusion of fusion are *committed* to confluence, not merely adapted to it. They depend on it.

A qualification is that persons who have been under the full delusion of fusion but have now corrected that stop at the preliminary phases instead of quick-circuiting to the final confluence. When they have corrected their readiness to fuse desires, they quick-circuit from spontaneity through anxiety and anger to a stopping point at guilt and self-hatred. When these latter have been worked through, they focus on anger; and when anger is managed more successfully, anxiety becomes the figural problem in their oppressive social relations.

This view of the quick-circuiting process will be helpful when attention is directed to the undoing of identification with the aggressor and projection upon a primed vulnerable other. If my speculation is correct, it means that no new process must be created for the undoing to succeed. Instead, a slowing down of the quick-circuiting is called for so that a reworking of the social emotions can be accomplished. It is not necessary, for example, to artificially create anger when a reversal of the quick-circuiting tendency uncovers an anger that has been experienced in each new transaction, even if it was only a minimally experienced and greatly feared anger. Neither guilt nor anxiety need be induced; they must only be discovered, amplified, and then transformed.

Furthermore, the order of undoing the identifications and projections is implied by this conception of a quick-circuiting process. The final stage of faulty identification and projection, or the preliminary phase the person has come back to and stopped at, is what is central in the present and must be confronted. First to be achieved is awareness of and transformation of the effort to fuse desires; when progress has been made in this respect, attention can center on guilt and self-hatred; later anger becomes figural and still later, anxiety. The slowing-down process moves backwards, from the later phases to the earlier ones. But before I proceed to elaborate on the undoing of faulty projections and identifications, I want to make a general statement that differentiates self as agent from self as agency.

Chapter 6

Self as Agent, Self as Agency: A General Statement

In *all* social relationships persons are self-regulating in two distinct senses: 1) they organize their various desires in respect to each other so that they *assert* in their actions as much of their complexity as possible; and 2) they organize their desires in order to take into account others in the relationship; that is, they *accommodate* so that their actions connect them with others as complexly as possible. Individuals are constantly balancing self-assertion with social accommodation, aiming to satisfy self and other at the same time. I take this as a matter of fact, not as some ideal that persons are striving to reach, and I have argued the matter in *Psychoanalysis: Radical and Conservative* and in *Getting Even: The Equalizing Law of Relationship.*[1]

In *mature, psychologically healthy* social relationships, the self-regulating processes of a person clarify, organize, and express the distinctive, separate, current desires of the self and the needs and demands of others in the relationship as well. The person searches for, discovers, modulates, and asserts his or her active desires. These are seen as the person's own unique desires and in their assertion the person construes self as agent. "It is I who am doing this in order to satisfy my desires." Simultaneously, the person searches for, discovers, and in the shaping of actions tries to accommodate to the true needs and demands of others in the relationship. Here again the person construes self as agent; the accommodation to the others is controlled by the separate, autonomous intention to satisfy one's own desires while also satisfying the needs and demands of the others. These conditions are characteristic of all participants in a healthy social relationship, and a community of agents is the result.

In social relationships that involve the *delusion of fusion*, the self-regulating processes of the person mix, confound, organize disjunctively, and fuse the current desires of the self and the needs and demands of others in the relationship. The person mixes together and obscures his or her own desires and the needs and demands of the others. The result is that what is asserted in action is a combination of vaguely perceived own desires and what are imagined — that is, projected — as being the others' needs and demands, not anything solicited and received from the others. The person construes self not as agent but as agency, the relatively nonresponsible instrument of own desires (which are experienced as forcing their way into the person's actions) and of the needs and demands of others (which the person believes have been thrust upon him or her). In the assertive aspects of action, self and other are fused within the person so that the person cannot know if he or she is satisfying own needs or others' needs. Simultaneously, as the person accommodates to others — shapes own actions to account to the needs and demands of others as these are imagined — the person is unclear whether he or she is accounting to the true needs and demands of the others or merely to desires projected onto others.

A major difference between healthy relationships and those based on the delusion of fusion is the intensity, or force, of the influence exerted by the participants. In healthy relationships, each participant responsibly asserts and accommodates with minimal coercion and manipulation. It is sufficient influence to openly discover one's own desires and others' needs and demands and to share these discoveries in a mutually communicative fashion. In distorted, confluent relationships, each participant is actively obscuring his or her own responsibility while asserting and "accommodating" with strong coercion and manipulation. The coercion and manipulation may be intentional, or they may be acted out yet not experienced, that is, may be an expression of unconscious forces.

The person believes that it is necessary to presume that own and others' desires are similar or complementary, or to insist that distinctive strong differences between self and others in this regard be disallowed, denied, or avoided. The coercive, manipulative facets of the relationship appear differently according to who are presumed superiors and subordinates, but the intense influences move in both directions. In an identification with an aggressor, the inferior person acts to control the superior as well as to submit; and in projection upon a primed vulnerable other, the superior person is heavily influenced by the subordinate as well as apparently dominant.

These strong coercive and manipulative factors create divisiveness *within* participants as well as *between* them. What the identifying person has taken in from the other in the identification process is hard to assimilate. The conflict between persons has been made into an internal confict. The molested child fights internally about which desires he or she can safely allow into action without again being overwhelmed by the other and without feeling guilty from what has been introjected from the molester. The projecting person must mobilize himself or herself to control the other, efforts which divert from direct satisfaction of the original desire. The child molester, because he or she feels guilty or is afraid of being exposed, is unable to obtain deep, emotionally rich and unconflicted sexual pleasure in those encounters that have frightened the child and brought about identification with the aggressor. The lack of full satisfaction causes insatiability of desires, restlessness, discontent, edginess, and alienation.

Persons who have strong forces pulling them away from direct satisfaction of their desires are prone to becoming agencies. Agents, because they are less internally conflicted as well as less socially abrasive, are more fully alive.

Chapter 7

Cautions on Taking Psychological Ideas into a Social Action Arena

I now turn from theory toward psychological suggestions and ideas that may usefully inform social action. In doing so, while I want these suggestions and ideas to be important and helpful, I am keenly concerned to keep it clear that in social action the psychological issues are seldom primary. Social efforts are carried out in groups and collectivities under the rubrics of political organizing, community organizing, trade union activities, the work of managerial associations, and cooperative struggles within bureaucracies. Social action is *social* action, not psychological action. Organizing workers or citizens or fellow executives is not group therapy,

I believe these obvious statements merit articulation because from my reading of socially committed mental health activists and my own experience, two differing strategies for using psychological ideas to strengthen social action seem to have been followed and to have demonstrated their limitations. One of these lines of action, followed over an extended period of time, has put psychological issues and leaders in the foreground and has led to the community mental health movement. This movement, like the public health and progressive education movements, has attempted to directly make people into better human beings, into agents, by psychotherapeutic services, therapeutic communities, and the introduction of ideas about mental health into schools and other small social institutions. Like these other movements, the community mental health movement has been quite dependent upon the powers of the existing society — for legitimation, for financing, and for social respectability — and has therefore been limited in the structural social change it even intends to produce.

Primary exemplars of leaders who employed this strategy are the social democrat Alfred Adler,[1] who had much to do with the rise of the child guidance field and efforts to reform child rearing through education, and Wilhelm Reich,[2] who for a time put his ideas and energies into the service of left-wing political groups, setting up mental hygiene clinics for workers and suggesting strategies for political mobilization of German youth that were primarily psychological in nature, this in the early 1930s. Adler and Reich were towering figures, ambitious to be leaders, exceedingly talented and widely recognized, and their very strengths caused them to place the psychological first in actions aimed at social change. But while social struggle needs to incorporate the insights and techniques of the psychological world to be as effective as it can be, I have come to believe that to work thoroughly and well, dealing primarily with psychological functions requires that social conditions have changed first. A social climate that encourages experiencing and sharing intense social emotions is needed before any critical mass of individuals will risk openly attending to very vulnerable sides of themselves. I discuss such a social climate later in this essay,

The clinics started by Reich and Adler and the social services developed inside trade unions by Bertha Reynolds[3] were intended for anyone in the population who had personal problems and was willing to try a course of psychotherapy or counseling. Reich aimed to reach working class individuals, Adler was successful with parents who were socially and politically progressive, and Reynolds reached out to trade unionists. A second strategy for the integration of the psychological into social action was foreshadowed by their attention to persons who represented potential political allies in radical social action. This strategy is to provide psychotherapeutic and social support services for people engaged in social action. There are now, for example, several centers in the world that cater to individuals scarred by torture when they were political prisoners. William Beardslee[4] has suggested that room be made in social-action movements for meeting the personal needs of activists during their engagement in social struggle. Friends are killed or die from natural causes, marriages are heavily strained, unfinished business from childhood cannot be bracketed forever. Activists have personal as well as social lives, and their personal needs require sophisticated attention. As the military has psychological services to deal with war neuroses, so should there be therapies and other support services available to political and community actors, including leaders as well as citizens brought into action. This second strategy for using psychological ideas has much to commend it — as I know from my own experience in the early 1970s in several political movements — and I would hope that any social movement that persists over time and organizes large numbers of people would incorporate psychotherapeutic and support services, not as luxury, but as a central offering of basic welfare provisions. Such services need not lead to the fostering of unwholesome dependence or political demobilization, as some political activists fear. This is a fruitful direction for the practical implementation of psychological insights in social action, though in my experience it is limited in the number of people it can serve and is therefore somewhat inefficient.

The psychological considerations I will primarily put forth, however, have a different supportive role, much like musical accompaniment in a motion picture. The story and characters are foremost in a movie, while the music may set the mood, enlarge the story, identify characters, alert the viewer to trouble coming, let us know that help is on its way, help us be solemn, or control our attention for other purposes. In this essay, some psychological matters may on occasion rise to more prominence, more like the music in an opera than in a motion picture, but seldom, in the purpose to which I have held psychology here, is it to be considered as sufficient unto itself. My aim is to improve the effectiveness of political and community organizing by introducing relevant psychological insights into these ongoing endeavors.

I can say this another way. Insofar as political organizing, trade union work, and the like engage people in social relationships, they touch upon motivations, resistances, and social-emotional capacities and habits. Every political organizer carries a psychological theory, a conception of human functioning, that guides the organizing process. Too often in the past, the theories that have been applied have been commonsensical in the worst sense: naive and narrow. The costs to the organizing effort have seldom been tallied, but in my experience over the years — as an activist in the civil rights, antiwar, educational, and feminist movements and in developing organizations for the support of progressive groups — these costs have been considerable. People whose needs are ignored may strive mightily to continue in collective effort, but they invariably burn out, become cynical, feel defeated, and utilize poor methods of expressing angry feelings, and gradually they cause the collective effort to become lifeless. I hope that in the struggle before us to create a just world of free and equal peoples throughout the earth, we can use psychological sophistication and be much more effective than we have been till now.

Chapter 8

The Angry Weak and
the Angry Powerful

"We have been asked, 'How do you cope with the apathy in this country?' We are stunned by the question and must reply, 'You must be hanging out with the wrong people.' "

Holly Near and Ronnie Gilbert[1]

When political organizing is being discussed, it is common for someone to remark that most ordinary citizens are rather apathetic, that there is abroad a strangely quiet acceptance of a burdensome fate. This tendency — of many peasants who support the dictators who oppress them, of the unemployed who believe they are the ones responsible for doing something about their unemployment even when they do not hold themselves at fault for this unemployment, of workers who vote for right-wing political candidates when these candidates are openly scornful of working people and their efforts to organize on their own behalf — is a confusing tendency, one that doesn't make a great deal of sense. At the least, it violates ordinary common sense that people should admire and support the very persons who are main instruments of practices that hurt them.

Alan Buss has commented that this tendency among the proletariat has been a major problem for the theory and practice of Marxists:

"Thus, the failure of orthodox Marxism was due to its ignoring the psychological importance of bourgeois ideology in reducing the revolutionary potential of the proletariat. What was needed now was a social psychological theory to explain the hidden, covert, or subjective forms of domination that had emerged. In other words, overt repression and exploitation had been replaced by more subtle mechanisms of psychological control brought about by the internalization of capitalist irrationality. The exploited now accepted the exploiters and their own exploitation. What was required was theoretical analysis, and an even more powerful and radical critique than Marxism was able to provide."[2]

Of course, those who are burdened by vicious social policies and practices do experience profound, often intolerable rage, but it is hard for them to focus it. For example, Schlozman and Verba, in their studies of the unemployed reported in *Injury to Insult*,[3] remark that there is a good deal of anger in the unemployed but there is no focal explanation of general unemployment to mobilize and concentrate that anger so as to make it useful in social and political confrontation. On the same subject, John Garraty has written:

"The Polish autobiographies revealed still another aspect of the political passivity of the jobless. Lazarsfeld and a Polish sociologist studied them carefully; they remarked on the 'inert' aggressiveness displayed in their accounts. The authors frequently manifested their rage and a desire for revenge but often directed these feelings at their fellow sufferers, i.e., at themselves."[4]

In another context, the civil rights movements of the 1960s gathered up the anger that blacks had personally internalized or alternatively directed at their fellow blacks, and turned that anger against racists and those who defended racist practices. As the civil rights leaders mobilized and organized in the ghettos and small black communities in the South, the crime rates of blacks venting their antagonisms upon each other diminished directly and sharply. Frantz Fanon[5] described the same phenomenon in Algeria when the uprising against the colonizing French took hold. However, these socially useful translations of anger from self-destruction to the creating of positive structural changes are the exceptions. Usually, the anger is reflected back upon the self by those who are oppressed.

I interpret the more usual happenings by placing them in the context of the delusion of fusion. When such major disrupting problems confront a society that the social scene is confusing and overwhelming to the citizens, the trend to fusion takes hold in the psyches of those most immediately affected by the crisis — the victims and, also, society's leaders. Identification with the aggressor and projection upon a primed vulnerable other become widespread. When unemployed people or abused children or oppressed ethnic minorities or battered wives are in the presence of those who dominate them, or when they are approached by political organizers or clinicians who wish them to confront those who are dominating them, they identify with the aggressor, become passive, self-negating, guilt-ridden, wishful of submergence into the desires of their tormentors. This is a lack of outrage that surprises observers. It is a *committed passivity*, a holding in check that derives from great fear of the destructive urges that arise in relationships involving the aggressor. Because these destructive urges occasionally break through, we have conflicting pictures of an angry *and* apathetic citizenry.

When the unemployed and others in their oppressed position are neither in the company of those who tyrannize them nor in a situation in which they can expect to have to deal directly with their exploiters, they are likely to live out the other side of the equation, to project upon a primed vulnerable other. The classic stereotype of this is the working man who cannot vividly oppose his employer for fear of losing his job, who gets drunk and comes home to beat his wife and children; but there are also many milder versions. Whenever the oppressed mistreat their spouses, children, neighbors, elders, and others who cross their paths and who are in the role of weaker in the relation, they are projecting this way. In a broader context, we see oppressed persons and whole groups display racism, sexism, and ethnocentrism in dealing with others among the downtrodden. They do so precisely because they act under the delusion of fusion and, as is always the case to some extent, identification with the powerful aggressor is paired with projection upon primed, vulnerable, weaker others.

When we are faced in our social and political endeavors with lack of outrage where outrage would be expected and appropriate, we do well to look for the committed passivity that is a sign of identification with the aggressor. This may appear as protection of the aggressor by the weak, too ready an assumption of helplessness, avoidance of the matter of domination entirely, or some attack upon the persons who diagnose the need for political action. And where we see these or other indications of committed passivity, we will usually also find exaggerated hostility with a displaced quality signifying that there is projection upon a primed vulnerable other. *We can thus make ourselves aware that rage is indeed present and that it is misdirected but, like all rage, potentially available for productive use,* I believe this insight to be a practical contribution from theoretical psychological study. Although it is a long way from such an insight to the gathered and energized use of anger in social struggle, as political activists we will get assurance from observing a known process that we are aware of; and observing it, we can use our awareness to help those going through the delusion of fusion become aware themselves of their identifications and projections.

When driven by the urge to fuse, persons tend to be submissive to the powerful, tyrannical to the weak. When political organizers try to mobilize victims such as the unemployed to oppose the powerful who are the instruments of an exploitative system, they face two particular problems. First, they must be wary of themselves being introjected improperly when they act to undo faulty identifications. Second, they must beware of fostering projections that are also faulty.

If the organizers are too powerful or persuasive themselves, they may win followers among the weak by creating new versions of the delusion of fusion. The weak may simply shift their identification from the old superiors and introject the political organizers. They will not grow into selves as agents, but will transfer from being tools of the status quo to being agencies of the political movement. Some of the political movements of the 1960s, such as the Student Nonviolent Coordinating Committee (SNCC), recognized this and tried to prevent any one leader from becoming too powerful. The Green Party in West Germany in the 1980s seems to have tried this also. Whether the specific solutions of these groups were successful or not — there has been disagreement about this — the concept of not allowing a leader to become so powerful that a new identification with the aggressor develops, focused now on the political leader, is a valid idea. In left-wing circles the problem is known by the phrase "cult of personality," which applied clearly to identifications with Stalin and Mao Zedong.

Preventing identification with the aggressor from appearing within a democratizing political movement does not mean preventing identifications. As Freud[6] showed, identification is basic to group cohesion. Healthy identifications enable the group members to grow and develop in their individuality while merging with significant others. It is possible to act as agent and be individualistic (as Ellen M. Wood has argued in *Mind and Politics*[7] in distinguishing bourgeois and socialist individualism), and still be submerged within a political group. The coherence of individual effort and collective striving is what democratic practice is about, so that political groups that promote dialogue, communication, and reflection among their members, groups that foster challenges within and questioning of group goals, also act to encourage healthy forms of identification.

An important need for political activists confronting the delusion of fusion, then, is to prevent or attend to new tendencies to identify with any aggressor and to transform such identifications, if they do start to develop, into healthy identifications with a democratic group in which all members are striving to become agents rather than agencies. Another need is to avoid projections upon primed vulnerable others and to translate any such projections that do exist into empathy, including empathy with one's enemies. The victims of exploitation must not be led to victimize their oppressors, to simply shift self-blame to blame of the powerful, to live out the process of projection upon a primed vulnerable other by making the powerful into vulnerable others.

Organizers who dehumanize oppressors fail to address the problem of the delusion of fusion. In the late nineteenth century and early twentieth century cartoonists and political agitators tended to do just that. The rich and powerful owners of industry, managers, and superintendents and foremen were portrayed as fat cats, as greedy, self-serving, ugly, monstrous figures. There was a certain amount of truthful portrayal in those cartoons and speeches, since these powerful individuals had dehumanized themselves in becoming self as agency of the capitalist system, and it is wrong just to "understand" people who hurt others and not hold them responsible for their actions. I in no way wish to diminish critical appraisal of harming persons. But those who dehumanized the powerful overlooked the factor of *identification*, which made the victims see themselves in the powerful persons, and so the weak, paradoxically, came forth to defend rather than attack the powerful; and the same dehumanizers overlooked the factor of *projection*, whereby the weak wish to live out their rage safely against vulnerable others, not fearfully against strong others.

The alternative to projection upon a primed vulnerable other is empathic assessment of others in their strengths and weaknesses so that realistic actions can be instituted and cooperative goals achieved. Wilhelm Reich[8] encouraged strikers to imagine when the police were harassing them that the policeman they saw was home in bed with his lover or walking around in his underwear. Reich was suggesting that in the midst of intense confrontations we do well to humanize those we are encountering. We will not project our own rage into them, nor are we likely to evoke their excessive violence, if we are forceful but realistic.

But because I have attended only to the victims in the hurtful situation, I have addressed only part of the story, of anger, the part in which the weak redirect their rage against still weaker others — or against themselves, that is, against their bodies in the form of alcoholism, headaches, stomach troubles, and so forth. Also to be observed and reckoned with are the strong members of the relationship, those who are administering the events that lead to the harm and hurt.

If little outrage organized directly against the structural bases of their suffering is seen among the victims in a hurtful circumstance, much anger and readiness to rage against the weaker and against their rivals is to be found among tyrannical persons. This seems strange because they are the persons who presumably gain advantages from their situation or at least maintain their privileged position.   On the other hand, given the frequency of angry outbursts among tyrannical leaders, their relentless searching for and suppression of dissent and resistance, their affinity for the use of violent force, their criticism of and contempt for their followers, and their facility in intimidation, I also find it remarkable that relatively little is said in the technical psychological literature and in the writings of political organizers about this anger.   It is reactionary leaders in political circles, men and women who are quite well off materially, who fuss and fume about taxes being burdensome, welfare overwhelmed with fraud, young people being too pleasure-oriented, enemies from without threatening us with imminent destruction of all we hold dear, labor unions being dangerous and divisive.   There seem to be no end of matters large and small that arouse the negative, angry feelings of those who are powerful.   And it is important, I am convinced, that the rage of oppressors be observed and studied in and of itself.   We must look closely at that anger and not be too readily distracted by its justifications, rationales, effects, or purposes.   For when we do look closely, we will realize there is much to be observed.

Why is this common rage of the oppressors overlooked or discounted when the misdirected and rebellious anger of the weak has been carefully and repeatedly diagnosed?   A first reason we attend less to the anger of the tyrant is that it tends to be controlled rage rather than helpless rage, giving thereby an appearance of rationality.   While the weak feel overwhelmed by their anger and react to it as a force acting upon them as much as within them or for them, the powerful insist upon their self-control even in the matter of strong emotions.   The powerful do not recognize that their anger is problematic for them because if they did, they would have to accept that they do not fully command their social-emotional lives. Not only do they strongly avoid any internal perception that their anger has underlying meanings; they also shield themselves so that others do not make diagnoses.   Other people who understand character armor will in fact readily see the tension and frozenness associated with controlled rage — by looking at the stiffness of body posture, the steely-eyed, sternly set face, the jerky body loco-motions, or the very aggressive physical games played. But most people do not have this kind of insight.

Further obscuring of the anger of oppressors is facilitated by the merging of personal rage and the instruments of the social institu-tion or social system. The powerful can wield the impressive influ-ence allocated to the system: workers can be fired for union orga-nizing; soldiers can be tried for insubordination; children can be punished by their parents or teachers for disobedience; junior staff members can be hassled by superiors around the rules or practices of the organization. With the backing of most elements of the so-cial system, including many of the isolated weaker person's peers, tyrants can vent their rage and be found threatening but not be as-sessed as themselves having personal trouble dealing with their anger.

But the main reason that significantly less attention is directed at the angry feelings of the powerful is that they successfully project so much of their rage. Up to a point, people in power roles experi-ence and express their anger, and they produce results as a conse-quence. Then, when angry feelings pass beyond the level at which the self-control and system supports will allow acceptable mastery, the powerful do not feel overwhelmed; that is to say, they do not process in their direct awareness the devastating internal feeling of helplessness and its partner, depression. Instead, they project their intense rage by producing helpless rage in the weak or by shifting attention to that rage. Their psychic resolution is less intrapsychic, as in themselves feeling helpless and depressed, and more social-psychological, as in doing that which provokes others yet keeps them helpless in the relationship and attending to this rage of those they have provoked. Projection — more than identification — di-verts from the awareness of an inner difficulty.

Finally, commentators fail to reckon adequately with the anger of the powerful because anger is the social emotion tied to con-frontation with obstacles, and the deep assumption holds and guides commentators to believe that oppressors are well-off and meet only occasional threats of frustration when rebelliousness breaks out. Since the social system is assumed to be paying off to the powerful, little ground for them to be discontented is obvious. Partisans and other observers alike, then, tend naively to assume that of course the strong are relatively happy, so that their anger could not possibly be derived from accumulated unmet needs, which it emphatically is.

Here we need only remember that the powerful are fused with the weak, dependent on narrowly defined forms of social relations, in short, living as agencies rather than as agents. This is the source of the rage in the oppressor, and it is little wonder that there is so much of that rage and so considerable an amount of psychic energy bound up in controlling that rage. Despite appearances associated with material wealth and social perquisites, the powerful are unfulfilled as persons and are consequently very angry. Thorstein Veblen[9] described this fact many years ago. *It is vital that we make ourselves aware that the rage of the powerful, like that of the weak, is indeed present, misdirected, and potentially available for productive use.* I believe this to be a second practical contribution from theoretical study.

Chapter 9

Intense Social Emotions Are Key

Identification with the aggressor and projection upon a primed vulnerable other are psychological tactics adopted in dealing with relationships characterized by the appearance of overwhelming social emotions. The unfolding of the delusion of fusion in a person's life is a culmination of these tactics that are meant to resolve or somehow contain these intense social emotions, which spiral upward and come to dominate interpersonal activities. I am referring here to great anxiety; awesome rage, whether a person's face is flushed crimson or drained pale; tormenting guilt; powerful self-hate and self-contempt; deep antagonism toward another person or persons; and the despair underlying a full delusion of fusion. These emotions come about in the deranged social relations of oppressors and their victims. And both the intensity of the emotions and the fact that they are *social* emotions, feelings bound up with specific happenings, must be reckoned with in undoing the resultant delusion of fusion, or confluence, among these people.

Here a major challenge confronts political organizers as it does also psychotherapists: unlinking destructive fusions entails the revival and reworking of these painfully strong and frightening emotions. In changing, the weak or the strong person must necessarily reawaken and re-experience the social emotions themselves, and *experiencing this time* must do something different in behavior and in the social relation than was done earlier.

The profound resistance to change characteristic of persons in oppressor-oppressed relations comes from a dim sense of the intensity involved in this process and their reluctance to have these awful emotions once again spread over their being. Perls et al. develop this point in an analysis comparable to that which guides my argument. They are discussing introjection, an important component of identification with the aggressor:

> "When one looks upon the introject as an item of 'unfinished business,' its genesis is readily traced to a situation of interrupted excitement. Every introject is the precipitate of a conflict given up before it was resolved. One of the contestants — usually an impulse to act in a given manner — has left the field; replacing it, so as to constitute some kind of integration (though a false and inorganic one) is the *corresponding wish of the coercing authority.* The self has been conquered. In giving up, it settles for a secondary integrity — a means of surviving, though beaten — by *identification with the conqueror and turning against itself.* It takes over the coercer's role by conquering itself, retroflecting the hostility previously directed outward against the coercer. Here, although actually defeated, the victim is encouraged by the victorious coercer to perpetuate his defeat by forever rejoicing in the deluded notion that *he* was the victor!

> "Though admittedly unpleasant, there is no other way to discover what in you is not part of yourself except by remobilizing disgust and the accompanying urge to reject. . . .

> "Disgust is a *natural barrier* possessed by every healthy organism. It is a defense against taking into the organism what does not belong there — what is indigestible or foreign to its nature . . . . Full remobilization of disgust for what *is* disgusting calls a halt to further introjecting, but it does not forthwith cause to be spewed forth what has already been introjected . . . . This takes time and a transitional period of more or less frequent or chronic nausea."[1]

Feelings of disgust and nausea are indeed a part of re-experiencing and casting out from one's psyche elements that have been improperly taken in and acted upon as if they were truly of one's nature, and so it is important for people trying to help others undo the delusion of fusion to be sensitive to these feelings. Instead, how often we hear the phrase "I am sick and tired of . . . ," for instance, without listening closely and facilitating the experience and expression of sickness contained in the remark — not just the words, but the nausea and bitterness that give bodily-emotional stuff to those words. Although we hear the phrase frequently, we seldom act in such a way that we *hold psychologically* the person asserting it so as to enable the feeling behind the words to surface and be reworked. We are inattentive to the psychological needs of the individual, and in our oversight we inhibit the undoing of faulty identifications.

Selma Fraiberg has remarked upon how those who were abused as children, who are prone to identification with the aggressor, need to re-experience intense feelings. In a report on a round table on *Maternal Attachment and Mothering Disorders* is recorded:

> "Professor Fraiberg . . . said that although nearly all her [abusive] parents remembered actual abuse in their childhood in stunning and chilling detail, they did not remember the affect of the experience, i.e., being abused and injured. If they were only able to help the parents reach the point of saying 'Oh, God, how I hated him when he would get that strap and lay me out and begin to beat on me. Oh, how I hated him!' When her group helped their parents remember the anxiety and the sense of terror that had come over them with the abuse of a powerful parent, they could demonstrate the parents' behavior toward their own children changed. Thus, she concluded, changes did not occur with just the memory of what happened, but with the actual re-experiencing of the terrifying feelings involved."[2]

In the Chinese revolutionary movement in the first half of this century there were "speak bitterness" sessions in which women relived their oppression by men and peasants recaptured their antagonisms toward landlords. These sessions demonstrated ways to overcome self-negation. They did not rely upon trained psychotherapists, but they were based on what I would consider sound therapeutic principles. Central to these activities was a revival in the here and now of old situations, peasants confronting directly landlords who had abused them, wives facing their dominating husbands and asserting their pain and their demands for new, more equal relationships. In these encounters old patterns in the relationships were often transformed; the confrontation enabled oppressed and oppressor alike to come into a new way of dealing with themselves and with each other, the oppressed asserting themselves openly, the oppressors acting more humbly.

Jack Belden, in *China Shakes the World*,[3] illustrates this point with "Gold Flower's Story." Belden interviewed a woman named

Kinhua, or Gold Flower, for eight to ten hours a day over a week's time and then set out to "tell her story just as she told it to me in a flood of bitter tears, angry imprecations and emotional outbursts of despair, frustration and hope." First came the story of her love at fifteen for Lipao, a boy she knew she could not marry, a story of desire held back, of adolescent fantasy and dreams, of social correctness and personal denial. On the eve of her wedding to an older man she hanged herself, only to be rescued and brought back to life by her parents. And she was married the next day to a man twenty years older than she, a man ugly and hateful.

On her wedding night, because she resisted, her husband raped her. For three years her husband and other members of the family beat her and mistreated her in other ways, even while she acquiesced and tried to please. Then her husband went off to a city to become a merchant. He left her behind in the control of his family, and life for Gold Flower did not improve.

Next, a unit of the 8th Route Army entered Gold Flower's village and set about organizing a Women's Association to work toward equality of women and men. A friend of hers, Dark Jade, was elected to leadership in the Women's Association and came secretly to meet with Gold Flower. "We must release ourselves from the domination of men," Dark Jade told her. "But we cannot do it individually, we must all stand together and release ourselves as a unit." Soon Gold Flower shared with Dark Jade and another friend an account of her suffering. "The speaking aloud of what had been going round and round in her mind for so long brought a rush of feeling such as she had not experienced since the days she had known Lipao."

The women's group then came to her father-in-law and Dark Jade told him, "Our investigation department has found out that you are treating your daughter-in-law badly." He responded, "Go away! Get out!" Dark Jade began to request that he change his ways. He refused and again ordered the women to leave. The group of women, who had clubs and ropes, then bound him and took him away to the Women's Association. As they were doing this, Gold Flower experienced fear and called out to the women not to hurt her "dear father."

He was held a prisoner for two days, and then, on the third, there was a general meeting of all the women in the village, who were to decide what to do with him. After a cadre from the district spoke eloquently about the plight of women and Dark Jade spoke, a bit more clumsily, about life in the village for women, Gold Flower's father-in-law was brought before the women and asked to tell of his bad treatment of Gold Flower. "I have done nothing," he said, trying to bluff his innocence; but Gold Flower was persuaded to denounce him and cite the details of her mistreatment. Intimidated, the father-in-law confessed his sins and vowed not to repeat them.

Gold Flower experienced now not only her suffering but hope as well. She became a leader, helping other women to reacquaint themselves with their pain and to challenge those who had dominated them. She worked to help young couples marry freely and for love, as she had not been able to do. She wandered in the fields at harvest time, matching boys and girls, encouraging them, arranging meetings in the homes of friends so that resisting parents would not interfere. But after a time, and it was a happy period for Gold Flower, she realized that not until she settled affairs with her own husband would she be really free.

She lured her husband home. On his return, her father-in-law complained to his son and told of his travails and of Gold Flower's new attitudes and behavior. That night she fought verbally with her husband about their whole life together, determined even to die rather than give in to any more brutality from him. They argued deep into the night and fell asleep exhausted, without making love. The next morning Gold Flower sought help from the Women's Association. Dark Jade and fifteen other women went to Gold Flower's home. They told her husband that he would speak of his treatment of Gold Flower or he would taste their fists. He tried to shrug them off. They tied him with ropes and took him and locked him in a room of the Women's Association. At a meeting the next day, to which Gold Flower came, the other women urged him to confess to mistreating her, and when he refused, they beat him. Under their blows he finally confessed to mistreating Gold Flower and promised never to do so again. Then he was allowed to go home, and Gold Flower was instructed to prepare food for him and take care of him.

Although her husband appeared chastened, that night when they were alone, he reasserted his dominance. They fought again. Then, tired from all the events, she allowed him to make love to her, but this served only to bring to her awareness the depth of her hatred for him. The next day she vented her rage upon him; he responded with attempts to beat her. She ran back to the Women's Association, the women of the village were summoned by calls through a megaphone and came prepared to tie him up again. With Gold Flower in the lead, forty and more of the women in the village ran to find him, but he had already fled. He was forever after that out of her life.

This impressive story that Jack Belden has recorded is one that was repeated many, many times in the Chinese Revolution. Central to this and the other tales is a re-experiencing of rage, fear, anxiety, and a confusing love and compassion for one's tormentors that always seems to accompany identification with the aggressor. Gold Flower not only denounced her father-in-law and husband. As one learns from Belden's full recounting of her story, she protected both of them as well. She alternated between attacking and denouncing them and lovingly trying to bring them into new ways. We know this seeming paradox well in respect to abused wives throughout the world. The reowning of their loving feelings toward their abusive mates is never easy, never simply undertaken, yet without the vividness it brings, whatever changes these women need to make in their lives cannot usually be accomplished. This emotional fullness of hate, compassion, and love side by side is typical for people with faulty identifications they want to resolve.

There is even more to be dealt with in the way of social emotions for people undoing the delusion of fusion, since there are harmful projections as well as identifications to be mastered. Although the clinical literature is less specific in describing the feelings that come up in the course of correcting faulty projections, the clues are there in the psychopathologies of people who make much use of this manner of avoiding their own lives. Centrally, as persons undo their projections, or "take them back" or "reown" them — as they acknowledge parts of themselves they have attributed to others — they will re-experience in profoundly upsetting ways feelings of suspicion, distrust, and lack of safety that the process of projecting was mitigating. Such persons will no longer say, "They deserve my suspicion and mistrust, but instead will acknowledge, "I am suspicious and mistrusting in my insecurity."

Along the way to this kind of recognition, there may even be a transfer of these social emotions from enemies to friends, that is, from members of one's outgroup to members of one's ingroup. Feeling that friends are not to be trusted, that one's familiar environment is an unsafe place, that those who profess their love and admiration cannot love one, is deeply disturbing, frequently promoting the sense of the uncanny. It is eerie and disorienting to distrust just those people one has been relying upon as caring, dependable friends. Yet when such affects exist, they must be lived out if faulty projections are to be undone. This is true even though the fact that they must be engaged poses serious challenges to social and political organizations dedicated to fundamental social change. For example, as Gayle Graham Yates has noted:

> "Susan Brownmiller writes of the enemy within in which she places the blame for women's incapacity on their own suspicion and distrust of each other and themselves."[4]

The delusion of fusion exists only in the context of social relationships and so can be rectified only in social relationships. Beyond this, mastering an intense social emotion, as must be done repeatedly in undoing the faulty identifications and projections that lead to this delusion, is better done when the person experiencing the feeling is with others. Whether the individual's companions share the same emotion and by this commonality stimulate its revival and make it less awesome, or are just available to protect the individual from living out extreme guilt, self-hatred, rage, or some other difficult emotion in a destructive and self-limiting way, they can make possible the bearing of unpleasant affect as part of the process of harnessing the emotion for new behavior.[5]

Although sharing anger may amplify the tendency for strong rage to become helpless rage, it may equally well lead to productive collective action in which the anger is directed inward actual frustrating or oppressive restraints. Sharing guilt, similarly, may lead to fundamentalist, punitive religion, but it may also lead to a sense of community responsibility and forgiveness, forgiveness of self as well as of others. Projected self-hatred in the form of outgroup hatred — e.g., racism, sexism, ethnocentrism, antiprogressivism — is a group-sustained process and can be undone when shared group norms are changed. Plain old self-hatred and self-contempt can be alleviated, once known openly and collectively, by the discovery that many others feel exactly the same way, as we witnessed in women's consciousness-raising groups when their attitudes toward their bodies were opened to the light of day. Each person in turn can be nauseous, suspicious, or panicky if secure in a collectivity which tolerates intense emotional life and devotes collective wisdom and energy to enabling the revival and reworking of traumatic past experiences.

Political and social movements in our society, possibly emulating bureaucratic norms, have been remarkably sterile in respect to finding ways to allow and work with the intense social emotions that appear in activities promoting social change. As William Beardslee has observed, activists in the civil rights movement sang together when they felt vulnerable, even created group singing rituals for that purpose, but they did not cooperate as well in mourning their defeats or dealing with the deaths of their fellows. They failed here to integrate the effects of social struggle on their private lives; like the system they opposed, they left individuals to their own devices. Beardslee presents the ideas of Reverend Caldwell, a movement organizer, on this subject:

> "In many people's lives in the Movement, there came a time when support was needed, and in some cases there was no support. To be more specific, while a person was trying to understand himself, maybe he turned to his

childhood for support, to make himself strong enough to deal with what was happening to him. Maybe he didn't find it there. He needed somebody to help him put it together, but there was no reinforcement from the predominant society or his family. A person in the Movement during those times was most likely just out of adolescence, suffering from the wounds that adolescence leaves. Maybe something in the Movement was not going fast enough for him or maybe his livelihood was threatened. He had a crisis because he didn't have the resources or the reassurance that he needed. If he was not able to deal with that particular crisis, it had a domino effect and shattered his image of himself. Many people left the Movement because of that.

"A crisis also came in many young guys' lives in the Movement when they felt that all they had done was in vain. . . . My analysis of it is that they weren't able to regroup and devise new ways of living at that point. I advised people to find a way to take care of themselves while there was still a chance."[6]

Engagement with deep psychological issues in the process of political action is neither a frill nor a luxury, neither digressive nor diversionary. I do not believe that social change is to be achieved by the reconstitution of character among all citizens via therapeutic (or religious) endeavors – changing people one by one, or changing families and the rearing of children. I am convinced, however, that efforts to achieve political change of any substance arouse basic problematic personality tendencies, such as tendencies to introject faultily, project unsoundly, and retroflect what deserves to be directed outward, and their arousal entails intense emotional experiences. These tendencies and some of the emotions they bring up serve as defenses against or resistances to social change, which suggests that change can occur only if the tendencies are acknowledged and methods are created for attending to them.

Beardslee describes the positive side of social actions that incorporate the undoing of the delusion of fusion as experienced particularly by black activists in the civil rights movement:

"A . . . major theme in the people's descriptions of what sustained them is a new consciousness of their own worth and of their power to bring about change. The whole of the segregationist culture had as its goal the passivity and acquiescence of Blacks: any action might threaten the status quo. Involvement in the Movement was involvement in action, action which broke the pattern of ingrained acquiescence and acceptance. There was a great joy and sense of accomplishment in this. Taking action, not being passive, was the visible expression of this new consciousness. Moreover, all of the workers had become angry, many enraged, by their own humiliation and oppression. . . . Taking part in the Movement was a positive way of dealing with this anger and rage. . . .

"What is remarkable about the workers is that they were not overwhelmed by their rage and they did not lash out blindly. Just as the capacity to grieve and keep working was a necessity for the workers, so was the capacity to be angry and feel outrage, and at the same time put those feelings into action toward the goals of the Movement.

"In reading over the histories, it is clear that the historians [activists] underwent inner psychological change.

"What is emphasized by the experience of the civil rights workers is the importance of relationships with others, at stages other than childhood, in enabling people to change. The intense relationships with others, which for a time superceded those even within the family and were among the most intense that the person had experienced, were a necessary part of the process of change."[7]

Recognizing that decisive political action requires and, as Beardslee so clearly indicates here, creates intense personal experiences, I would distinguish three contexts in which they will take place, each of which has a special contribution to make: 1) collective action in which there is direct contact between oppressed and oppressor or representatives of the oppressor; 2) ingroup activity of the people acting in common cause, especially activity preparing for contact with the opposition or reflecting upon contact with it at some time in the past; and 3) individually working through one's inner life as it has been affected by participation in collective action around one's role as oppressed or oppressor. Transformation of one's way of being in the world can take place in each of these contexts, but only when the transaction or introspection does not repeat the established patterns of submission and tyranny.

In the direct contact between the dominating strong and the weak, anger that once led to helpless rage and submission or to controlled rage and domination can become the anger of complex and integrated self-assertion and can become connected with true perception of the other's anxiety and defensiveness in such transactions. In these new angry encounters between persons in the weak position and those in the strong role, guilt and self-hatred may be washed away in the tides of collective support of the self-assertion. Persons may get fully in touch with their anger, find ways to use it productively rather than helplessly or in overcontrolled fashion, and begin to recognize the distinction between their own, naturally arising needs and desires and those that have been taken on for the express purpose of managing the oppressed-oppressor relation. Each person comes to his or her individuality and chooses to act as part of a group in interactions that now achieve socially defined goals happily for all. The delusion of fusion is broken.

Developments in clinical practice and theory point up the importance of lively direct contact for change in human life. From psychoanalysis comes the theme that the transference and its interpretation are central to therapeutic change. The patient lives out with the analyst, here and now, the patterns of behavior and chains of thought that distort his or her life, and this time — if the analyst interprets well — they have a different course. This time they are worked through to mutual satisfaction and then let go as they were not earlier in the patient's life. The transaction with the analyst is transformative. In existential therapy, reliance is similarly placed upon the encounter between client and therapist, not upon solving the client's problems outside the therapeutic setting, and the authentic meeting of client and therapist is deemed to be the vital factor. In family and marital therapy, it is thought to be best to have the participants actively engage each other in their typical disruptive modes so that these modes can be altered here and now, which is more likely to lead to far-reaching corrections than is restrained discussion of the disruption.

Change takes place 1) when relationships recapitulate the conditions prevailing when the delusion of fusion first developed; 2) when the recapitulations are lively, present, concrete, and importantly felt; and 3) when new and different resolutions of conflictual relations bring immediate, self-evident, surprising satisfactions. It is obvious fact, not promise, not wishful hope, when persons effectively assert and define themselves in collective engagement. To return in a vivid way to approximations or equivalents of the circumstances that produced a self-denying or self-limiting solution and resolve them differently now has often been found necessary for the alteration of habitual patterns of resignation and exploitation. Gold Flower, whose ultimate step in transformation was her confrontation with her husband, clearly illustrates this process.

From the vantage point of the oppressed, the intense social emotions that must be aroused for transformation to occur are precisely those that were conducive to the establishment of identification with the aggressor: anxiety, anger, guilt, and self-hatred. Workers become again afraid that they will lose their jobs, and their anxiety becomes intense. Medical students fear they will be failed in school if they openly oppose their instructors. Strikers know deep anger and bitterness when confronted with scabs or the police. Ethnic groups turn against each other with a hatred that is best understood as the projection of self-hatred. Followers who fight with those in authority find themselves unaccountably guilty. And those on the underside continue to exaggerate the rationality, the self-possession, the power and assuredness of those on top — another form of self-hatred. All these experiences appear and reappear and are the stuff that must be worked with in transformation of oppressive relationships.

The transformation that will follow from the successful management of these intense social emotions in encounters with the other side will *this time* result in acting as self as agent rather than instituting the emergency pattern of fusing with the other. The transformation will include changes in the ideas and beliefs of the weak about the strong — they will be more acutely aware of and attentive to the particular truth about the strong, less susceptible to myths and appearances. At the same time, those who have been dominated will arrive at new ideas and beliefs about themselves, about their strengths and possibilities, their participation in their own disempowerment, their capacity as individuals to act cooperatively in new ways. The revival of intense social emotions in contacts between the oppressed and oppressor risks a repetition of identification with the aggressor, but at the very same moment it opens the opportunity for personal growth and social change.

By simply reviewing what projection upon a primed vulnerable other does for the powerful, I can predict what the weak will learn from them in transformative encounters. Take, for example, the common tendency, known from Hitler and Stalin through Reagan, for leaders to try to get common folk to focus on an enemy out-group rather than on the current internal problems of society. The leader is projecting self-hatred and guilt in such an endeavor and is encouraging followers, through their identification with his or her leadership, to project theirs also. Even if we know of terrible childhood experiences endured by such leaders and that these may lead them to have great doubts about themselves, and indeed to feel guilt and self-hatred, we follow their projections by imagining that such confident people could not be self-hating and guilty. They don't act as we do when we feel those feelings. Of course they don't; that is what projection is about. In transformative encounters, as when Senator Joseph McCarthy was subjected to intense public scrutiny by representatives of the people of the land, the weak — here the citizens living in a fairly authoritarian social scene — discover a disparity between how real the threat is in fact and how the threat has been pronounced by the leader. The communists of the world were not about to take over the United States government as McCarthy had been screaming. Projections were being unmasked and identifications with an aggressive — indeed sadistic — leader undone in the McCarthy hearings.

The use of scabs, informers, repressive police, and the military by dominating persons oppressing the weak can be seen not only as the application of force but also as a factor promoting projections by the weak. Projection is often the result of lack of support. One projects negative qualities of one's own upon a person or group that might be expected to be supportive but is not. Here, the groups being used, after all, are themselves oppressed people. They have chosen, however, under the influence of their own identification with the aggressor, to fuse with the oppressor, to become instruments of domination, and they have forfeited in the process some degree of their own development as agents in their lives. The unaccepting oppressed — those acknowledging they are in the weak position and trying to change that — need to perceive and to take into account the faulty introjections that help make it possible for these others persons to act as agencies of the oppressor. If the struggling weak merely blame, scorn, and hate these intermediaries, they will forget that they too have identified with the aggressor in the past and indeed are presently trying to undo such identification. In thus dehumanizing scabs, informers, repressive police, and/or the military, they will disown their own tendencies to identify with the aggressor. Instead of recognizing themselves in these adversaries and thus accepting in awareness their own proclivities for submitting and identifying and so probably learning how to overcome these, they will passively discharge these proclivities via projection upon these people on the other side. As an example of how the psychological processes involved here affect actual social struggle, repressive police and military forces and scabs generate anger and hatred directly because they frustrate strikers and other agents of social change, but there is an added intensity to the anger and hatred, a sign that those being repressed are warding off consciousness of their own wishes to retreat and submit.

In direct confrontations between the weak and the strong, the weak can learn two distinct lessons concerning anger. First, they can discover that the strong are trying to turn the anger of the weak into helpless rage so that they will become ineffective in their struggle. Using whatever power they have — greater strength, the power of their authority in an institution, the force of their own threatened rage — the strong work to insert the feeling of helplessness into the anger of the weak. Watching this use of anger as a power mechanism will strengthen the weak in their self-regulation and thus enable them to become more like agents in their endeavors. It will help them to tame their anger and use it forcefully.

Second, the weak can become aware of the desperate need for control of their own anger that characterizes the strong, along with their projection of that part of it they can't control. Then the weak will begin to humanize the other, in two distinct ways. First, they will start to see needs and desires as separate — for example, "This boss of mine's needs are not my needs and his oppressive anger does not have to become mine." Second, the weak will start to discover that powerful people are also insecure, are pushed by anxiety they cannot fully master, fears they pretend do not exist, doubt within themselves. Leaders, kings, and dictators are hardly as rational, self-satisfied, clever, and productive as they are imagined to be. Hitler came to be seen as an indecisive leader who periodically made hasty, rash decisions. Ronald Reagan came to be known as a passive person. The people on top are simply people, a few among the many.

Here follow some things the oppressed may learn about themselves in transformative contact with oppressors:

While the oppressed will continue to see themselves as victims of domination in a faulty system, they will also see that they are contributors to that system, that they play a part in their own victimization. Then a new compassion for self, a nurturance of self in one's weakness, a forgiveness of self for one's vulnerability, a support of self will unfold and enable the oppressed to be less hampered in their self-assertions. Accepting openly not only that they are weak but also that they help make themselves weak, that part of the strength of the powerful is what they give over, permits the oppressed to choose to apply that strength to their own welfare and comfort. The support they supply to others can be redirected toward themselves. Acknowledgment of participation in one's own domination can serve a curative purpose; it need not lead to devastating self-blame.

Concomitantly, oppressed people are likely to discover that they carry excessive guilt. While there is "real guilt"[8] in the sense that they have participated in their own domination, a guilt which is relieved by self-forgiveness, there is also the guilt taken on by turning anger back upon the self when one fears the consequences of living outwardly the anger. This is an important part of the guilt of the first stage of identification with the aggressor. It is diminished and the oppressed person relieved of its burden when he or she becomes aware of its origin and redirects the anger toward its original target.

The oppressed person also becomes aware of self-hatred as an unawares introject, as a taking on of the influence of the oppressor. The remarkable extent to which self-hatred leads weak persons to subject themselves to self-criticism and to self-abuse and attenuated suicide — by means of drugs, alcohol, and accidents — will become clear and the urges in this direction less insistent.

In self-assertions in the context of dealing with oppressors, oppressed persons learn not only the needs and desires that are active within themselves, but also that they have been willing to avoid defining these in their identification with the aggressor. The fusing of needs in the past is contrasted with the individuated and self-articulated needs of the present, and pride in ownership of own needs comes forth.

Similarly, in the interplay of angers, oppressed individuals become aware that they have contributed to the helplessness factor in their own anger. In their anxiety or their great haste to resolve the conflictual situation, they have underestimated their own capacities and opportunities and in this way made themselves helpless. Their helplessness wasn't all produced by the dominating other. Directed, productive, controlled but not overcontrolled rage feels good to the angry person, whereas helpless rage is quite unpleasant. Discovery of one's part in becoming helpless is liberating.

In transformative relationships between oppressed and oppressor, there is increased tolerance for anxiety, ambiguity, and ambivalence. There are tension and doubt, confusion, contradictions, risk, error, and imperfection in all intense experiences, and the capacity to bear the weight of these without reverting to faulty identifications and projections enters a person's consciousness and excites and rewards the person.

Compassion for the oppressor comes too in the transforming transaction. As an oppressed individual gains self-mastery, the real other becomes more vivid as a human being with his or her own frailties and drivenness. A healthy form of identification and a healthy form of projection, empathy, enable oppressed persons to undo their idealizations (positive and negative) of oppressors and learn about their particular humanity. This is coming to love one's enemy, not in a shallow, moralistic way, but with a deep and sorrowful understanding. The opposition to oppression continues, but the individual oppressor is separated in the mind of the weaker person from the system of domination that hurts all participants.

Not only oppressed people are transformed in direct encounters between themselves and those who dominate them; so too are the dominators. New awarenesses appear for them as well, awarenesses associated with the undoing of projection upon a primed vulnerable other, paralleling those experienced by the underdog who is rising to equality. Here follow some of those new understandings, first in respect to self, which is harder to understand for the dominating person, who has relied heavily on projection and control of others, then in respect to others, who have been greatly misperceived in the processes of oppression.

The dominant persons become aware that they have been functionaries. They have paid the price for power by fusing with the system, by becoming agencies while imagining that they were agents. On the one side, oppressors begin to develop sensitivity to the fact that they are instruments of an oppressive system. They experience discomfort performing those acts of the system which damage the weak, and they come to see that they as well as the weak have been victims. No longer seeing themselves merged in the system, they can see the system for what it is — an oppressive arrangement of social relations. On the other side, oppressors begin to rediscover their own needs and desires as distinct from the inclinations fostered or demanded by the system in which they have submerged themselves. They learn that their true wants are different from what they imagined them to be.

Oppressors experience and work productively with their guilt, which once they mainly saw in its projected form. Their self-control had tended to hide their guilt from themselves. They come to experience real guilt and the regret that goes with it in respect to those they have oppressed, and they reform and experience forgiveness, their own and that which the downtrodden regularly provide to tyrants who reform. They also become aware of existential guilt, in that they see how much of themselves they have negated or failed to realize in the operations that were implementing domination.

Those who have been the strong in power relations become aware of the depth of the self-hatred involved in their control of unwieldy desires. The distaste they regularly feel for internal processes that are hard to handle can be quite intense, which is one reason why the strong are typically reluctant to use psychotherapy. Now they experience with a new intensity hatred for that part of themselves which has been self-controlling. When we remember that a person who is self-controlling is also one who is controlled by self, we can comprehend this hatred. It is a feeling on behalf of denied desires, hatred of the rigidly self-controlling part of one's functioning. And now also hatred of other unruly desires that the person has avoided experiencing directly by projecting them becomes anger at self-victimization and a new determination to be true to one's own wishes.

The full experience of suspicion, distrust, and feeling unsafe in the vital contact is aroused and is lived through without devastation, adding an appreciation of one's capacity to be self-supportive in the midst of high tension. The feelings of distrust and suspicion are seen to be what the person brings from the past and may not necessarily refer at all to dangers posed by the oppressed — "It is I who am suspicious," not "They are out to hurt me." The dependence of the oppressor upon the oppressed for dealing with his or her own psychological problems is consequently lessened, and feelings of relief and self-confidence emerge.

In place of controlled rage there may temporarily appear helpless rage, a stage on the pathway toward owning the full extent of the anger that oppressors carry. Dealing with the helpless rage and surviving it leads to a useful taming of anger.

Like the oppressed persons who are collaborators in the transformative relationship, the oppressors develop an increased tolerance for anxiety, ambiguity, and ambivalence, and in addition gain understanding of and compassion for those on the other side — the oppressed. Again, healthy identifications replace unhealthy ones, and empathy supplants unawares projection, so that the strong come to see the weak and themselves as joined in common effort and more alike than different. The vitality that characterizes relationships of equals in close contact is allowed and appreciated. Among the more particular awarenesses about the oppressed that take hold when projection upon a primed vulnerable other is mastered are the following:

The shift of responsibility to the oppressor by the weak is an active step as well as a submissive response to power; the oppressed are actors in allocating responsibility and in divesting themselves of power. Their giving it over is, indeed, an act born of a series of painful emotions starting with anxiety and helpless rage, and is thus not under their cool, rational control, and yet it is an act: a choice and decision are involved. Crucially, the weak legitimate authority, as Elizabeth Janeway[9] argues, and thus can also pull back or withhold that legitimation. The weak, who seem to be only victims of their own fate, are understood to be more powerful than they themselves believe.

The weak, though they sometimes appear willing victims, are submissive ambivalently. Even when they wish to be unthreatening, their needs push them toward self-assertion, and their assertiveness then contradicts their efforts to be self-negating. Further, ready submissiveness shields a great deal of rage. White racists talked about the contentedness of blacks until there was a lifting of too ready submissive tendencies and the long-term struggle for equality was revived; then the rage that lay behind the submissiveness came clearly into view. Along similar lines, oppressors become aware that the oppressed are not genetically lazy and incompetent; rather they have been *selectively* irresponsible.[10] Under the pressures of perceived domination, the weak become lazy, live by a different sense of time, cannot delay gratification, and so forth. Without those pressures, however, they seem like respectable and responsible folk. The weak too use power, and this is observed and appreciated when oppression is overcome.

Oppressors discover that when the weak are relieved of guilt and self-hatred and when they are self-forgiving for being party to their own victimization, they are safer, less likely to seek revenge upon their oppressors.

When the helpless rage of the weak is developed into productive, controlled anger, the feelings of anger from the weak that enter into transactions appear less threatening to all, and can be understood, respected, even welcomed by an oppressor. Tamed anger is less likely to arbitrarily erupt upon the oppressor and can be useful in moving all collaborators in the new relationship to new achievements. Tamed anger helps identify present needs, helps move people toward collaboration, and keeps relationships lively.

Oppressors begin to experience the weak as tolerant of their own anxiety, ambivalence, and ambiguity, and this lifts the oppressors' sensed burden of excessive responsibility for them. And events confirm the new situation: the weak no longer call upon the strong to save them from fear and doubt or to relieve them of their hostility, but instead become responsible for handling these themselves.

Finally, the strong discover that the separate needs and desires of the weak are interesting, social, exciting, and informative to them in their own living processes. How the underclasses manage their lives is impressive, given the hardships they must deal with, and when these skills are applied in transformational relationships, the aesthetics and craft of such management are wondrously educational to oppressors, who have believed they have nothing to learn from the subdued.

I have been sketching some awarenesses that can be expected when contacts between the powerful and the powerless result in the undoing of the delusion of fusion and corrections of faulty identifications and projections that support this delusion. These awarenesses are products of *transformative encounters* between oppressors and oppressed, and it is wise to remember that while there are many, many interactions between them, only a few of these are transformative encounters; the remainder are either continuations of the oppressive conditions or neutral task-oriented dealings without any exploitative ingredients. Transformative encounters are few and far between and usually result from considerable prior preparation. On occasion spontaneous actions are transformative, though close scrutiny of these may show considerable accumulated fantasies and imaginary scenarios among the protagonists.

Preparation for contacts that are transformative is less likely to occur in the frequent usual interactions between oppressor and oppressed — where the participants are heavily burdened by the mechanisms of the delusion of fusion — than in peer groups, where it is possible to experiment with building trust, developing motivation for change, and creating the capacity to be aware of what demands attention. In the peer groups of the oppressed (one thinks of unions, the civil rights groups with their church or political bases, antinuclear groups, students as a body vis-a-vis teachers, tenant organizations. and families as well) and in those of the oppressors (boards of directors, country club groups, "citizens" groups, Chambers of Commerce, and again families), the anticipation and exploration of possible encounters goes on all the time. More often than not, such preparation is unplanned and unsystematic. The oppressed, traumatized by their oppression, are preoccupied with their oppressors, indeed, fascinated by them, as Hallie has keenly noted,[11] and in their attempts to work through their pent-up rage, their "unfinished business," their need to repair their self-esteem, or simply their confusion about what is happening to them, they are ever imagining possibilities for turning the tables on their exploiters. In their peer groups, they seek support for bearing the tensions of being dominated, but they also consider ways for changing their life circumstances.

Less noticed but equally active is preoccupation with the weak in the circles of the strong. I have already pointed out that oppressors are dependent upon those they oppress for dealing with their own psychological problems, and I have noted their intrusiveness upon the lives of these others, their inability to stay clear of these human beings they hold in great contempt. It is a further ramification of this preoccupation that oppressors are often to be found talking about their dealings with those whom they dominate as if rehearsing for encounters. They too have "unfinished business" and seek to resolve their delusionary condition time and time again within their peer groups.

Inside the very peer groups themselves, however, problematic patterns of confluence, faulty identification and projection, guilt and self-hatred, helpless and overcontrolled rage, and divisive anxiety surface anew. One source of these patterns is external pressure applied to the group of one's peers. Unions are hounded by industry and government, and in turn unions challenge management; change-oriented political groups are harassed by police forces; civil rights organizations are intimidated by racist coalitions and in response fight back and become threatening in their own right. These pressures are very real, and they induce stress in the peer group, stress which is regularly followed by activation of the defensive maneuvers leading to the delusion of fusion. Indeed, the ineptitude and downfall of many social groups can be traced to divisions within them that parallel, even imitate, the divisions between the social group and its external opposition. Even when external pressure is not actively being applied, its frightening anticipation is evident in peer groups.

A second source of the problematic patterns in the peer group is history and tradition. In a large social system that is governed by patterns of domination and submission, the subsystems mirror the larger whole; the organizational principles of smaller groups are heavily influenced by the most prominent principles in the larger group. If the workplace is organized in an authoritarian manner, the families of workers and management both are likely to be run in an authoritarian way; if the military is primary among national governmental functions, educational institutions are likely to have a militaristic cast. And the rigidity needed for the maintenance of oppression leads to rituals, proprieties, rules, fashions, and traditions within the peer group which have a continuing life of their own. For example, the unvarying hours of work for parents in a family lead to unvarying routines and rules about meal times. The rigidity from the workplace spills over into family life.

A third source of the problematic patterns is the character structure of the members of the peer group. This has been so deformed by experiences of domination and submission that they bring with them dispositions to function by faulty identifications and projections. Indeed, their lives have been so colored by domination and submission that they believe these are the normal ways of relating. There is thus little facility in handling anger within the ingroup or in affirming self rather than hating self for having needs that bring one into difficulty.

In short, every peer group reflects the dynamics that transpire between oppressors and oppressed because the members of the group carry over their accustomed methods for managing anxiety, anger, and guilt and self-hatred and the disowning of needs that might be provocative. There is antidemocratic tradition in labor unions; splits between blacks and whites destroy the unity of the civil rights movement, a unity forged in dangerous common struggle; feminists who are angry with all men divide from feminists who are intolerant of any sexism including that focused upon men as an undifferentiated grouping; domination and submission flourish within the ranks of the well-off. Every peer group in an exploitative system is bedeviled by the delusion of fusion.

Accordingly, inside each peer group in a system of oppressors and oppressed, a dialectical situation arises: the group serves as a support system for individuals, and the group threatens to institute its own form of oppression. The tension of this dialectic, whether at any given time the group is actually being supportive or oppressive, makes of the group a potential training ground for undoing the delusion of fusion. Because the tendencies to recreate oppression within the peer group appear over and over again, the impetus toward the delusion of fusion is a regular event for the members; because the group is supportive, indeed exists because it has taken on the responsibility of sustaining its members, the undoing of the delusion of fusion can be carried out in a relatively safe environment (A peer group that wasn't supportive wouldn't really be a peer group.) The struggle to clarify the confluences, introjections, and projections that are personally and socially harmful can proceed in the relative security of the peer group, and through that struggle individuals can change themselves while simultaneously preparing to engage in transformative encounters between oppressors and oppressed.

The slowing down of the quick-circuiting process is helped along by the relative security the peer group provides; by contrast, rapid transition from spontaneity to anxiety to anger to guilt and self-hatred to full identification with the aggressor or full projection upon a primed vulnerable other is likely to occur when destructiveness is expected in social relations. The group can help members who are trying to slow down and change themselves. For instance, to come to realize that one's desires are confounded by introjections or projections is quite disorienting. One's sense of self is shattered, and even though it was a false sense because the self was fused, it gave one some stability. The peer group offers a new stability. Similarly, people are more willing to own their guilt and self-hatred if they feel safe, secure that others will not abandon them, remove support, or condemn or belittle them, secure also that they will not destroy themselves in their self-hatred. It is no simple matter to recover and forgive guilt and self-hatred, and a sympathetic, tolerant, and receptive group can provide support of this process.

At the same time, for the peer group to serve its transformative functions, attention must be paid to the various ways in which the delusion of fusion manifests itself in dealings with external groups and in internal affairs, including the influence of the character structures of the group's members. The full range of social-emotional confoundings will have to be brought to the surface and worked with. There will be occasions to deal with anxiety and anger as well as with guilt and self-hatred — anxiety and anger caused by the opposition or due to the presence of oppressive tendencies or merely differences of a strong nature within the ingroup. By this reading of what is necessary for the ingroup to be a transformative influence, it is not the case that the ingroup by itself is peaceful and placid while encounters with the opposition are stormy and unsettling. If the ingroup is merely comforting or simply quiets social-emotional storms, it acts to further the delusion of fusion rather than transform it. Only when the group is able to provide for the working through of the social-emotional experiences associated with the undoing of faulty confluences is it also able to prepare its members to act in politically productive ways when encountering persons and organizations not of the group.

All the lessons that can be critically important to basic change in the struggles of oppressors and oppressed can be learned within the peer group. Tendencies to divide anxiety unevenly and to create contrast between helpless rage and controlled or projected rage; guilt and self-hatred from faulty introjections as well as moral judgments and hatred of others from projected guilt and self-hatred; reliance upon the other for the determination of one's desires — all these appear within peer groups. Similarly, new awarenesses I have described as characterizing the outcomes of transformative encounters between the weak and the strong arise inside peer groups too, as when helpless rage is made into useful anger, projected guilt is taken back, responsibility allocated more in line with reality. The needed lessons can be learned, however, only if the group is alive and receptive to working with the personal concerns of its members, if the inner psychological and the interpersonal social-emotional factors are considered to be important and pertinent political concerns.

Attention is most profitably given to these issues at times when they rise to lively importance in the group process. When anxiety fills the room or anger flashes through the group, when a peer group member is vividly expressing self-hatred or guiltiness is clearly present, the group can pause in its work and devote itself to making sure that the emotion is handled in such a way that no member weakens himself or herself and no other member becomes more powerful, things which happen in a group when social emotions aren't being faced and dealt with clearly. One function of good leadership is to promote such attention and encourage this kind of psychological work, but anyone in the group who is attuned to these issues — such as a member who might be influenced by this essay itself — can take it upon himself or herself to bring the group to deal with them.

Now, every organizer knows that it is vital in political struggle for there to be solidarity within the ranks of allies, that divisiveness makes for vulnerability when dealing with the opposition. How do I square this need for solidarity in the peer group with the need for active and lively social-emotional contestations? Does not solidarity depend upon cooperation, congeniality, loyalty? Should not the group be as free from strife as possible? What political wisdom can there possibly be in having intense, contentious relationships unfold within the group?

The answer to these questions is that support and security in the group do not mean peace of mind or calm interpersonal relations; support and security mean bases of trust and care from which the difficult work of undoing delusion can progress. It takes trust in others to allow oneself to experiment with ways of being angry with them, and it takes also the actual expression of the anger for the trust to be meaningful. When one has, fearfully, tried a new way with anger, or tried an old way and let it be changed by others, the solidarity with those against whom the anger was directed can become deeper. To be angrily self-assertive in a nonblaming way rather than helplessly frustrated and blaming often leads to communion with the other toward whom one's anger has been directed. Or when one has been self-controlling in anger and enabled by others who feel confident and self-supportive to let go of the control, here too new bonding often happens. To explore one's guilt and not be condemned but find new acceptance and forgiveness ties one more closely to those who know the truth about one. Cooperation, congeniality, and loyalty are functions of difference and its resolution, rather than of the absence of difference.

In political groups that are successful, provision is made for psychological understanding and work on personal issues as preparation for transformative encounters between oppressors and oppressed. The interpersonal factors are foreground, not background, and not luxuries. Gold Flower's growth depended upon many discussions with Dark Jade and other women about her shame and humiliation and her fear of opposing her husband and father-in-law, and, not to be forgotten, depended upon her loving care of these men who mistreated her.

Here is another example of such accomplishment from the area of brutal political repression. Cienfuegos and Monelli describe as a psychotherapeutic instrument the testimony of individuals tortured by the Chilean military after the overthrow of Allende:

> "People who have undergone a brutal, humiliating, and degrading experience often find it difficult to speak of the subject. They are afraid to cause pain to loved ones, and they also fear being devalued for having gone through such an experience."

In such cases, these writers note,

> "The mere idea of remembering the experience produced fear and anxiety, but at the same time 'telling' was the only possibility for release from painful and humiliating memories.

> "The therapeutic effect of the testimony is mainly linked to the relief of anxiety and depression resulting from the traumatic experience. . . . The testimony acts by restoring affective ties, by orienting aggression in a constructive manner and by integrating fragmented experiences. . . . The communication of the painful experience, once considered impossible, is achieved when patients become aware of the therapist's interest and, consequently, their own ability to tolerate such horror."

Cienfuegos and Monelli also refer to former political prisoners in a nontherapeutic context:

> "Those who had the opportunity to talk spontaneously to others about their pain and torture, later felt comforted by the receptivity and understanding of fellow prisoners. Later studies have demonstrated that political prisoners sentenced to long periods of imprisonment left jail in better emotional condition than those who served short sentences that left them little opportunity to share their feelings with others."[12]

These quotations suggest the political usefulness both of dealing with intense personal experiences inside the peer group and of individual working through of one's inner life as it has been affected by oppression; and Cienfuegos and Monelli illustrate how psychotherapy may help in the latter process.

In thinking on the relevance of psychotherapy to political organizing, I am mindful of programs that have been developing in recent years in industry, employee assistance programs in which counseling for troubled members of the organization enables them to continue to work and contribute to the organization, and I want to elaborate on my statement in Chapter 7 in favor of psychotherapeutic services for social activists. I want to suggest that every political grouping which engages in serious social struggle should have its own therapeutic teams. These specialists would be available for crises, as they have been for soldiers in wartime in the prevention and treatment of war neuroses. They would be on hand for enabling grief to be worked through. People can sometimes handle grief and other personal problems by themselves, but if they can't, they should have this help available to them. Specialists who provide such assistance could pick up whatever fallout occurred from intense interpersonal encounters within the peer group that failed to carry to completion the issues that had been raised.

But therapy for individuals under the auspices of the political group need not be directed only at transitory or situational upheavals. It can also usefully be made available for the personal growth and development of members who have been primed for significant change by successful transformative encounters in the ingroup. The most complete slowing down of the quick-circuiting processes associated with the delusion of fusion can take place in a psychotherapuetic context. Here the sorting out of own needs and introjected or projected needs can occur with the greatest safety and support. Here the ego functions of introjection, retroflection, projection, and demand for confluence can be studied and made awares as processes. Here the subtleties of anger and anxiety can be seen most keenly.

The focus of such therapy would be guided by its larger purpose of enabling individuals to participate more and more successfully in transforming oppressive social relations. It would help them work through their inner lives and interpersonal relations, especially as affected by previous participation in collective life around conditions of oppression and as relevant to future engagements around these matters.

Given my belief that effective political action involves intense personal experiences, I consider it only responsible to develop therapeutic services that are readily available to activists and that are positives in the eyes of their organizations — services that can be valued and used without shame, and that will be for growth as well as management of trauma, yet modest in their promises and secondary to political purpose.

Chapter 10

The Quick-Circuiting Process and the Delusion of Fusion

I have been saying that a quick-circuiting process exists when the delusion of fusion is in place and characterizes the interpersonal social-emotional activity of an individual. This means that the person experiences rapidly and in turn spontaneity, anxiety, anger, guilt and self-hatred (or their projected versions), and then settles into trying to merge her or his own desires with those of the other or others in the relationship. The delusion can be corrected if the quick-circuiting is slowed down so that the person first becomes aware of each social emotion and then learns to express it more productively or give it up for a livelier emotion. In this process, after the person has basically worked free of efforts to merge desires with the other, guilt and self-hatred become focal; when guilt and self-hatred are experienced directly, fully, and not too rapidly, then self-forgiveness becomes possible and the retroflection, or turning back upon the self, of anger can be dispensed with; when projected guilt and self-hatred in the form of blame and contempt for the weak are reowned and re-experienced as own guilt and self-hatred, also fully and slowly, then again self-forgiveness is made possible; if anger can be known and held in personal experience long enough, then better deployment of it in social relations where it is pertinent can be realized; if persons can accept their anxiety and stay with it on the way to preparing themselves for danger, then they are also on the pathway to transforming their anxiety back into the excitement of spontaneous encounters.

Reacquaintance with social emotions and alternative use of them necessitates that the quick-circuiting process be slowed down considerably. Oppressed and oppressors alike can be said to live too hurried an existence, while they are actually engaged in maintaining the status quo. This is another paradox: hurrying, scurrying, rushing . . . to maintain what is.

The process of quick-circuiting the social emotions can be modified in a group through two different approaches. The first focuses awareness on the process itself and its speediness. People who are confluent in oppressive social relations are helped, by the leader or another member who is attuned to social-emotional processes, to become aware of the miniscule moments of anxiety, anger, and guilt and self-hatred that regularly follow the unexpected spontaneous impulses that arise in them and threaten to enter their behavior. Simply by pointing to successive signs of emotions, the leader or other knowledgeable person can lead persons to recognize their flickers of anxiety, the ever-available touches of rage that rise up and are squashed, those flashes of guilt that course through their lightly known consciousness. This makes awares the quick-circuiting process itself. Then attention to how rapidly the persons experience these many feelings, how speedy and unlived their lives have become, gives them a sense of the complexity of their experience, a sense of how much they have going on. It enables them to become interested in their own processes — a vital step in recovery from oppression.

The second approach to slowing down quick-circuiting, and undoing the delusion of fusion, is to make awares in its own right each of the phases of the whole social-emotional experience that culminates in the delusion, beginning with the final phase, in which persons are confounded as to whether the desires that activate their behavior are their own or a mixture of own and other's, and working backwards step by step toward spontaneity. If we can enable individuals to know and to own the depth of their identifications with the aggressor and their projections upon a primed vulnerable other without their feeling criticized, we can expect that they will be alive to their guilt and self-hatred; and if we can find means to foster awareness of guilt and self-hatred along with forgiveness and commitment to change, we can anticipate that these persons will again become angry; and so on back through anxiety to natural spontaneity.

Since all groups are heterogenous, we can expect that in any group seeking to go through this process together, some members will be involved in working through one social-emotional phase while others are working through another. For instance, some will be ready to see the confounding of own and others' desires and available for dealing with their projections of guilt and self-hatred, some will for a long time need to sort out what they want and how what they thought they wanted was burdened by their accommodating to others' demands, some will be exploring new ways to use their anger in confrontations with their allies and with their opponents in the oppressive situation. It is no simple matter, therefore, for a group to undo the delusion of fusion by working from the final phase back to spontaneity in social relations.

One key to making the whole process work is to continue to attend to the deeper, later phases while working on the earlier ones. For example, groups can center upon the confluence in which individuals' own desires are confounded with introjected and projected desires; then they can focus upon confusing guilt and self-hatred while continuing to acknowledge tendencies to merge desires; then they can turn their corrective attention to new experiences and uses of anger while still working with introjected and projected standards causing confusing guilt and self-hatred and with the tendency to compound and confound what individuals identify as their needs and desires. By always devoting some time to the deeper phases, even when most members of the group have moved away from the fusion of desires and the introjections and projections associated with guilt and self-hatred, the group assists those still struggling with these issues and fortifies against regression into a fused condition those who have moved on toward becoming agents. In this work each of the phases is still attended to as a discrete phase, which in itself is a means for slowing the quick-circuiting tendency.

In the chapters that follow, I expand on the theme of undoing the delusion of fusion. I take up in reverse order the stages of the journey to the delusion and offer suggestions for working with the distortions of functioning that are found in them. First, I attend to the full delusion of fusion in which oppressed and oppressor confuse themselves about whose desires are being tended to. Then I turn to problems with identification. Next, I have suggestions for working with faulty projecting activities. After that, there is material on being angry — how to transform ineffective angry ways into effective ones. Then, before concluding this work, I take up anxiety and making it useful,

Chapter 11

Working with the Full Delusion of Fusion

Oppression is maintained when the weak and the strong in social relationships obscure their own ego boundaries and fuse with each other, or enter into unhealthy confluence. Playing either tyrannical or submissive roles, persons avoid defining clearly for themselves and for others what they need and want, especially as their wants might cause differences with others. They steer shy of clear definitions because the appearance of differences would mean that they would have to take responsibility for their actions, stand behind them, be vividly self-assertive, risk isolation.

Perls, Hefferline, and Goodman describe the situation of unhealthy confluence this way:

"Persons who live in unhealthy confluence with one another *do not have personal contact.* This, of course, is a common blight of marriages and long friendships. The parties to such confluence cannot conceive of any but the most momentary difference of opinion or attitude. If a discrepancy in their views becomes manifest, they cannot work it out to a point of reaching genuine agreement or else agreeing to disagree. No, they must either restore the disturbed confluence by whatever means they can or else flee into isolation. The latter may emphasize sulking, withdrawing, being offended, or in other ways putting the brunt upon the other to make up; or, despairing of restoring the confluence, it may take the form of hostility, flagrant disregard, forgetting, or other ways of disposing of the other as an object of concern.

"To restore interrupted confluence one attempts to adjust oneself to the other or the other to oneself. In the first case one becomes a yes-man, tries to make up, frets about small differences, needs proof of total acceptance; one effaces his own individuality, propitiates, and becomes slavish. In the other case where one cannot stand contradiction, one persuades, bribes, compels or bullies.

"When persons are in contact, not in confluence, they not only respect their own and other's opinions, tastes, and responsibilities, but actively welcome the animation and excitement that come with the airing of disagreements."[1]

We do not usually think of marriages and long friendships as being oppressive relationships, yet unhealthy confluence appears in them, and when it does it makes them similar in tone to the relationships we call oppressive. The difference is that spouses and friends are more able to change than people in these other relationships when resentment of unhealthy confluence becomes pronounced.

The cure for oppression in a peer group bedeviled by unhealthy confluence can be stated with surprising simplicity: the cure is democracy in social relations. The democracy I have in mind more than permits group members to express their wants in the manner of one person, one vote, however; I am coming out for *democratic social practices that are guided by sophisticated psychological understandings and that encourage group members to explore their own wants and to discover what these are.* It is not enough that each member have the right to enter her or his own desires into the governing deliberations and resolutions of the group, because that assumes that each individual knows well what those desires are. Knowing clearly one's own desires is precisely what is missing in unhealthy confluence, that is, under the sway of the delusion of fusion. Thus, democratic social relations which will undo the tendencies to the delusion of fusion that maintain oppression will be social relations that promote the examination *and discovery* of individual desires, the searching and studying by each member into what are true desires and what are introjected and projected desires, wants that are untrue to self.

I want to say this another way. Democracy that can correct tendencies to the delusion of fusion depends upon creative endeavor, creative not only in the special ways that different persons with different desires influence each other but also creative in the process by which members of the democracy are facilitated in becoming themselves through self-discovery as well as self-assertion.

A concept from the clinical literature concerning parenting of young children is pertinent to this formulation of democracy. It is an idea articulated most clearly by D. W. Winnicott when he talks of the mother as a "holding environment" for the child. As Winnicott explains, a mother with her infant is a holding environment because the infant is importantly merged with its mother and in the process of building on its nature while separating into a distinct human being. The mother is a source of consistent provision from the environment, not a magical source, not one that knows too well the infant's needs and provides for them, but an empathic source, one that is responsive to signals and indications from the infant. The limitations of the mother are as important as her powers, since from the limitations comes the necessity for the infant to articulate its own needs and from her powers comes the provision for satisfaction of those needs. The mother as holding environment "contains" the infant while it is becoming aware of itself and its needs and capacities, enabling the infant to become a separate other person; then the mother acts to foster gratification of the infant's needs.[2]

A democracy functioning as a holding environment is a group that encourages its members to discover, explore, and reveal their interests and their purposes, as well as a group that finds the means to satisfy these. Its members tend to merge with one another both in healthy confluence, when a group goal has been reached and members are finding their individual satisfactions through the group goal, and in unhealthy confluence, when members blur their boundaries in the interests of keeping peace or avoiding responsibility. The democracy surrounds its members, protects them, and offers satisfactions to them as they define themselves in their separateness and uniqueness, and it helps them to overcome unhealthy confluence by supporting them in expressing themselves authentically. Such a democracy encourages the dialectic of union and diversity, building unity from diversity and also building diversity from the communion that is attained.

Cheryl Hyde has stressed the importance of such a supportive environment for women activists engaged in community organizing:

"Knowing that others care often comforts an individual when confronted with derogatory comments, hecklers, etc. Fears and concerns can be addressed within a supportive environment. . . .

"Women stressed that a 'safe' environment was essential to developing [the] interpersonal sides of organizing. A safe environment is one in which trust, respect, equality and validation of an individual's experience takes place."[3]

Donna Warnock, in an interview about organizing the "Women's Pentagon Action," similarly referred to the need for "providing a safe place for women to express their deep, hurtful emotions" and told how such a "place" worked in that endeavor:

"So I said 'Look, why don't we just figure out how we *feel* about all these different issues that we want to address, and then try to group these feelings together and move through them and within each one deal with the issues that are appropriate to these feelings. I know some of the emotions that come up for me are grief, anger and power.' That really got us rolling. As soon as we decided that we were going to develop the thing emotionally we realized how significant that was and that this way each individual could find her niche."[4]

In discussing efforts to ameliorate the nasty "post-traumatic stress disorders" that have plagued veterans of the Vietnam War, Donald R. Catherall has described a similar kind of holding environment:

"Dealing with the effects of trauma is largely a social process and occurs in the natural social groups in which people live . . . . The groups constitute a social context that can provide a sense of community for the survivor. A facilitative social context contains two elements: 1) a consistent system of values and beliefs in which the survivor can move through a process of self-examination; and 2) a sufficiently supportive affective environment such that the survivor can feel safe engaging in the process of self-examination and grieving."[5]

A second contribution from clinical work that is important to a democratic group interested in undoing the delusion of fusion is understanding of the crucial importance of attending to process in group interactions. As Irving D. Yalom has said:

> "Process focus is not just one of many possible procedural orientations; on the contrary, it is indispensable and a common denominator to all effective interactional groups. One so often hears words to the following effect: 'No matter what else may be said about experiential groups . . . one cannot deny that they are potent — that they offer a compelling experience for participants.' The process focus is the power cell of these groups; it is precisely because they encourage process exploration that they are potent experiences. . . .

> "Process commentary undermines arbitrary authority structure. Industrial organizational development consultants have long known that if a social structure openly investigates its own structure and process, power equalization takes place. High power individuals are not only more technically informed but also possess organizational information which permits them to influence and manipulate. They not only have skills which allowed them to obtain a position of power but, once there, have such a central place in the flow of information that they are able to reinforce their position."[6]

Most helpful for the correction of the delusion of fusion, then, is for people to find themselves in a holding environment that permits attention to internal states and to interpersonal processes. This is most easily accomplished in a therapy context, in which the therapist is a very personal holding environment for the client. It is next most easily carried out in peer groups of political and social actors, since central to the groups' functioning is their commitment to serving the needs of their members. It is with the most difficulty carried out in the context of active opposition between oppressors and oppressed, since in this context process commentary is especially hard to achieve both for the oppressors, who must be in control and therefore are not open to discovering their fusion, and for the oppressed, who are threatened and intimidated by the strong who dominate them. Groups can develop ways to make their members better able to support each other in their difficult hours of confrontation with the other side. Generally, however, a full holding environment has to be developed away from active opposition.

Governments are meant to be holding environments. Governments are community systems intended to hold people and to provide settings, such as schools, in which they can unfold in their individuality as well as accomplish tasks that take many to achieve. That modern governments do not fulfill this obligation well is merely a reflection of the fact that they are not very democratic.

Within the fuller holding environments that people do manage to create, the practices that will counteract the delusion of fusion center upon a certain kind of inner experience. Writing specifically about the patient in psychotherapy, Hellmuth Kaiser has described it clearly and succinctly:

> "Three mental activities — very ordinary activities, indeed — seem especially conducive to producing this fateful inner experience: first, and perhaps foremost, . . . making a decision; second, . . . reaching a conviction by thinking; and, third, . . . wanting something. At least it looks as though whenever one of these mental functions is about to appear in sharp focus within the patient's attention, whenever the patient comes close to having it driven home to him that it is *he himself* who is going to make a decision; or that the conviction in his mind is really his, originated by his own thinking; or that it is he, and he alone, who is wanting something, a piece of delusional ideology rolls like a fog over the mental scenery, softening or even obscuring the lines of the picture.

> "Of course, what is necessary to make the inner experience of deciding, thinking or wanting so potent that it needs obscuring is the condition that the decision is not a routine decision expected and approved by the patient's environment; the conviction reached by the patient's thinking is not supported by authority; or, in the case of 'wanting,' what he wants must be something he is not supposed or not expected to want."[7]

These, of course, are exactly conditions that a group fighting organized oppression comes up against.

Erving and Miriam Polster have direct suggestions for working with unhealthy confluence which can be used when individuals are making decisions, reaching their own convictions by thinking, or discovering and expressing what they want:

> "The antidotes to [unhealthy] confluence are contact, differentiation, and articulation. The individual must begin to experience choices, needs, and feelings which are his own and do not have to coincide with those of other peo-

ple. He must learn that he can face the terror of separation from these people and still remain alive.

"Questions like, 'What do you feel now?' 'What do you want now?' or 'What are you doing now?' can help him focus on his own directions. Dealing with the sensations which result from these questions prevents him from buying in on a standard dream package which may or may not suit his needs. Stating his expectations aloud, first to his therapist, perhaps, and finally to the person from whom these satisfactions are demanded, can be the first steps in sorting out covert attempts at confluent relationships.

"By attending to one's own needs and articulating them, one can discover what his personal, unique directions may be, and he can get what he wants. He does not have to strike a bargain with some appeased power; he becomes an independent agent, in touch with where he wants to go and how he might go about getting there under his own steam."[8]

My final suggestion for working to counter the delusion of fusion comes also from Kaiser, whose whole theory of neurosis is drawn around the idea of this delusion. He learned through his painstaking observation and speculation that open communication was the key element in the struggle against the delusion. On the one hand, starved communication was the basis of the delusion of fusion; on the other hand, the delusion of fusion acted to keep communication at a minimum. The problem militated against its solution. This was the "vicious circle" that was the foundation of neurosis, he said. In turn, the essence of psychotherapy (and thus of a democratic group that facilitates the undoing of unhealthy confluence.) is to engage in relationships that are different from many relationships in the following way:

"The crucial condition which makes all the difference between psychotherapy which helps, and alleged psychotherapy which doesn't, is *that the therapist does not withdraw psychologically.*[9]

The failure of political and social groups that have been trying to introduce democracy into social institutions is that the members have tended to withdraw psychologically from one another in the tense struggles that engage them. They have withdrawn and so lost open communication, partly because of social conditions that are threatening and scary, but also partly because there are social-emotional conditions that are threatening and scary. These conditions are the presence in such groups of deep feelings of anxiety, anger, guilt, self-hatred, resentment, contempt for others, and the like. These feelings have led to, and been somewhat suppressed by, the delusion of fusion.

Persons under the delusion of fusion hold on to it tenaciously in efforts to avoid these painful feelings. And then, after this stage, it is no easy matter to stay with others even in a benevolent holding environment while trying to face up to, and win freedom from, such feelings. But it is vital to do so, if one's group is to win its struggles.

When a group is *successful* in undoing the deepest level of the delusion of fusion (the fullest identifications with the aggressor and the fullest projections upon a primed vulnerable other), the reward for such success is members' re-experiencing of guilt and self-hatred. Some reward! And beyond the revival of guilt and self-hatred lie anger and anxiety. No wonder that, knowing this intuitively, persons cling to the unhealthy ties of fusion.

But a new element can helpfully enter our understanding at this point, and it will also need to enter our practice. There are regressive and progressive forms of the appearance of guilt and self-hatred. When rage is being turned back upon the self, the appearance of guilt and self-hatred is a regression; it represents a deepening of the process by which the delusion of fusion is created, a move from person as agent toward person as agency. When a person is recognizing and affirming his or her own needs and undoing unhealthy confluence, however, the appearance of guilt and self-hatred marks a reversal of the quick-circuiting process and a progressive move toward the person's acting as agent on her or his own behalf. When the person can be shown that experiencing guilt is an achievement worthy of praise and encouragement because the person has been avoiding responsibility for his or her own behavior and is now acknowledging this, the conditions are present for the self-forgiveness that is so essential to mature functioning. Regret and that forgiveness become healing ingredients in the growth process.

Chapter 12

Noticing and Changing Faulty Identifications

When people come together in groups and act with common purpose, they are guided by their identifications with one another or with the goals they are pursuing collectively; good group functioning depends upon healthy identification processes within the group. After all, at its core, identification as a psychological experience exists when an individual shares some common quality with another person. That common quality may be a personal attribute — a way of walking, a manner of speech, a manner of dress, an intention or purpose, a value system — or it may be a social characteristic such as allegiance to a group, felt ethnic identity, or submission to a particular authority. Thorstein Veblen[1] importantly relied on the concept of emulation — to copy or imitate with the purpose of equaling — in his social theory, thus setting identification as critical to the establishment of social classes and the class system and, ultimately, to the whole makeup of society. Much of Freud's social theory[2] also is grounded in identification and its various forms. To be like another, to share commonalities with another, to have another as an ideal to be admired and copied — all speak to the notion of identification.

In groups, the pattern of all the identifications present is so rich that in order to notice and try to change identifications with the aggressor, we need to make a careful distinction between these faulty identifications and healthy ones. What must we look for in making this distinction?

To my way of understanding, there are two major differences between healthy identifications and these others — one an internal factor, something that goes on in the inner psychic life of the individual, the other an element of social relationship. I have been stating that identification with the aggressor is an internalization of domination such that a person becomes self-dominating — replaces his or her own values with those of the aggressor and tries always to allow only those needs into action which are acceptable to the aggressor. This is a self-conquest aimed at avoiding the other. The conflict *between* persons is obscured by becoming a conflict *within* a person. In that internal conflict, part of the person is lost or sacrificed. Insofar as the identification with the aggressor substitutes the aggressor's demands or wishes or values for those of the identifier, it eliminates or holds down the identifier's own demands, wishes, or values.

Healthy identifications proceed in the opposite direction. Instead of regulating one's needs and values in accord with what is required from the outside, instead of being in the shadow of the other, in a healthy identification process one articulates one's own needs independently or with others acting as a holding environment, and subsequently discovers commonalities with others. The social relation is a cooperative connection among individuals acting as agents, each with needs and values which are openly revealed and entered into a negotiating process. Self-regulation involves specifying one's desires and values, organizing one's diverse needs, and paying attention to others in the situation.

Internally, then, identifications with the aggressor lead to self-conquest, while healthy identifications lead to self-articulation and self-discovery or -invention. In the interactive sphere, the faulty identifications serve as defenses against relationship which threatens to become intolerably full of conflict; their aim is to create distance, a kind of psychological breathing room. Paradoxically, what actually develops is a fusion and the loss of access to oneself. In a group, identification with the aggressor arises when rage among group members is so great that they feel likely to destroy each other; the identification takes hold when both the weak and the strong individuals are constrained to remain in the relationship despite these murderous impulses. The weak adopt identification with the aggressor so that they minimize the depth of personal contact between themselves and the aggressive strong people in the group when some form of contact is inevitable. The weak believe that if they take on themselves the standards and values of the strong, if they reshape themselves in the image of the strong, they need not then be intimately controlled by the strong; they will have distanced themselves, they believe deep down, from active social domination. But they actually will have internalized that domination.

Healthy identifications, in contrast, create authentic intimacy with others without requiring the participants to obscure or deny their essential separateness and differences. In healthy identifications, the individuals in a group express the needs and interests that guide their behavior, and when there is an overlap of needs and interests, or when a common goal can be seen to serve different interests, the group members identify with one another as cooperators. The force of commonality brings the members closer together, lessens the psychological distance between them, and, even when they have very different desires, the possibility of satisfying themselves through joint effort promotes cohesion and contact among the group members.

The following example portrays an ambiguity below which can be either identification with the aggressor or a healthy identification. A meeting was held in which health care activists were trying to educate union rank and file about issues of occupational safety. In good democratic fashion, after an introduction addressed to the whole assembly, small groups were formed so that the union members would be actively involved in talking about their unique situations. Members met in clusters in corners and other niches in the meeting hall and formed their own circles.

In one of these small group discussions, it was not long before one union member, a small, balding, middle-aged man, began forcefully stating the arguments for the safety of working with formaldehyde that had been made earlier by management people when they had been confronted on the issue by the union. It seemed clear to observers that the man was accepting these arguments that had originated in management, and he was putting them forward as sound and appropriate positions. Here is the identification: a union man at a union meeting identifies himself with a management point of view.

What was ambiguous to other members of his circle, what would determine whether the identification was faulty or healthy, was whether he had reached his acceptance of management's position regarding a potentially dangerous chemical by his own critical study of the matter or was somehow automatically identifying with management. Had he systematically and autonomously evaluated the facts, or was he primarily responsive to the authority of management and taking on faith its view as descriptive of the facts? If he had conducted his own critical assessment of what management had given out, he was showing a healthy identification, a matching of his opinion, formed when he functioned as an agent, with the perspective of managers construable as thoughtful others. If he had merely taken in whole, swallowed without chewing, almost as a reflex, the orientation of management, then he was displaying an identification with the aggressor.

It was not considered relevant at that meeting to pursue psychological functioning, so we observers in his cluster were unable to determine whether this union member manifested a faulty or healthy identification. Time was not allotted for such thoughtful attention, and being psychological in one's concern was not an acceptable way of being in the group. As a corollary, the immediate rejections by some others in the discussion group of what management had offered to resolve the issue could not be checked out as to whether they were faulty projections or healthy, accurate readings of reality.

Suppose that the cluster had taken up and analyzed the identification patterns of the man who was putting forth management's position on formaldehyde and had discovered that he had identified with the aggressor. In the process he would have been encouraged to relate the method by which he developed his position, where he had gotten his facts, how he had worked with them, and so on. Suppose that he was clearly sincere but had little of his own to say about the issue, that he had obviously swallowed management's views whole, and, further, that as he talked it slipped out by the way that he feared he would threaten his job if he opposed management. Then some of the group might have discussed his reaction to the situation with him openly and straightforwardly but without hostility. But I would bet that some would have criticized the man with clear contempt or disgust. They would have felt that a company man, a fink, was in their midst, and they would have condemned him roundly.

Such condemnation would be contrary to the purpose of acknowledging psychological issues in social action, and it would probably also be a projection upon a primed vulnerable other. All of us in the meeting possessed some hidden tendencies to identify with the aggressor, and could have used the promanagement man's behavior to divest ourselves of responsibility for those tendencies by condemning him. The display of disgust or contempt — strong emotions indeed — rather than compassion for a frightened man would have been the giveaway of group members who took this route. In the future, these group members would be defensive rather than open, as well, for the interesting reason that they, having tendencies to identify with the aggressor like all the rest, would feel condemned in the very act of condemning their colleague. I cannot stress enough the importance of accepting others while striving to undo the faulty identifications, projections, and so on that afflict their behavior. The general principle of psychotherapy that one accepts the person while helping to sort out the healthy and neurotic patterns of behavior, ultimately helping the person cast off the neurotic ways, is vital in applying clinical insights to social action.

After it is established in a group that an identification with the aggressor is operative in a person's functioning, an effort to change that identification and the process of introjecting that invariably goes with it can begin. A first step in this effort is to bring the faulty identification into the person's and the whole group's awareness, to notice it and make it conscious. Here are some signs that point to problematic identifications:

- Frequent speedy agreement

- Lack of criticism in group activity

- Frequent use of "I should"

- Behavior without conviction or appetite for it

- Compliance without interest or enthusiasm

Speedy agreement with a proposal put forward by someone else can be appropriate if the proposal clearly will help satisfy an interest or goal that the person who agrees has already formed and perhaps has been independently pursuing. Usually, however, it takes time for a person to register what is put forward, to study how the proposal may facilitate the satisfaction of some needs and limit the satisfaction of others, and to judge whether there is enough in it to merit approval and agreement. Thus speedy agreement, especially when it is routine or has been insisted on by the other, will usually mean that consideration of these matters has been aborted. And frequent speedy agreement will almost always mean that the agreeing person too readily takes on as his or her own that which is decided by the other — an identification with the aggressor with plenty of introjection.

It is an old story in the struggles between those who are committed to preserving the status quo and those who foster change that the conservative side argues for efficiency and decisiveness while the progressive side calls for democracy even if it is to be time-consuming. Similarly, it is an old story within change-oriented groups that there are some who are in a hurry and others who are patient, and the difference may boil down to those who wish for quick agreement with few questions asked and much obedience demonstrated, a sign of faulty identification, versus those who wish for the change to be accomplished in the slow, painstaking, thorough activity which involves all the members in learning what they want and in saying that to the collectivity.

Failure to welcome criticism and promote critical and self-critical attitudes and approaches within a group also indicates, as well as stimulates, problematic identification. Criticism is the hallmark of difference, challenge, and negotiation, all of which are basic to healthy identification. Criticism in the group assures that individuals will not submerge themselves, give up their uniqueness, avoid their responsibility to be themselves while the group is doing its business. When criticism is missing, it's likely that at least some members are doing these things. Criticism means that persons are taken seriously and are deemed worthy of comment and observation, are valued and needed by their peers. In a group seeking social change, criticism is especially important to the sorting out of what are true needs and what are needs taken up in identifications with an aggressor.

There is also, however, hypercriticism — that criticism which comes quickly as a reflex response to assertive behavior in others, which does not allow ideas and emotions to percolate before judgment is made, which often is a put-down or indicates rejection of others, which can reflect a general tendency to depreciate. Hypercriticism is hardly a sign of healthy identification. On the contrary, this ready and rapid negativism is regularly a defense against identification, a refusal to hold in awareness for thoughtful examination another person's idea or suggestion lest one be tempted to agree with it and to that extent at least identify with whoever has put it forth. Paradoxically, rapid criticism of this kind is much like the firmly closed mouth of a small child someone is trying to feed — a refusal to taste.

Interrupting a speaker, whether in a meeting, a discussion group, or informal conversation, is a form of hypercriticism. Not allowing a person to finish her thought (it happens more to women than to men) is like disagreeing rapidly without open confrontation.

Both being hypercritical and interrupting can also be defenses against introjection: not letting something into one's psyche because one might swallow it whole and would not know how to digest it or get it out. In this connection, making sure that individuals are permitted to present their own ideas fully, without interruption, is a method for preventing introjections. If people are expressing fully what they have to say, they generally will not push their audience to introject what they say. On the other side, their audience, freed of the push, will get more to think about and will move toward thinking about the presentation, testing it, discriminating among its contents, and move away from swallowing or rejecting it whole.

Social attention to the frequency of interruption in a group is a useful device. I know a couple who decided to watch closely how they treated each other when they were in company as well as when they were alone. They agreed to announce regularly for a period of time every instance in which one of them felt interrupted by the other. They also committed themselves to each asking if the other was finished before they began to speak when there was any question about the matter. It was not easy for them, nor for those of us in their presence, but it revealed remarkably how frequently they interrupted one another, and it led them to increased patience with, and awareness of, each other. Their practice became infectious so that others who saw them in interactions began to do the same thing. Awareness of patterns of interruption became vivid indeed — and nervous-making too.

Use of the phrase "I should" suggests that conscience is being taken into account in the making of behavior. A person who says "I should" is likely to be asserting, "If I follow the values and standards that I hold, I shall. . . ." A person's frequent use of "I should" responses in group activity means that she or he keeps values and standards in the foreground of experience rather than in the background where they usually operate. Most of the time in social intercourse we do not draw directly upon our fundamental values to regulate our relations; we reserve focus upon these values for special events which have long-term implications, as when we form close friendships, marry, or commit ourselves to protracted, dangerous common struggle. When values are in the foreground with frequency, concern about differences in values must be lurking about, concern lest there be even minimal divergence that is undetected. This is precisely the condition that holds for the weaker persons in oppressive relations; they are concerned not to have values and standards that violate the preferences of the stronger person or persons. Frequent use of "I should" by anyone indicates that the values guiding behavior are introjected values. For an oppressed person, these introjected values typically do not accord with those the person would have created if only her or his own needs and desires had been taken into consideration. The person is saying that she or he is acting in accommodation to an other rather than according to own wants, is sacrificing self for other. An identification with the aggressor is in play.

The distinction between persons who are moralistic, who are very judgmental, who always see the world in terms of right and wrong, good and bad, and persons who are ethical, who, without judging others, conduct themselves with social concern and propriety, is another distinction between persons living by faulty identifications and those living by healthy ones. A man who is prudish because his parents punished him for his sexual curiosity, that is, who introjected their reproaches, is likely to be on the lookout for those adolescents who are finding their sexuality so that he can judge them and heap reprimands upon them.

Finally, when we see behavior without conviction or appetite for it or compliance without interest or enthusiasm, we are observing action that has minimal drive from the desires of the actor. Ordinarily, a person feels rising excitement stemming from desires and is moved into action when something in the environment is soon after perceived as available for gratification of the desires; or a person is stimulated by the environment so that lively needs are tapped and the action follows. When the individual is moved by external forces *without inner-desires' being mobilized*, we have identifications of a faulty sort and behavior without conviction. The motivation does not receive the amplification that attachment to desires would promote. The individual moves on the energy of someone else and not at all on the energy of needs pressing toward satisfaction. A group member may start to carry out an uninteresting task such as stuffing envelopes for a political rally on the urging of a leader but, without added inspiration, soon become listless and distracted, thereby showing compliance without enthusiasm. In many social groups a few people end up doing most of the work because others drop out after being asked to do things that lack intrinsic interest, and these others only comply and live on the energy of leaders for a short period of time.

These various indications of faulty identifications are not difficult to observe, but in our social groupings we have not paid much attention to the psychological functioning of ourselves and our compatriots. Making ourselves and our fellow actors aware of these identification patterns is part of the process by which we can begin to undo them. It happens also to make interpersonal relationships more interesting.

In addition, group leaders and members can create a culture that discourages actions that express or encourage identifications with the aggressor. It can be made a group norm, for example, that behavior without appetite is to be watched and even distrusted. When interactions among members of the group lack excitement, when individuals seem to be going through the motions rather than investing themselves intensely, when people are lethargic from fatigue, when boredom sets in, group processes can be fostered that enable members to nourish each other and themselves, to cease from goal-directedness and turn to replenishment, to look at what is happening and find ways to invigorate each other.

Sometimes a simple acknowledgment that there is in ascendance behavior without appetite suffices. For instance, it is often successful in the classroom, when students are bored or preoccupied and not attending to what is going on, for the instructor to call for a break or to stop the instruction and ask where people are. This calls upon class members to check into themselves, to discover their needs, and to affirm their individuality in the midst of collective endeavor. Persons who have lost contact with one another or with the group as such are brought back into connection. Social-action meetings can be kept short enough to engage members fully. Group dynamics can be regulated, as in the occupational safety illustration, so that large groups break into small groups to engage all members in active participation; lectures can be replaced by dialogue, sermons given up in favor of Quaker-style individual participation, in which all members are encouraged to speak their thoughts.

In the forming of identifications, no group phenomenon is more important than leadership behavior and style. From the time of Freud's *Group Psychology and the Analysis of the Ego*,[3] group cohesion through identification with a leader has been known in the technical literature as an essential component of group life and collective behavior. The leader who is on the side of promoting healthy identifications gives voice and presence to what is happening among members who may not be in communication with the rest of the membership so that all will become aware of all that is alive in the group and can identify with what meets their own needs. This leader also creates conditions that foster individuals' self-expression and articulation. This leader then does not take credit for their contributions, but praises and amplifies what they have given to collective life. Similarly, this leader does not disclaim errors and let subordinates shoulder blame. In short, the leader who is likely to promote healthy rather than faulty identifications practices democracy.

The leader who does not practice democracy, but on the contrary is self-aggrandizing — for instance, *does* take credit when it is due to others — promotes faulty rather than healthy identifications with himself or herself, the chief among them being idealization. The "cult of personality," with its attribution of godlikeness to the leader, and the abasement of self and of other group members in deference to the glory of the leader are signs of idealization. It is identification gone awry, in that this kind of elevation of leaders diminishes the responsibility of members, obscures the contributions of the many, and suggests lowliness or weakness of the average participant in the group.

A clue to dealing with such harmful practices lies in E. Y. Harburg's ditty

> "No matter how high or great the throne,
> What sits on it is the same as your own."[4]

The way to prevent or correct idealization is to humanize the leader, to reveal him or her to all group members not only in strengths but in weaknesses, to show failures as well as successes and let each member take from the leader only that which is bona fide, attractive, and useful in the member's life. Setting social norms and practices up so that the leader cannot obscure and the members cannot avoid noticing the leader's limitations is part of this. When students are empowered to critically appraise a teacher's competence without fear of retribution, they are encouraged to note how the teacher can improve, and they usually find things that need improvement. While it is valuable for the leader to be gently glorified with recognition and praise when he or she is developing group process in a good way, in order that the collective life of the group be exalted, it is also necessary that the leader be treated as a person, not any kind of god, for idealization will ultimately destroy a group.

In the early days of his work, immediately following the Russian October revolution, the renowned Soviet educator Anton Makarenko illustrated the power of democratic leadership in his work with severely delinquent adolescents — young people who roamed the streets in bands, acted entirely outside organized society, and promised to be trouble to the new society. As he described events in his *The Road to Life: An Epic in Education*,[5] Makarenko, making up his treatment plans as he went along, transformed an anarchic group of young ruffians into an exciting, orderly communal group, and the major part of his success was the leadership style he exemplified and developed in his colleagues and his charges. Makarenko led by making strong demands upon the young people but also by making forceful demands upon various authorities higher in the hierarchy than he himself and facing up to leaders in the surrounding villages who came to ask him to punish his charges for their invasions and pillaging, defending his people against the townsfolk even when they were taken to task for clearly delinquent acts. When he went to deal with higher-ups, Makarenko took with him, as observers, selected members of his group of delinquents, who could see for themselves that he manipulated, lied, exaggerated, beseeched, and otherwise did what had to be done to obtain basic necessities for their community in a time of great scarcity. Since he negotiated in front of his youths, they could see his failures as well as his successes. He played in their games and took his lumps as well as handed them out; he acted in their plays.

They weren't changing, weren't trusting, weren't letting him help them. He gave up in exasperation and despair and came close to committing suicide, only to be given courage again by some of the young men who were beginning to understand how much he cared for them. After this, he created small groups within the community in which leadership positions rotated among all members. Each could have a turn as leader. The community flowered.

The story of Makarenko's democratic and equalitarian functioning in the early days of his work is all the more poignant because he was more naturally quite autocratic and militaristic, hating the "progressive education" that was dominant at the time in his controlling ministry, and because these authoritarian qualities eventually came to dominate the community. Makarenko instituted in the community a much more authoritarian leadership style, and predictably, faulty identifications in the form of idealizations resulted. He was idealized, the community itself was idealized. Eventually it was ruled by the secret police. Yet in its early days the community had a leadership that humanized and lifted up children and adolescents who were extremely troubled.

More recently, Steve Burghardt illustrated the democratic approach to leadership through the words of a Brooklyn group worker who told him about what had developed in her social service agency after clients and staff created a parents' group whose purpose was to fight the possible closing of a neighborhood school:

"You know, this last year fighting to keep the school open has actually been one of the best in terms of getting closer with clients and clients becoming more a part of the place. We all set up the parents group together . . . and together tried to work on strategies for keeping the school open. Since they were the ones who could prove the benefits of the program and of the school, they *had* to have a real voice in things, and so they were always viewed by themselves and us, as being as powerful as any of us in what happened. They also saw us in action and under stress, and saw a lot of nervousness before meetings, our own tensions and fears — there was *real* equality on that, let me tell you. . . .

"Our group and individual work seems to be growing better . . . people hold back less. They refer to themselves and their problems, but they are starting to connect some of their problems to larger issues, too . . . they seem to be less uptight about us and what we're doing — they trust us more, I think. The talking is a lot more honest, a lot more painful, but they don't seem to worry that we'll screw them with what they say. I've been under a lot more pressure on my job . . . and yet I love some parts of it more."[6]

I turn now from group processes that are useful in preventing or undoing identifications with the aggressor by members of a group and attend to guidelines and concerns when focus is upon an individual whose experience is seen to be importantly shaped by introjection. Because being with an individual who is under the sway of introjection can be tricky and undoing or inhibiting the process is subtle, I can offer only some basic themes to be kept in mind. These are themes that guide a trained therapist, and I do not expect group members to "therapize" their comrades; yet the themes are also clear enough and sufficiently coherent with what I have said about group process that they may be useful to readers of this essay. Most of the ideas that I will present in the next paragraphs have been culled from notes taken when listening to the Gestalt therapist Isadore From.

First, the aim in counteracting a person's introjecting ways of shaping experience is to enable the person to risk experiencing what was interrupted by means of introjection. Thus, the person was once excited, striving to meet his or her desires in the environment, then ran into conflict about those desires, and then introjected the standards of the other in the conflict. If the introjecting is now undone, there will be a revival of the excitement, plus anxiety, frustration, and anger, and, it is to be hoped, this time the person will stay with the experience, exert his or her capacities more completely, and achieve an experience which is quite satisfying while at the same time he or she is becoming more self as agent.

Second, two distinct aspects of faulty introjection can be isolated and attended to. One of these can be labeled "right now introjecting." In the ongoing processes of group activity, the individual can be seen to be introjecting — taking on an idea, an emotion, a gesture, a viewpoint without making it his or her own; complying prematurely; or avoiding choosing, deciding, believing his or her own thoughts. The second aspect of faulty introjection can be called "living now the influence of past introjections." The individual is acting on the basis of internal commands that were originally someone else's, and now the person acts *as if* they were his or her own. If the union member adopted management's position on the safety of formaldehyde because he felt he would threaten his job were he to oppose management and he felt this way because some relative long ago told him time and time again that those who complain get fired, then presenting management's views as his own was a case of living now the influence of past introjections. When a woman is acting as her mother insisted she should, she also is most likely living now the influence of past introjections. If I do something *only because I should*, I'm surely living now the influence of past introjections.

A series of tactics which promote a person's acting as an agent may counteract right now introjecting. For a start, it is important to have the person *experience* in the present doing something that seems like introjecting, not by telling the person "You are introjecting," but by making appropriate observations. Just to tell someone that he or she is introjecting runs into the paradox that you seem to want the person to stop introjecting by introjecting your interpretation. This is like antidemocratically demanding that persons act democratically. A better approach might be an observation like one of the following, depending on the situation.

- "You seem to agree without being convinced; are you aware of that?"

- "You appear to like this idea very much; what don't you like about it? Is it hard to dislike it?"

- "Our leader's statement is wise; let's see if we can also know its limitations."

- "Let's share what we appreciate and what we don't appreciate about each other."

- "Before you agree to do it too quickly, give some thought to it; are you aware how quickly you were ready to accept this task?"

- "What would it be like to say no in this group?"

- "Is anyone here unenthusiastic about what is going on?"

In trying to have a person experience himself or herself as introjecting, it is wise to take little steps. What is critical is not what the outsider can observe, but what the person can hear. Learning to experience oneself as giving over one's role as agent is sensitive and scary business which can only take place in a context of respect and thoughtfulness.

Not to shame is especially important when relating to persons who habitually introject rapidly, because such individuals are easily wiped out by humiliation. This, after all, happened to them in the past. A parent, a teacher, or other powerful authority who "knew it all" demanded introjection — was intolerant of disagreement and shamed the weaker one into taking in what he or she was putting forward. Authoritative behavior that brings about introjections is often of a blaming, shaming nature. Persons who rapidly introject would rather internalize the conflict than feel the pain of humiliation. Avoidance of shaming and sensitivity to feelings of humiliation have high priority in overcoming introjection and thus oppression.

When a person is right now introjecting, it is helpful to encourage his or her "no function":

- "Do you want that?"

- "Are you satisfied with that?"

- "Is that enough for your needs?"

A too ready and unconvincing "Yes" can lead to the next observation:

- "You seemed to say that without checking it out with yourself."

At bottom, this involves not only the observer's taking the individual seriously, but the individual's starting to experience his or her own process with interest and respect.

Another theme in attending to introjecting actions is discouraging "mere adjustment," that adaptation to the environment which gives power and force to the external and disempowers or diminishes the internal. Adjustment, or adaptation, is double-sided. There are demands or attractions from the environment that must be answered to, and there are one's own needs and desires that must be met. Introjection highlights the former and hides the latter. Countering introjection, consequently, calls for a balancing act, a revival of "selfing" endeavors, a putting of one's needs, one's person, one's requirements, one's preferences into active play in any relationship with the outside. Someone who is too adjusted to circumstances needs encouragement to throw in these ingredients and stir up the pot as a means of undoing introjecting proclivities. Although such a person is likely to meet the encouragement with anxiety or annoyance, that will have to be accepted if introjecting patterns are to be changed.

The aim in dealing with a person who is living now the influence of past introjections is to enable the person to contact an introject, become aware that it is the voice of someone else which he or she has taken on, and move the conflict that flourishes within back to a conflict with the environment. If conquering oneself with the standards or beliefs of another has served to alleviate a serious interpersonal conflict, one fraught with destructive urges, then the undoing of the self-conquest will revive that conflict. The difference this time will be that the person can be helped to manage the conflict productively in relation to people who are in his or her present environment, being angry, assertive, and scared in a way that does not lead to helplessness and resignation.

Living now the influence of past introjections is essentially experiencing as part of oneself that which belongs on the other side, in the environment. Thus, contacting the introject proceeds somewhat as in the following dialogue:

A: "I shouldn't be aggressive."

B: "Who told you that?"

A: "Well, I was punished by my father for hitting my sister and at school for roughneck play at recess."

B: "Oh, that belongs to your father and teacher. Let's see if it belongs to you."

The goal is to help persons know what *they* want, what *they* believe, who *they* are now, and to enable them to realize that they have more scope and possibility than their "shoulds" permit. They must experience their self-conquest, however, and they must hear the voices within as those of one or more people in their past history if they are to demolish the effect of their introjects upon their current way of being.

At a training session for psychotherapists an exercise on revising introjects was carried out. Trainees paired off and gave each other lists of "I shoulds" and "I shouldn'ts." After they had developed a catalog of their dominant introjects, person B in the pair was instructed to help person A undo an introject — contact it, speak to it, find ways to soften it, destructure it so that anything in it that had been and continued to be useful could be kept as a standard while what was not useful could be discarded. The trainees became engrossed in the exercise and went at it with enthusiasm.

After roles had been reversed and the exercise repeated, so that each trainee had been helped to undo an introject, the trainees were asked to describe their experience in the exercise. R.L. said she was surprised to find that she became angry. This should be no surprise to the reader, by now, since the act of introjection was meant to quell rage in the basic progression into identification with the aggressor presented in this essay. R.L. had, in effect, gone back to where she was at the time she introjected and had contacted an emotion she could use now. B.T. said she did not feel anger, but rather fear. When I asked what she was afraid of, she said she feared she would be as abusive as her father had been to her as he molested her when she was a child. Her introject, his prohibition against revealing or otherwise reacting to what had happened, sat on her wish to be abusive toward her molesting father and was still inhibiting her in her adult life. A different reaction was described by B.R. She fought to hold on to her introject, to claim it as her own, even while acknowledging that she had internalized others' commands. K.S. said he recognized a feeling of loss and the giving up of another who had died and whom he had carried inside himself during intervening years. The mourning, however, seemed incomplete, and K.S. not free of values not his own but introjected from this important other person. The latter three reactions can be seen as holding on to the particular introject to avoid experiencing at this time the excitement, frustration, anxiety, and anger it squelched. They may also be seen as continuing investment in introjecting as a way of containing the present, whether that be avoiding separateness of self and other (K.S.), holding down assertiveness (B.T.), or merely not becoming a discrete, risk-taking, creatively adjusting human being (B.R.).

In noticing and acting to change problematic introjections, groups must be alive to all the emotions that accompany the un-doing of such introjections including disgust and nausea. It needs constant reminding that individuals identify with the aggressor when they feel weak and helpless in a relationship which they can-not avoid. Accordingly, when these persons begin to recover from the darkness of their participatory submission, they will re-experi-ence their weakness, sometimes as simple helplessness, sometimes feeling childish, sometimes in despair, always with a least some dis-gust and nausea. They will need heavy doses of social and personal support. If a group makes such support available, the group will become sophisticated in respect to the undoing of introjections as it attends to the psychological processes experienced by members.

It is my hope that in the course of social-change activities it will become more acceptable for individuals to openly reveal the unsettling and strange sensations that arise with the dislodgment of introjects, and groups will more and more become knowing, supportive, and benevolent holding environments. The processes both of introjecting and of undoing introjections will be of interest to members as they learn about themselves and their compatriots.

Chapter 13

Discovering and Undoing Projections

In attending to a person who is projecting, it is helpful to keep in mind that people push outside themselves only those experiences of their own which they feel unable or unprepared to master internally. If they could maintain and handle the tensions of their rage, for instance, they would have no cause to disown their rage and to find it coming upon them from external figures. Persons are unlikely to project upon primed vulnerable others unless they perceive their own psychological happenings as excessively burdensome. Remembering this makes it easier to empathize with a person who is projecting. Projectors often fail to generate such empathy because they gain power via their projections and they appear to others as self-contained or self-satisfied and not in need of our compassion.

Sometimes the perception of what is too burdensome is emotionally cheap. In long-established power relationships, for example, where one party is always in command, he or she may have the psychological capacity to manage the internal social-emotional convections of the relationship, but the primed vulnerable other is conveniently available and it seems to the commanding one on the face of it easier to project than to grapple with the feelings. In such instances a kind of intrapsychic and social laziness prevails. More often, however, the individual who is in the position within the relationship that permits or facilitates projection is personally quite disturbed by the feelings that are aroused by certain encounters, and projecting these social emotions can make it seem like the other is carrying the weight they impose.

In order to overcome this inability or unwillingness of the person who is projecting to manage internally the aroused social emotions, others must enable this person to feel capable and desirous of supporting the emotions. He or she needs to be supported and helped to create a sense of self-support so that self-management of anxiety or self-hatred, disgust, weakness or helplessness will seem possible and promising, indeed desirable in some way. A person is unlikely to take back and experience directly as his or her own a feeling which has been projected onto an other unless the person has a sense of inner energy and strength and social safety. Accordingly, a basic requirement in modifying projecting maneuvers is to increase the support felt by the projector. This support is needed whether this person is an oppressor, a troubled member of a group fighting oppression who is, say, trying to feel some power by projecting on another weak person, or someone not personally involved at all in struggle between the strong and the weak.

What do I mean by support? Following Erving and Miriam Polster,[1] I define support as any element or collection of elements, internal or external, that makes for the ability to proceed with a sense of integrity through an experience that is novel. That which preserves and encourages a person's felt integrity in the presence of new and thus challenging conditions can be taken as support to that person. I have said that projection upon a primed vulnerable other, in common with identification with the aggressor, is installed when social emotions in transactions between persons seem overwhelming and destructive. Necessary to the undoing of such projection is making the apparently unbearable in fact supportable and supported. Reviving in awareness old situations in which the social emotions were indeed overwhelming from lack of adequate support in the encounter and *this time* providing the needed bolstering and assurance that integrity will be preserved is a basic strategy for undoing projections upon primed vulnerable others.

We can look again at Selma Fraiberg's work with parents who were themselves abused as children and who now abused their own children, referred to in Chapter 9. As she noted, when they were small and mistreated, they hated their parents but could not live out their hatred; neither could they carry it with them and still go about living, so they retroflected it — turned it back upon themselves — and it seemed to disappear, only to return, among other places, in their projections upon their children when they became parents. In discussing her work, Fraiberg suggested that with support from therapists these parents were enabled to re-experience intensely their hatred of their own abusing parents, along with the anxiety and terror involved in being abused, and that with this re-experience they became able to give up their projections upon their own children and their abuse declined.[2] This, it seems to me, is a basic model for undoing projections upon primed vulnerable others.

Anyone who has tried to overcome prejudice when it is overtly expressed in relationships will be able to attest to the inadequacy of trying to undo this form of projection by reasonable argument or objection. A common example is the making of racist or other prejudiced remarks at family gatherings such as Thanksgiving dinners. Many holiday gatherings of families, oddly enough, bring out projections upon other social groups as a signal of family cohesion; that is, one or more family members try somehow to base ingroup loyalty on jokes or directly hostile remarks about a favorite outgroup. These comments may be antiblack, anti-Semitic, anti-Catholic, anti-Polish, anticommunist, or anti- any other despised group. Those members of the family who do not have the prejudice being aired find themselves uncomfortable because they don't want to upset the family but also don't want to let the negative remarks go by unanswered. Few of these persons deal with their discomfort successfully. Some simply hold their thoughts inside and feel miserable, discontented with themselves and angry with their prejudiced relatives. Though this is fertile ground for undoing projections, those who speak up tend to use ineffective methods: they usually speak rationally to the unreasonableness of racism, for instance, to its inaccuracy, to its socially harmful effects; or they express outrage and demand that family members not make racist remarks in their presence; and they usually end up frustrated, helpless, and feeling guilty.

Here is an illustration from a twenty-eight-year-old woman who has been active in the peace and feminist movements:

"My father and uncle are racists and sexists. They have often made provocative comments about women, for example, such as 'Women should learn their place and stay in the home.'

"I used to argue with them, but that only made them do it more, and it frustrated me a great deal. So I have learned to deal with their comments by not reacting when they are provocative. I am angry with them, but I want to relate in a family way with them. Over the years they have begun to quiet down on these issues. They know how I feel and what my positions are, and they are not going to influence me to believe as they do. I think they are becoming a bit more tolerant.

"I can do that in my family because I relate to them over time and I want to be on decent terms with them, but I find it hard to do the same thing with strangers. With them, I get mad and end up feeling awful."

The key to such failures in dealing with the projection in racism, sexism, or other prejudice is the lack of support for the person projecting. By not recognizing and attending to the anxiety and rage and felt weakness behind the prejudiced behavior, those who try to contravene it lack a foundation for influencing the prejudiced person. If they persist in their efforts without providing the necessary support, they inevitably do find the rage, but they come upon it in an unhappy way, because now it is directed at them. In turn they become angry and the interplay of identification with the aggressor and projection upon a primed vulnerable other moves onto a new stage, even characterizing the relations within one's family if that is where the issue of prejudice has arisen. The person who has tried to fight the prejudice but has failed to do so effectively becomes identified with the aggressor through suppressing anger and internalizing the social conflict. In the example above, the young woman, after being frustrated and made angry, stopped reacting openly when her father and uncle were provocative; she quieted down and tolerated their racism and sexism. Internally, she joined these men's aggression against her for challenging these traits. She aggressed against herself by stopping her angry feeling, which was a form of identification with them. Thus, in relation to her father and uncle, she came in a sense to live out the dictum that "women should learn their place and stay in the home."

At this point the reader may be forgiven for feeling some rage as well, since my argument suggests that the weak must support the strong who oppress them if projecting by the strong is to be undone. Women who are oppressed by men, blacks who have been put upon by racist whites, Indians who have been mistreated and maligned by the majority American culture, children who have been abused by their parents, poor people who have been degraded and hurt over and over by the wealthy, students who have been mistreated by their teachers — these are all to support those whom they are opposing? How dare a serious and sincere thinker suggest such a course of action! What nonsense psychological thought brings to real social struggles! Away with such speculations and recommendations!

I ask the reader's forbearance so that the full argument can be realized. I too was stopped by what seemed to be the logic of my argument. But I am not about to ask that those who are suffering the most obviously be called upon now to shoulder even more responsibility. I would simply be joining in the oppressive endeavors if that were the upshot of my considerations, and my whole purpose is to labor toward the ending of exploitation and oppression for all involved in such relationships as I have been describing.

Clearly, those who are the weak in the relationship, those who have identified with the aggressor, are already supporting the strong. It is this very support that is the mark of their oppression. They do the work demanded of them, they protect the batterer from discovery and community control, they nurture those who dominate them — is it not remarkable how much nurturance is involved in the life tasks of those who are oppressed? They provide the physical, material, and spiritual support required by those who are projecting for the maintenance of their personal welfare. As Harriet Lerner has said in discussing the relations of men and women:

"Sure enough, those old dictates to 'play dumb,' 'let the man win,' or 'pretend he's boss' — are out of vogue. But their message still remains a guiding rule that lurks in the unconscious of countless women: *The weaker sex must protect the stronger sex from recognizing the strength of the weaker sex lest the stronger sex feel weakened by the strength of the weaker sex.* We learn to act weaker to help men feel stronger and to strengthen men by relinquishing our own strength."[3]

My conclusion is not that the oppressed should take on *more* supportive activities; they should rather change the manner of the support that they render. And they need to find ways to support and oppose at the same time.

The support to be given to the strong is not support of projections themselves. The weak must not accept strong people's projections, absorb them through identification, encourage them through behavior communicating that they, the weak, are not a threat. Instead, they must — and can — discover the fact that the strong are projecting and both support the strong and oppose the projecting activity in such a way that it is not needed. What is required for this is to elicit the experience from which the projecting comes. As the experience is remembered and elaborated, the conditions for the projection become clear and the possibility of meeting them differently arises. The strong projector affirms the experience; a weaker person trying to get rid of the projection confirms the experience and provides a truer, more grounded sense of its meaning, allowing for a new management of it, including the undoing of the projection.

Such a process can be realized in a psychotherapist's office much more readily than in the direct encounter of oppressed and oppressor because in the office there are an established base of trust and a common task of promoting the welfare of a person who, while seemingly weak as client or patient, is projecting like a powerful person. This is not to say that it is an easy task in psychotherapy to have persons find and undo their projections; on the contrary, it is not at all easy, which is one reason so little has been written about it. But it is nonetheless considerably simpler to help undo projections as therapist than it is as a weaker person in contest with a stronger.

The idea that the strong who are dominant from projecting must be supported if their projecting is to be undone takes me back to the beginning of my writing this essay. As numerous others have been, I was then perplexed that those who are exploited and kept down very typically can be found to be supporting those who oppress them. In the course of writing this essay, I think I have come upon the wisdom of the oppressed. *Their support for those who oppress them has a function beyond self-preservation and the avoidance of responsibility — the function of attempting to provide the grounds for the strong to give up their projecting endeavors.*

Of course, the activities of the weak in this respect are not all wise; otherwise we would not speak of oppression, but of mutually fulfilling human relationships. In fact, the support that the weak offer is in general provided at their own expense, by means of self-denial and the loss of their own inner guides, their will, and ultimately their sense of their own needs through fusion. The different support that is required for the undoing of projections involves self-affirmation. The task is to affirm self in the face of a projection and to oppose the projecting while supporting the person who is doing the projecting. AFFIRM SELF — SUPPORT PERSON PROJECTING — OPPOSE PROJECTING PROCESS.

These actions are carried out by the weak in transformative encounters with the strong. Why do not the weak more regularly implement such a program in their transactions with the strong? The answer, I believe, is that they feel their weakness, their isolation from means to improve their lot, their threatened condition; in short, they find themselves in a situation in which they are lacking support. There are situations in which an individual may be the object of a hierarchical or tyrannical projection and not feel threatened; one is the situation of an able therapist working with a client who projects. In social situations also there are occasionally individuals who have a firm sense of self and are able to preserve their integrity in exploitative encounters even when they are in a weak position in the social relationship involved. These are the exceptions, however; more commonly, even relatively grounded individuals will respond to hierarchical or tyrannical conditions with fear and uncertainty. This is the psychological state to be expected and thus one not to be denigrated. It should be predicted, made awares to the individual experiencing it, and shared among those in the community who are similarly affected.

The felt weakness of persons in the weak role in a relationship is triply difficult because some of the weakness is from the objective circumstance, in that the strong have access to social powers; some is personal, in that each of us carries a sense of our own frailty through all the moments of our lives; and some is projected from the strong onto the weak. This latter aspect is often critical to the whole division of power. The combination of intolerance for their own weakness of those in the strong role and excessive acknowledgment of weakness by those in the weak role is basic to power relationships, and this combination is fundamentally the definition of projection of weakness.

To find their way out of this morass, the weak need to find their own support as they try to support in a self-affirming way the person or persons projecting. That support is most likely to be found in community, in collective caring and tending. It is an old and established political understanding that the strength of the weak is in their organization. Labor unions, community organizations, and political entities have long relied on the solidarity and unity of their members. What is now needed is an understanding of solidarity and unity that promotes support in the collective via sophisticated psychological insights as to both what is happening in the membership, that is, inside each member and between members, and what is happening between the collective and those whom it is opposing. What I am suggesting here is that social and political organizing seems to have had all the right instincts in its focus upon collectivity but has failed to integrate psychological insights into its efforts. The psychological insights most needed, I believe, are those I have been detailing in these pages — awareness of introjections, projections, the tendency to fusion, flight from anger and anxiety, helplessness in rage, excess responsibility in relationships, and others. Feeling supported in a group, even with one's strangest, most private, or secret fears right there with one, is basic to beating or avoiding projections oneself there and to helping undo them in the other members. With strong psychological insight present in the group, it becomes more possible to question one's fears aloud — "Why am I so anxious in this meeting?" — and to question other group members both honestly and intelligently in efforts to undo their projections — "What is it about the manager that makes you so angry?"

Relatives or friends or other associates of strong and powerful people can work to undo their projections. This may not be simple for these life partners of the strong to try, since they tend also to be persons given to projection in the circumstances involved and are likely to be trapped in their identification with the projector, but the possibility is there. Consider again the family together during a holiday gathering. When racist or otherwise prejudiced remarks are made by their parents on these occasions, young adult children seem to see themselves as helpless or inadequate to the task of confronting the slurs in a productive manner. They fear to challenge, and later argue often that they want to preserve family harmony, that it is useless to try to change their parents, that they have tried and failed.

Yet they are by no means subordinates, except in their imaginations. What might they do to carry out the formula of AFFIRM SELF - SUPPORT THE PERSON PROJECTING — OPPOSE PROJECTING PROCESS? They might assert that they see things differently and inquire into what their father or mother experiences in respect to those who are being belittled:

- "What is it like for you, Mother, to be in a black community?"

- "Dad, what happens to you when you are with someone who seems to be sympathetic to communists or who is openly socialist in commitment?"

- "Have you been mistreated by someone who is Jewish?"

Being clear about one's own position — interested in and accepting of others and their experience yet able to differ with their beliefs and convictions — is sometimes much easier than we are accustomed to thinking. What is called for is curiosity about the experience of another and humility in one's approach to reality. Also called for is freedom from the urge toward fusion. Willingness to stand alone without fear of isolation and be an agent in social relations is central for the overcoming of projective processes.

After affirming oneself and offering support to the other person, the next order of business is to bring into awareness the fact of projection. Some signs of problematic projections are:

- Frequent use of the impersonal "it"

- Frequent use of "you should," "he" or "she should," or "they should"

- Easy blame of others

- Avoidance of one's own part in negatively valued events

- A sense of being watched

- Excessively admiring others for doing well what one can do well oneself

- Assigning the energy behind events to external forces

A person who uses the impersonal "it" with frequency is tending to disclaim responsibility for his actions or hers by projection. Perls et al. have articulated this most clearly:

"The prevention of outgoing motion and initiative, the social derogation of aggressive drives, and the epidemic disease of self-control and self-conquest have led to a language in which the self seldom does or expresses anything; instead 'it' happens. These restrictive measures have also led to a view of the world as completely neutral and 'objective' and unrelated to our concerns; and to institutions that take over our functions, that are to 'blame' because they 'control' us, and that wreak on us the hostility which we so carefully refrain from wielding ourselves — as if men did not themselves lend to institutions whatever force they have."[4]

They recommend an experiment that both shows the presence of projection in "it" statements and suggests a way to recover what has been projected:

"Translate, as if they were in a foreign language, those sentences in which 'it' is subject and you are object into sentences in which 'I' is subject."[5]

For instance,

"It is hot in here and making me too drowsy to talk about our struggles with authority"

might become

"I feel hot and drowsy as we talk about taking responsibility in our struggles with authority."

Or,

"It seems to me that your ideas about dealing with projections are naive"

might become

"I don't like your ideas about dealing with projections."

The examples I have just used are mine. The reader will find it simple to discover "it" statements that strike closer to home, and I encourage attention to these as a method for sensitizing oneself to the presence of projection. Members of groups that are alive to social action may wish to use the experiment recommended by Perls et al. to foster the taking of responsibility for their own actions and reactions by all individuals in the group. When too many "it" statements are heard during discussion or speeches, a call for the translation of these into "I" statements would be appropriate and useful.

In the same way that introjection is expressed by "I should" do such and such, projection is carried forward, especially projection of guilt and moral preoccupation, through "you should," "he" or "she should," or "they should" do such and such. When one or another of these phrases becomes common in discourse or is the organizing principle for a group's purpose, projective processes are sure to be operative. For example, antiabortion groups believe pregnant women should carry their fetuses to term under all conditions; antiwelfare individuals argue that people on welfare should work no matter how difficult and painful their life situation; and middle-class folks think poor people should be tidy no matter how degraded they may feel. Projection is active in each of these instances, as we can often see not only from the use of "they should" but also from intense emotional investment in the matter at hand.

The other side of "they should" is blaming "them." No group is blamed more than the victims of oppression, as William Ryan[6] ably demonstrated. The phrase "blaming the victim," which he coined, is essentially interchangeable with "projecting upon the weak" or my "projecting upon a primed vulnerable other." To blame is to place the responsibility for a fault upon someone; both elements, allocating responsibility and finding fault, are key to the projection process at work here. Whether the fault in the picture is a moral one, tied to some "ought" or "should," or simply a human limitation or casual error, if it is hard to carry, it can be seen in the other and the self can be freed from its weight. Easy blame of others, thus, appears when penalties for any fault are severe.

When individuals typically avoid acknowledging their own part in negatively valued events, they are similarly engaged in projection. The self-righteousness that is so common both among the well-off and among those who are attempting to counter exploitation is a prime manifestation of this tendency to avoid one's own part in disvalued activities. Many powerful people cultivate the tactic of seeing and pointing out limitations in others but reserving for themselves freedom from open negative evaluation, and this tactic becomes an underpinning of their projection tendencies. This is the case with those teachers who give negative feedback in returning students' exam papers but refuse to accept evaluation of their own performance as teachers from their students. These teachers don't get information from those they've been controlling, leaving an empty place in the relationship which they go on to fill with projections.

A sense of being watched in a hostile way is a sign of projection activity. To be admired and looked at positively is desirable, but to be spied upon, to be scrutinized closely in the search for weakness or blameworthiness, is not. Focus upon being watched this way may be an indirect expression of self-criticism that is not bearable. If I am basically severely judgmental about a characteristic people have and find that the characteristic could rightly be associated with myself, I may refuse to hold criticism of it in my consciousness but be tempted to find that criticism in other people: they are watching me to find this thing that at some level I know to be there, and when they find it, they will use their knowledge malevolently.

Projection is not only associated with negative phenomena. Anything that serves to lighten the load of responsibility that one feels may be connected to projective processes. Thus, persons may excessively admire others for doing well what they can do well themselves. By admiring others this way, they seduce these persons to carry forward activity that they like seeing and to bear responsibility they do not wish to own. Persons who make themselves weak by abasing themselves before those they fear use such projections to create glorifications of the figures they fear. A similar diversion of responsibility from self to others occurs when people assign the energy behind events to external forces rather than to themselves.

I have been discussing various signs of projection. When one of these signs clearly appears in a participant in a social relationship and the person is made aware that he or she is projecting, the undoing of the projection has begun. Awareness of the present operation of projection is a vital component of the undoing process. But it is only a start. Also to be recognized are how the projection is done and what in the world or in the situation is promoting the projection.

The how of projection can be illustrated by typical aspects of racist behavior. Persons who are racist do not look closely at those they discriminate against, and this lack of pertinent visual contact promotes projection. Racists frequently say, "They all look alike"; such a view can only come about from not looking closely. Within the black community, within the Asian-American community, within the Hispanic community, people vary tremendously in personal appearance, and not seeing this variety can come only from not looking or not looking closely enough to individualize the person. The extreme, as we know it from housing and school controversies, is to avoid direct personal encounters with those one is prejudiced against. Never encountering fosters never seeing, which fosters projection.

At a symposium on feminist therapy I witnessed the practice of undoing projections. Five black feminist therapists conducted a workshop in which they asked the group to look at them closely and to answer a series of questions, such as which of them would be preferred as a therapist, which of them was most typical of black people in general, and which of them the observer would wish to have as a friend. The very task of looking closely and responding to particular issues quickened our sense of stereotyping and projection.[7] Their procedure pertained directly to how projection is put in place. Every psychotherapist knows that lack of eye contact between client and therapist is ground for projections by the client onto the therapist. The same kind of ground is provided by not hearing others, and in fact by not perceiving *oneself* clearly, for example, by underestimating one's own kinesthetic sense when relating to persons who seem strong and graceful.

Projections are almost never all wrong; there is usually something in the world that encourages or promotes or tolerates the projection, and in dealing with projections, it is helpful to find what it is. Care must be taken to locate truths about victims that are harmful to them — their part in the projecting process. The truths may thereby be made better per se and/or may help in the undoing of the projection. Are American Indians physiologically extremely vulnerable to alcohol and thus ripe for alcoholism? If so, they — and other Americans — need to know it. Are some or all Indians also more communal, more tribal, than the majority culture, and less competitive? If so, anyone who has to deal with the prejudices of projecting representatives of the majority culture needs to know it. If someone is generalizing from the smells of a group of persons, deriving from the food they eat or their anxiety in relating, to project bad character or general nastiness or unpleasantness onto them, knowing the truth about the smells may unlock the projection.

Along the way, care must be taken not to blame either the victims or the perpetrators of projection. Apart from the fact that not all real factors that enable projection are negative, the finding of a truth being used by the projector is likely to be helpful only if that truth is taken up in a supportive rather than a blaming framework.

Undoing projections is not easy, and I do not wish to give the impression that it is. I have already referred to the problems, such as various intense unpleasant feelings surfacing, that can be anticipated. When a person is helped to become aware of what was unawares being projected, that person may experience, for instance, weakness, disorientation, and jealousy of the imagined sex life of the person or persons who have been projected on, so that the helper doesn't know that positive assistance has been given or what to do next. At such a point the antiracist or antisexist actor in a family will see that she or he has aroused difficult emotions and will be tempted to retreat. Other feelings I have mentioned earlier as surfacing when projection is being counteracted are suspicion, distrust, and a sense of being unsafe, including sometimes a sense of being among enemies even when among friends. These feelings are not easy to own, nor are they simple for even a well-disposed observer to see and accept, which means that neither the projecting individual nor the person acting to undo the projecting process has an immediate sense of comfort.

In the antiracist effort, when a projection is being undone and anger, anxiety, or distrust is aroused, with luck and much support the powerful feelings are recognized, accepted, and dealt with, and the rupture in social relations is not allowed to proceed. In the place of what threatens to be a full revival of destructive urges is put caring and acceptance. Is this not the essence of what Martin Luther King, Jr., was able to do during the high days of the civil rights movement? He resurfaced the fury of the racists in the country and found ways to calm it while building community between oppressor and oppressed. He was engaged in loving the enemy. The oppressors could not but see the humanity of the blacks and white supporters opposing them, but they were angry that their position was being threatened. King did not back off or allow his own fear to turn into helpless rage, and the critical moments when this was transformative were precisely when the anger of the racists was greatest. When policemen turned blasts of water from fire hoses and dogs upon people demonstrating in a peaceful manner, the excess of their fury was vividly clear to the whole nation and to the police as well. Since their power was not being challenged, only their irrational views and actions, these authorities slowly came to take back their projections. Others, equally racist, who saw the extraordinary contrast between the behavior of the nonviolent marchers and the response of the police more quickly undid their projections. Both the police and the others then began to treat blacks more equitably.

As this example suggests, nothing underscores more than the undoing of projection the assertion that the process by which the delusion of fusion is rectified involves enabling and tolerating personal experiencing of intense, fearful, and strange social emotions.

Chapter 14

Recovering and Reorganizing Anger

". . . the warm pleasurable (and angry) destroying of existing forms in personal relations often leads to mutual advantage and love, as in . . . the breaking down of prejudices between friends. For consider that if the association of two persons will in fact be deeply profitable to them, then the destruction of the incompatible existing forms they have come with is a motion toward their more intrinsic selves — they will be actualized in the coming new figure; in this release of the more intrinsic, bound energy is liberated and this will transfer to the liberating agent as love. The process of mutual destruction is probably the chief proving ground of profound compatibility. Our unwillingness to risk it is obviously a fear that if we lose this we shall have nothing; we prefer poor food to none; we have become habituated to scarcity and starvation . . . .

"In general, anger is a sympathetic passion; it unites persons because it is admixed with desire."

> Perls, Hefferline, and Good-
> man, *Gestalt Therapy: Excite-
> ment and Growth in The
> Human Personality*[1]

When adult persons in an oppressive relationship are made fully aware of their introjecting and projecting activities and the guilt and self-hatred that are interwoven with them and all these are reduced in power so that they no longer control relationships, the next emotional experience for these persons is not joy, but rather it is rage. They meet again anger once so intense it seemed it might be literally annihilating; at that point it was suppressed, though far from fully pushed down; now it becomes figural again. Persons who have carried through the weak role in social relations know a new upsurge of great anger at their oppressors, and those who adopted the strong role once again experience great anger at the oppressed, for being not quite manageable — and now indeed at the whole social system for not quite providing satisfactions it seemed to promise. The next task in the process of normalizing relationships that have been oppressive is to turn all this anger into warm anger which releases the "more intrinsic selves" of the participants and produces love. The task is not to discharge or dissipate the anger, as if it were a familiar but now unwelcome interloper in psychic life and in social relations, but to bring it into experiences that bond rather than divide the persons.

In the passage quoted above, Perls et al. assert that this can be done — angry persons can destroy existing forms in personal relations and still unite with the other persons who are the objects of their anger. Although angry encounters sometimes create emotional distance between the actors, they may also serve to bring people closer together to mutual advantage. Let me underscore this point, with which I agree: *being angry can rewardingly unite persons who are in conflict with one another.* This is easier to accomplish in socially equal relationships such as friendship, invoked in the quoted passage, than in relations between socially advantaged and disadvantaged people, but it is possible in the latter also.

An exercise in expressing anger that I have used in small class and study groups and that can be tried informally by as few as two people illustrates how anger can be uniting. Persons in the group are asked to separate into pairs, one person being A and the other B. Then A is instructed to act angrily toward B in a blaming way. I have found that though group members may not know each other at all, they are generally quite willing to project their own angers and reactions to anger into the situation and carry out the exercise with conviction and liveliness: "You did this terrible thing to me . . . ." "You are troublesome, because . . . ." A may blame B for a specific act that A can creatively imagine, or not specify an act but blame B for "causing me all this pain and difficulty." Then roles are reversed for a time, so that everyone has the experience of being both A and B. Then in the group individuals relate their experience. Usually what I have found is that persons in the B role either distance themselves — for example, look away, try to get on with their own business, or just look through A — or retaliate with blaming assertions of their own. In either case the distance between A and B increases, because in counterattacking, B pushes A away.

Then A is asked to act angry again, but this time is instructed not to blame B, but to make only "I" statements. "I do not like to be ignored," "I was angry when you did that," and so on. Typically, now, B becomes angry in return, but also A and B find themselves talking sincerely and intensely to each other, hearing each other and developing empathy for each other's experience. This mode of being angry makes for contact between the persons rather than separation. These results are common and clear, even in such a situation as this exercise in which people are being artificially angry.

In the first part of the exercise, when B is avoiding A's blaming by counterattacking with blaming, a major function of anger can be perceived. B blames A so as not to introject — not to take in and accept the blaming that is coming from A. Considerable anger among those who are weak is in the service of *this time not introjecting* what is being put upon them by those who are strong. In the second part, B doesn't get mobilized to withdraw or otherwise defend against blame, because no blame is coming from A. Instead, B falls into the "I" mode of speaking also. The result is an exchange between two people who share the responsibility for their anger-fed relation.

Thus far in my investigation I have focused upon divisive anger, the helpless anger of weak persons and the overcontrolled and projected forms of anger of the strong. I have done so because the personal relationships of interest to me have been the destructive ones of the weak and the strong. Now, however, I am looking at the anger that surfaces when their introjections and projections are undone. This is potentially a positive and constructive anger, because of the situation now of the people who bear it. People who have thrown off introjections and projections have a sense of being in charge of their lives and so have the strength and will to express their anger directly and openly; and for people to be able to do this has great positive importance in our world. Alice Miller[2] has

strikingly suggested how great and how positive. She has persuasively argued that the child who is permitted to experience feelings
of anger and express them to an adult, and is respected in the
adult's response, is the child who does not become violent. She
calls for dealing with angry children not by domination and repression, but by hearing them, allowing them to know their own needs
and angry feelings freely, and making these significant parts of the
relationship between adult and child. She also documents the cruelty and child abuse that are associated with not permitting such
ownership and expression.

Approaching the subject from a different perspective, James R.
Averill has studied anger and aggression systematically, and he has
concluded that anger is often constructive. For him the motives of
constructive anger include asserting independence, asserting authority, trying to strengthen a relationship, and trying to get someone to do something for you. And each of the motives he lists can
be seen as pertinent to the situations we are addressing.

How, then, can we be brought to disregard the parental admon-
ishments, so in contrast with what Miller recommends, to not show
anger which many of us were subjected to and learned so well to
comply with? How can we use this usually forbidden or unwel-
comed emotion and at the same time be listened to by others and
accepted by them? Because our parents insisted that anger is
childish, disrespectful, unsocialized, improper, we as adults almost
always find that situations marked by overt anger make us feel uncomfortable and that to express our own anger would be inappropriate. Yet there is something attractive and inviting about acting
angrily; we feel it would be wonderful to be able to accept with
comfort the anger we often find in ourselves.

Averill helps in this regard when he notes that

"on the sociocultural level, anger functions to uphold accepted standards of
conduct."[3]

He asserts that though the general cultural directive is that one
should avoid becoming angry, there are conditions under which any

reasonable person is appropriately angry and allowed to be angry. Especially when anger is in the service of maintaining the social system as it is or the accepted standards of conduct is it permissible to be angry. Thus, anger seems to be permitted to the upholders of current power relationships and not to others. But we can read this conversely, too: having the courage to mobilize and utilize anger can be empowering, since by doing so, one puts oneself in the stance of defining standards of conduct.

In his biography of John L. Lewis, Saul Alinsky,[4] the political organizer, has presented examples of Lewis at his finest as a labor leader, and among them the following account of one episode in Lewis's career stands out in respect to the power of well-controlled anger. In the 1930s the C.I.O. was being built through struggles with big industry, and victories had been won with U.S. Steel and G.M. Alinsky notes that

> "Lewis singlehandedly won collective bargaining with U.S. Steel without a strike..."

and bested General Motors, and then was called in to deal with Chrysler Corporation, in early April 1937. There was a sit-in at Chrysler. Lewis liked and respected the head of the firm, Walter Chrysler, whom he called a "just, decent man." But

> "This time it was the humane, warm-hearted Walter Chrysler and his hard-boiled, anti-union production boss, K. T. Keller."

Also present for the company was Nicholas Kelley, general counsel.

As the negotiations proceeded, Keller, speaking hardly at all, sneered across the table, looked disdainfully past Lewis, stared insultingly at the other C.I.O. leaders, and in general infuriated them. So Lewis decided to break down this man. By the next day Keller had made all the union people uncomfortable and conscious of his aloofness, with grimaces that unnerved many of them, though not the "impassive chief," who sat in complete silence. Across from Lewis "sat Keller with his manifest scorn becoming more obnoxious to the CIO spokesmen with each passing minute. To Lewis and his associates, Keller's face began to symbolize the attitudes and position of a giant corporation toward its employees."

The tension heightened. Suddenly Keller broke a silence of his own. Turning to Lewis, with a sneer in his voice he said:

" 'Mr. Lewis, you haven't said a word about this situation. Do you happen to have any comment or contribution?'

"Lewis very slowly rose to his feet and with a murderous stare at Keller softly replied, 'Yes, Mr. Keller, yes I have. I am ninety-nine per cent of a mind to come around this table right now and with one fell swoop wipe that damn sneer off your face.'

"There was a dead silence in the room. Governor [Frank] Murphy [of Michigan, who had called this meeting] hastily cleared his throat and announced a brief recess. The Governor got up quietly, nervously looking at Lewis and Keller. Keller seemed to be in a state of shock. Suddenly he shook his head and came around the table toward Lewis. Lewis deliberately turned his back on him and began to walk over to the other side of the room. Keller followed him, then put his arm around Lewis's shoulder. Everyone heard Keller in a pleading voice say, 'I'm really not as bad as you make me out to be, Mr. Lewis, really I'm not as bad as that. Believe me, I'm not as bad as that.' "

"Lewis turned to Keller and still with complete dignity said, 'Well, Mr. Keller, in the heat of controversy, one is bound to be indiscreet.' Keller's resistance cracked after this episode."

The labor leader Lee Pressman was sitting in on the negotiations, and Alinsky quotes Pressman's assessment of that moment:

"It is impossible to put into words just what everyone felt at that moment. Lewis, the man, was not threatening Keller, the man. Lewis's voice in that moment was in every sense the voice of millions of unorganized workers who were exploited by gigantic corporations. He was expressing at that instant, their resentment, hostility, and their passionate desire to strike back. There just was no question that Lewis's threat was not against Mr. Keller as a person, but against the Chrysler Corporation and every other giant, soul-less corporation in this country. It was a moment of real greatness, because Lewis transcended his own person and was speaking out the deep yearning of millions to force a great, sneering, arrogant corporation to bend its knee to organized labor."

And it was a moment when Lewis was defining standards of conduct.

Then Lewis took on general counsel Kelley. As Alinsky writes:

"The next day Lewis cleared the decks as he demolished Nicholas Kelley . . . . Lewis went on and on and on developing his denunciation in low, cold, withering words. Lewis continued driving and driving into him until everyone thought that Kelley was about to have a fit of apoplexy. Finally Kelley leaped to his feet and screamed, 'STOP IT, STOP IT, Mr. Lewis!' After a good deal more in this vein he finally ended up by shouting, 'Mr. Lewis, I want you to know, Mr. Lewis, that I-I-I am not afraid of your eyebrows.' Lewis's laughter rolled Kelley out of the fight and Chrysler gave up."

For a hot and angry situation like this one to become warmly productive, the individuals involved must stay in contact with one another, complete their striving actions, and find some satisfaction of the goals they want to reach out of the conflict. Because the persons involved may be enemies, may have old grievances, may be fearful of each other or even of their own rageful tendencies, staying in contact may be no easy task. In the Chrysler-C.I.O. confrontation, as in many others, of course, it was managed. There was heat and there was warmth. At the end, Lewis had won important concessions from management, and Chrysler had won a contract and continuity of its operations. As J. Raymond Walsh summarized the outcome:

"Sole bargaining rights, strictly defined, were denied the union. But the contract contained a promise that the company would abstain from all support or agreement with any other organization which purposed to undermine the U.A.W. effort. In effect, if the U.A.W. [the auto workers' union in the C.I.O.] was sufficiently popular to prevent the appearance of another bona fide union, it would remain sole bargainer for all employees."[5]

New let us look at a range of other situations in which anger is in one way or another focal, to see various ways it can be dealt with in them.

An extreme situation among these is psychotherapy with deeply disturbed persons. For example, in his book *Modern Psychoanalysis of the Schizophrenic Patient*. Hyman Spotnitz[6] asserts that hatred can be a therapeutic force of compelling character for the deeply disturbed. He says that hatred binds the schizophrenic patient to his or her therapist even more firmly than does love, so that the patient is willing to work as long as necessary to master aggressive and angry impulses provided that the danger that he or she will act on them destructively is kept to a minimum, which is likely in the usual hospital setting where schizophrenic patients receive therapy. Often the therapist will be called upon to help the patient discover the anger and bring it into the relationship; whichever introduces it, the successful revival and expression of anger is central to the treatment of the disturbance, Spotnitz says.

Barbara Bender,[7] who has treated children who were battered by adults, comments upon a kind of misplaced compelled loyalty to the batterer evidenced by such children — for example, one boy who, when a rare angry and hostile comment came forth from him and was noticed, pretended to be hurt rather than stand behind the anger and take the hostility as his own. Similarly, Pennie Cohen has noted that victims of violence in a family are exceedingly loyal to those who have hurt them, and in their loyalty refuse to become angry at their violent spouses or parents. She then proceeds to an important therapeutic aim in work with these victims:

"A final important aspect of therapy related to helping the victim shift the blame from self to perpetrator is the process of enabling the expression of anger. Typically, clients who have experienced childhood violence are angry with themselves and have difficulty experiencing anger with parents . . . .

"It is frequently helpful for the therapist to express her/his anger at the client's family for permitting or perpetuating the violence. This has a permission-giving element for the client. Permission-giving probes such as 'What do you do with your anger?' are also helpful. These kinds of probes assume that anger is normal and expectable."[8]

When the clients are "angry with themselves," of course, they are demonstrating their identification with the aggressor, and when therapy with these victims of violence is successful, it undoes introjections and surfaces rage that they point outside of themselves.

Klaus D. Hoppe, writing of working with survivors of severe persecution by the Nazis, tells us that if the therapist is willing to be seen by his or her patient as like the persecutor of the past (typically like an SS officer),

> "then the patient may transform excessively destructive drives into constructive ones."[9]

Seeing the therapist as persecutor causes the patient to bring out old anger that would have been self-destructive if expressed in the past, then to let go of it and become able to be angry and express anger at the therapist and others in the patient's present life.

David M. Berger,[10] who also worked with survivors, notices in his report their difficulty with anger. He makes the astute observation that the anger of such survivors is diffuse rather than object-related and dealing well with the anger involves connecting angry expression with real objects, either persons the survivor is connected with at present or persons from the past. The main thrust of Berger's therapy was to bring the patient back to the period of persecution as often as possible and have the patient give detail after detail of what was experienced and the affects that accompanied the experiences. Invariably, of course, hatred of the Nazis surfaced in these explorations, and this was encouraged, which helped the patient focus anger past and present. It was also found useful for both therapist and patient to acknowledge that the patient had identified with the aggressor, and for the therapist to say that this identification was a normal response to a severe situation. This relieved immobilizing guilt and shame.

Some sense of how difficult it is to go back to scenes of persecution can be gotten from the following exercise, which indicates it is often hard even to re-experience a parent's anger at one as a child. People are asked to close their eyes and remember a time in childhood when a parent was strongly angry with them. They are then asked to describe what it felt like to be a child in the presence of an angry parent. Typically, they don't find this easy to do; they have trouble coming up with details. Then they are asked to comment on whether it was hard to remember the episode. They acknowledge it was hard. Finally, they are asked to look at whether they have protected the parent in their remembering and in their reporting. They generally begin by saying no, sometimes adding that they deserved the parent's anger, but then come to acknowledge on the spot that they have protected their parent. This has a freeing effect on them. They have acknowledged something they couldn't acknowledge before, and this is relieving.

A moving incident that illustrates the same theme occurred in a class for social workers. The class was discussing a residential setting for drug-addicted mothers and their children. A student who was working there had observed a child making a switch, and when she asked what it was for, the child replied that it was for his mother to beat him. The student was appalled at this, but the child defended his mother. Another student in the class said that her mother had done this to her throughout her childhood and that it was common and accepted in their minority culture. The instructor responded by saying that it was child abuse to beat a child, whether or not it was a cultural phenomenon. The student, who had not only told of being beaten but also described hiding under a bed out of fear of it, defended her mother's method of discipline quite strongly. The next week the student did not appear for class. She had withdrawn from the instructor and from the class. When she did return in another week, the instructor approached her and asked if something was wrong. She replied that she had been offended by the attack on her culture and her mother, that it had felt racist. The instructor worked with her around the issue, and they came to a mutual understanding and to friendship by agreeing that something could be culturally dominant and yet hurtful and harmful, and that race had nothing to do with the instructor's position. The student came to understand that she had experienced her mother's brutality with some terror and, at times, with some excitement — an admixture of pleasure that her mother was attending to her and some sexual arousal from the physical experience. The instructor learned that there was some love and some thrill in these encounters that were primarily painful.

A therapeutic setting with which Carol Roman[11] was connected provides significant occasions for the productive unfolding of anger. It is a residential setting for treatment of persons with drug and alcohol addictions. Clients are seen to go through stages of anger, first of an unproductive sort, later of a valid kind. They enter the program from drug-ridden urban streets and have street behavior in place. Rage is on the surface and is regularly called upon. Anything may be taken as a provocation, and provocation leads to expressions about previous angry-making circumstances:

> "If you did that to me on the street, I'd stick you. Don't push me or I'll take you out."

As the client progresses in therapy, anger becomes more focused. A client who is feeling angry will overreact to rule setting, but the expression of anger is carefully focused on the rule or rule maker, while denial of other sources of intense anger the client finds in his or her quite restrictive living situation remains in place. In other terms, whereas at the beginning of treatment anger is directed at all people and covers all situations, in the middle of treatment the client points anger at the confining structure of the residential program and fires it off bullet by bullet. At the end of therapy the client becomes angry only occasionally and at well-delineated objects for well-delineated reasons — e.g., angry at someone for making a noisy disturbance in front of a TV the client wants to watch.

As some of the above stories indicate, with people who have suffered extreme domination such as former abused children or victims of the Nazis, the revival and successful handling of anger turns out to have significant positive results for the victim. A similar story is told by those who have studied the psychological side of the civil rights movement and the women's movement. As the psychiatrist William R. Beardslee said of activists working in the civil rights movement:

> "Just as the capacity to grieve and keep working was a necessity for the workers, so was the capacity to be angry and feel outrage, and at the same time put those feelings into action toward the goals of the Movement."[12]

Similarly, in a study of psychodynamic factors associated with the sit-ins of the civil rights movement, Pierce and West conclude:

> "In summary, it may be said that the surprising sense of power of the sit-in demonstrator, and the benefits that he derives from his ordeals in large part are related to the way in which the experience couples genuine ideals with psychological drives into an acceptable mode of expression. Reinforcement comes from identification with key adult figures, *gratifying discharge of hostile feelings*, rewards in terms of status in the group, a sense of inner strength through the successful exercise of self control and the realization of self fulfillment through working and suffering to achieve a worthy goal [italics added]."[13]

One more psychiatrist can be called upon to support the view that successful anger is productive of the welfare of the oppressed individual. Sheldon Cohen[14] discusses desegregation from the perspective of a southern psychiatrist. He refers to the "retroflexed rage which had built up over generations" in southern blacks, rage which was not available to the awareness of the individuals. It was expressed in violent intraracial aggression — slashings, rapes, and murders in the black community — and in psychosomatic illnesses such as hypertension; but these signs were interpreted, until the civil rights movement came along, as simply part of the life of the community, the way things were. The marches, nonviolent demonstrations, and sit-ins mobilized this aggression and directed it into socially productive channels to the benefit of the angry persons and the movement to overcome racial segregation.

Elizabeth Janeway develops this same theme in her discussion of the "powers of the weak":

> "Groups of the weak, forced to comply with regulations laid down by those against whom they cannot hope to rebel, repress their anger . . . . We can see that the ability to let anger out is indeed a mark of progress on the way to daring to act for oneself, according to one's choice."[15]

And Gayle Graham Yates, writing of the women's movement, asserts that

"Women must learn the meaning of rage, the violence that liberates the human spirit. The rhetoric of invective is an equally essential stage, for in discovering and venting their rage against the enemy . . . women also experience the justice of their own violence."[16]

The predominant theme I have extracted from the thinkers I have just been citing is the need for the recovery and new handling of anger in social relationships. The writers with a political interest, particularly, reflect the fact that in regard to anger most attention of a psychological sort has been directed to those who are in the weak position in relationships and that the spotlight has not often been put on how those in the dominant role might be enabled to progress through new forms of anger activity. As I stated earlier, I believe that inattention to the rage of the strong is caused by the fact that it is controlled to a large degree, backed by the social system, and, above all, projected onto others, and thus is not so dramatic in its appearance as that of the underdogs. Nor is it much looked for by other members of society, since "what would those well-off people have to be angry about?" But I also believe that new dealings with anger are needed by, and would be beneficial to, those who are identified as strong most of the time in relationships — and that this is particularly true in politics, as I shall explain below.

Regardless of whether one chooses to look at the strong or the weak, the arousal of their plentiful anger is an established political maneuver. We can expect to find intensity and rage wherever political activity is being organized — inside right-wing anticommunist movements, among workers organizing into unions or preparing for strikes, among women struggling for their liberation or opposing "women's libbers," among blacks remembering their grievances and readying themselves for action, among nationalists of minority status or patriots. All thrive on the liveliness and immediacy of angry feelings. Political endeavor and anger go together like marriage and sex.

The usual explanation of the everpresence of anger in political life refers to grievances, but it also needs to be stressed here that anger is a contactful emotion. To be angry is to face forward toward a frustrating obstacle and engage with it, either directly or in fantasy. The fascination of victims with their oppressors, so aptly described by Philip Hallie,[17] is one manifestation of the contactfulness of anger. Anger is a social emotion. It brings people into communion with others in the form of shared anger toward a common opponent or frustrating object, or it brings them into contact with their opponents or representatives of their opponents. Angry people are not simply self-contained, not licking their wounds in the privacy of their shelters. They are available for collective action.

Yet the anger that is mobilized politically is most frequently misused. For example, among those who are activated from the weak side of a relation, instead of transforming individuals and helping them reach collective goals, the rage too often leads to further helplessness, often via debilitating projection. When women put all frustrations they experience upon men or when blacks see all their problems outside themselves in whites, they all too readily avoid their own part in the relationship and project upon the opponent. Unions who see in management all evil and do not boldly face themselves and their own methods of operation as possibly contributing to their union's problems must invariably attribute weakness of their own to management.

Projection aside, when anger is surfaced and the efforts to use it for social change are not well carried out, or when groups speak their grievances but do not act upon them, further helplessness is promoted. Here is an example of how things do not have to end this way, however. In her book *Despair and Personal Power in the Nuclear Age*, Joanna Macy[18] has developed a program with a series of exercises which work to bring to the surface the despair that people feel about nuclear danger and then seek to enable participants to go on to self-empowerment and commitment to try to end the danger. Groups in the program are led to experience and then deal directly and creatively with the helpless rage felt by the weak, in order to counteract the tendency to submit to the nuclear status quo. Macy's methods have been applied successfully in mobilizing people in peace work. First she provides exercises in "telling our nuclear stories," in guided meditation, and in "imaging with colors and clay," in which group members make paintings and shape clay in efforts to create the most horrible images of nuclear holocaust they can imagine, and there is a "despair ritual" derived from the "speak bitterness" sessions in the Chinese revolutionary movement which I described in Chapter 9. Then there are exercises seeking to stimulate a turn from despair to empowerment. These include, for instance, guided meditation again, brainstorming, and "opening pathways though movement" — an exercise in dance and other movements designed to give people a stronger sense of how they can use their bodies. Finally, there is work on "empowering our-selves," dealing with how people feel their own power, how they imagine it, and how others empower them, as well as consideration of how to build skills needed for social action and how to develop rituals for committing oneself to it. Personal experience in these workshops has convinced me of the immense creativity involved in them and of the emotionally intense quality they provide to life. Beyond this, people do, as Macy prescribes, commit themselves to one or another degree of action, as the culmination of their taking part in the program, and go on to honor the commitment.

It is vital to the successful political use of anger that activists dis-cover and analyze their better and worse ways of handling it in en-counters with their opponents. But training in productive ways of expressing anger is overlooked in preparations for making strong political assertions, e.g., striking, and so is making people familiar with the grounds of negativity in angry confrontations and how it may bring trouble, e.g., the feeling of utter hopelessness leading someone ragefully to swat at a counterprotester, bringing on un-friendly police action.

For those on the strong side in a political encounter, exclusive focus on the other, on the representatives of the weak, leads in-evitably to further projection. Such a process fails to promote lis-tening for, discovering, and attending to the human quality of one-self as well as one's opponents, a practice that is necessary for re-owning of what has been projected. In addition, unless the strong develop awareness of how angry they are, there is little likelihood that they will loosen their controls over their anger and hold it in awareness while still maintaining contact with their opponents — thus both gaining more confidence in themselves and bonding with others, sometimes including some of their opponents — and transform themselves and their relationships.

Let me develop this last point. The strong, with their powerful feelings of outrage, commonly intimidate others; one way or another, the others in the relationship find a means for distancing themselves. They may cease to argue, physically leave the scene, withdraw into themselves, identify with the aggressor, anything to free themselves from the threat of being severely hurt by the anger of the strong; it is probably the single most important cause of persons giving up being agents in relation. Unless a political encounter can facilitate attention to the depth of this outrage, attention that maintains connection, and can find means for enabling its expression without destroying contact in the relationship, transformation of the strong or the weak in the relationship is unlikely. Failure of the strong to deal with their controlled rage pressures the relationship to disintegrate.

As is the case with projectors in general, the strong will not revise their handling of anger without support of some kind, and in confrontations between the strong and the weak that support often comes from representatives of the weak, though it may also come from neutral observers or collaborators. John L. Lewis demonstrated for the leaders of the Chrysler Corporation how a person could be angry without either projecting or overcontrolling his feeling. Such modeling is one way the weak can help the strong. Another is their hearing and accepting the rage of the strong without being thrown by it or diverted from pursuing their own intentions. Acknowledgment of that anger can bring it to common awareness, while refusal to be cowed by it is supportive of the basic humanity of the other — who also now doesn't have to be terrified of being overpowering, as in fact many strong rageful people are — and is basic to the maintenance of connection in the relationship.

Because the revived anger of the weak is a result of the undoing of introjections, their new ways of dealing with anger are probably going to be a function of positive identifications. Three main themes along this line come readily to mind, themes derived from lessons learned in the women's liberation movement in recent years. First, sharing anger with others in a similar situation leads to positive identifications and subsequent encouragement and support. Second, learning to diagnose and then refusing to introject the projected anger of the powerful clears the way to healthy rather than disturbed identifications. Third, good ways of being angry help one to function as agent rather than as agency.

First, sharing anger. Griping, complaining, telling stories of humiliation, and gossiping about the hurt one has received are common characteristics of the community of the oppressed. In most instances these responses lack the fire of the anger felt in the originating situation, and in most of them as well there is a tendency to "ventilate" and dissipate the emotion. After all, these are painful experiences and the desire to rid oneself of their influence is profound. Yet there are groupings in which people respond to anger in a new manner, in which the individual is encouraged to expand the feeling and enlarge the description — to carry and express all the feeling, whether pure anger or anger, hurt, humiliation, shame, and timidity combined — and in the process reach into the experience of others. Soon another story is told and members of the group discover that they have a shared world and a shared fate. From this understanding can come new strength and commitment to action, since there is now an environment to help one deal with the oppressive figure or system. Women's consciousness-raising groups exploited this method during their early years just as union organizers did in earlier times and as radical political organizers have also done.

A variant on such consciousness-raising groups is personal counseling for women who are preparing to go to court in divorce proceedings. An experienced clinician can help a client to testify in such a way as to empower herself through a contactful use of anger in the court process. Usually, the client is already very angry but helplessly so. If this is the case, she can be helped to see that the judge and court officers will be available to facilitate her expression of anger if she focuses on it clearly and tries to mobilize their support, and that they can protect her from violent reactions from her spouse. She can be enabled to see how hurt and rageful her husband is as well. Good counseling will help her prioritize her grievances and achieve validation of her anger over incidents she catalogs. And her examination of past emotional traumas in the prioritizing endeavor can help her expel introjects, from her husband or from others in her present or past life, that may have contributed to difficulties in her marriage.

Second, as important as sharing — and corralling — one's own rising anger is learning how to diagnose and keep out projected rage. The reflex of a weak person faced with the power and the powerful rage of the strong is to get out of the situation unharmed. As discussed earlier, in day-to-day life oppressed people often introject the substance of what is communicated by the raging powerful, then slip away and use it to prop up their identification with the aggressor. At a time of confrontation the reflex may change, however. Now a danger for those fighting their oppression is that they will absorb, not the matter, but the manner of their raging opponents, desperately reflect it back, and thereby be hurt literally or at least fail to win ground in the encounter. What they must learn instead is how to stay in contact, observe the rage of the powerful, and not take it on at all. For instance, relaxation techniques can help subordinates to take care of themselves in the presence of an aroused other and not absorb his or her anger. In nonviolent resistance, going limp typically achieves this and also quiets the fearful anger of police or National Guard personnel. (Sometimes, we know, police vent their rage upon nonresisting folk, but this tendency usually passes when they discover how spectators condemn the cruelty involved.)

Groups can assist their members in observing and staying clear of projected rage. Part of my purpose in this study is to facilitate attention to projection as a tactic in power relations. Shared analysis of what is happening in the presence of the powerful can be used on the spot by persons on the underside of a relation to halt the tendency to introject the anger of an other, and what is thus learned can be reinforced later, in a group review of what happened.

My third theme from the women's movement is how good ways of being angry help one. In this connection, Harriet Lerner has written a powerful work on the nature and use of anger from a feminist perspective in her book *The Dance of. Anger.* She argues that ineffective anger, anger voiced "without clarity, direction and control," can be reassuring to the other because it may help the other to keep calm while the angry person fusses and fumes. Similarly, she notes, fighting and blaming

"is sometimes a way both to protest and to protect the status quo . . ."[19]

when the person is not yet ready to move in any given direction. And further:

". . . those of us who fight ineffectively are usually caught up in unsuccessful efforts to change a person who does not want to change."[20]

Too often, she has observed, persons try to change others into persons like themselves, not different from them, and thus to avoid being separate and responsible for self. Yet we do not in fact have the power to change other persons unless they want to change, and our efforts to do so as often as not protect them from changing at all. Our efforts rouse them to fight back and reaffirm themselves as they are. At the bottom of ineffective anger, according to Lerner, is a "deselfing" process, an avoidance of taking responsibility and being a separate individual — an obscuring of self as agent, as I would put it.

In my view, if ineffective anger is in the service of "deselfing," productive anger is in that of "selfing," in Lerner's phrasing — a making of self into agent. Indeed, productive anger is both the producer and the product of a person acting as an agent. Anger is a feeling that we cannot control having, though we may avoid recognizing that we are angry, and like all feelings it is something we have a right to. The first step in becoming productively angry is to experience oneself as angry and to accept that something vital and valid is happening to one. This is not always so easy. For instance, many men have been reared to understand that when they are under the authority of someone else, they must control their angry feelings preferably to the point of not even experiencing them. G. C. Lichtenberg had a wonderful ironic aphorism about such denial of selfhood:

"On K.'s advice, I got frightfully angry about that matter."[21]

By contrast, healthy, productive anger involves firmly asserting or protecting oneself, as the following definitions of anger all suggest:

Lerner: "Anger is a signal and one worth listening to. Our anger may be a message we are being hurt, that our rights are being violated, that our needs or wants are not being adequately met, or simply that something is not right."[22]

Carol Tavris: "Anger is ultimately an emphatic message. Pay attention to me. I don't like what you are doing. Restore my pride. You're in my way. Danger. Give me justice."[23]

Bach and Wyden: "It's a basic emotional and physiological reaction against interference with the pursuit of a desired goal; and an expression of strong concern when things go wrong."[24]

And finally, taking the self as agent into the broad social world,

Abraham Maslow: "Anger does not disappear with psychological health; rather it takes the form of decisiveness, self-affirmation, self-protection, justified indignation, fighting against evil, and the like."[25]

The second step in becoming productively angry is to get a clear sense of what one is angry about. Although this often seems simple to assert, when angry persons pay close attention to their angry feeling and to the circumstances arousing it, they may find that they are distorting the circumstances in such a way that they can sidestep being responsible for themselves in the situation. Thus, though it is no simple matter, it is important that time and attention be given to clarifying the true sources of anger, as well as where one stands in the whole situation. This last is critical because it leads one into such questions as whether one is blaming others, preparing to throw up one's hands in helpless defeat, getting ready for real changes, or spouting off and expecting little in the way of change.

The third step in becoming productively angry is to communicate to the object of anger that one is indeed angry and what the anger is about. This is no easy task either. Often, if we are not confusing the issue by divesting ourselves of our responsibility, we are blaming the other and arousing the inevitable resistance to fault-finding. When we are angry with a superior in a hierarchy, we are often scaring ourselves with the thought that we will be severely punished or indicating to the other that we are likely to back down if countermoves are made. Only when we can deeply own our feeling of anger and pinpoint as well its basis can we communicate through self-as-agent statements ("I" statements) what we wish to communicate in such a way as to maintain contact with that other and with the goal toward which we are moving. This may also take support from others, and it can use a strong and clear presentation. A wise piece of advice from Hendrie Weisinger about communicating anger:

> "When you direct your anger, make sure your voice level is not too loud and that you have good eye contact."[26]

Weisinger also has lively advice on handling the responses to one's anger from its target. He names a series of "blocking gambits" that people use in response to anger — laughing it off, the put-off ("I'll talk about it later" or "Sue me"), retaliation ("I'll get back at you even worse"), threats to do other unpleasant things, denial of having done what has made one angry, guilt ("with tears and the message that you are being mean and cruel", as Weisinger notes), squabbling (or trying to, since this takes two), "Why?" (professing not to understand why one is frustrated and angry). Similarly, he names ways to overcome these gambits — "playing it again," processing (talking about what is going on between you), hedging (appearing to give ground without actually doing so), defusing (putting off further discussion until the other has calmed down), and cut-off (responding to the provocative statement with only a short word and quickly getting back to the point).[27] The gambits are means for the target to ignore the grounds for one's anger; the counters to these are means for staying with one's anger and concerns while staying in contact. For instance, if the target replies, "You too!" one may "play it again" — reiterate one's initial angry statement — or refuse to squabble by saying "Whether I also do that or not, this time you did it and I don't like it." One thing that is needed here, obviously, is to be sturdy enough oneself to maintain tenaciously the contact with the angry-making other and to remove any and all frustrating blocks he or she may erect.

Persons who have mastered all the steps that make for productive anger are more able to pursue goals in a determined way and more likely to achieve them. As part of this, they are better able to take care of themselves, to protect self-esteem, to assert their own value, to defend their rights. Productive anger is a force for deepened and committed effort in the face of challenge from the outside.

Groups which are useful in endeavors to make awares individuals' tendencies to demand confluence, introject, or project are groups which become able to manage internal angry encounters. This ability is very important for these groups when they are engaged in efforts for social change. The frequent angry disagreements that characterize social-action groups are staging areas, as it were, for encounters with those who are not of the ingroup. To foster the expression of angry differences between members while still keeping them in contact with one another and with the overarching purposes of the group is thus a major opportunity as well as challenge for the group.

How does a union, say, foster difference and controversy and give voice to the minority while keeping a sense of solidarity? When practices do not foster fusion, introjection, and projection, such conflict is welcomed and handled adequately, including the expression and management of anger. This puts the union members in contact with reality and each other and strengthens their identity as union members — the opposite of the situation in many unions, where the union bosses "do it all" and so drive the workers away from each other. Thus there is a fertile field of social-change possibility in the reintroduction of emotionality into the workings of ongoing groups, including emotions of great intensity such as anger and anxiety.

I have been describing here the happy side of anger, the side which is productive of self-definition and, often, of a bonding between the angry person and others who are the object of the anger. I might summarize the ingredients of such useful and satisfying anger as follows. The angry person will be able to say:

"It is I who am angry.

"I am angry for me and my needs. My desires are important.

"Yet I am not trying to force change, to dominate those who are the targets of my anger. My wants are not more important to them than their own.

Rather, I hope to bond in mutuality with an equal if the other is willing, once having been informed of my desires; or I will take care of myself if the other is unwilling.

"I am an agent of my life."

When a person has become able to be angry in productive fashion, the emotion next in line for that person is anxiety, this time a lively anxiety with the potential for spontaneity and excitement if it is managed adequately. We are back in the area of the spontaneity of children who have not been hurt too much — children in whom we see excitement, joy and wonder, curiosity, and readiness for challenge and active engagement with others. This anxiety is close to what I have elsewhere called "being thoroughly alive."[28]

Chapter 15

On Anxiously Acting Assertively

Most discussions of anxiety in the clinical literature are of neurosis, anxiety disorder, panic disorder, or anxiety as emotion so distressing that the person develops symptoms such as obsessions, conversion reactions like tics, or delusions to make it disappear. In everyday life also, people tend to see anxiety as all negative, an attitude consistent with the uncomfortable feeling they have when they are anxious. To counter this slant toward seeing anxiety as an emotion not to be welcomed, I want to strongly affirm that experiencing anxiety can also be a positive matter and indeed that the ability to experience and tolerate anxiety is a sign of healthy personal functioning.

It is not posing a new idea to say this. It is a basic idea in most psychotherapies. For instance, the psychoanalyst Elizabeth Zetzel has argued that such an ability is critical to the success of psychoanalytic treatment in achieving psychological health:

"If anxiety . . . is defined as the response to an internal danger situation, the capacity to develop and tolerate anxiety, associated as it must always be with an unconscious conflict, is very closely related to the capacity to recognize and tolerate the instinctual conflicts and tension that constitute the internal danger situation that threatens. The more . . . an individual has been able in an internal, unconsciously produced danger situation to develop and tolerate anxiety as such, the more one finds in analysis that he is capable of facing and resolving the conflict that determined it. Conversely, the more the individual has tended to defend himself against anxiety, by the development of hysterical symptoms, severe psychosomatic symptoms, by the omnipotent denial of danger . . . the less will he be capable of tolerating insight . . . . I would like to suggest that . . . this capacity of achieving and tolerating the anxiety associated with insight is of decisive importance."[1]

Outside therapy also, the ability to experience and tolerate anxiety — that ability to take into awareness and stay with the discomforting feeling that is anxiety until it dissipates naturally — is a sign of health. The reason here is that with it a person can become and remain conscious of a danger that his or her needs will not be met or of a sharp challenge in the environment which must be engaged. This important aspect of anxiety is its so-called "signal function,"[2] which alerts the person and enables him or her to regulate actions so as to avoid frustration or pain or, better, achieve satisfaction in the presence of danger or challenge. Here, then, is one broadly applicable way of construing anxiety as a plus.

In considering hypnosis and anxiety, Brown and Fromm contrast the normal and pathological aspects of anxiety. (I would substitute for "normal" and "pathological" the notion of "manageable" and "unmanageable.") They have written:

> "The normally anxious person experiences optimal tension and prepares for the challenge of learning. The pathologically anxious patient is overcome by a debilitating anxiety state he is unable to master. These anxiety states are often attack-like in nature. The normally anxious person experiences an increased arousal appropriate to the situation, such as an examination or before an operation. The pathologically anxious person usually does not know the source of his anxiety, or if he believes he knows the cause consciously, his perception is often incorrect. Because the source is unclear, anxiety is accompanied by excessive worry."[3]

Zetzel[4] similarly distinguishes between what she has called anxiety reactions approaching traumatic experience and anxiety reactions that indicate initial active mastery based on toleration of this painful affect.

Another approach to a positive perspective on anxiety comes from Gestalt therapy theory. In this theory, anxiety is described as the experience of having difficulty breathing during that heightened energy mobilization which is called "excitement." Anxiety arises whenever that excitement is blocked. In reckoning with anxiety as an outcome of the blocked excitement, we may read that phrase (following Kenneth Burke's "dramatistic" method of dialectical analysis)[5] both as "*blocked* excitement," with an emphasis on the negative, and as "blocked *excitement*," with an emphasis on the positive. In the Gestalt therapy view a person who is anxious can be seen as blocking excitement, stopping himself or herself from being excited, negating or limiting his or her spontaneous being in the world, *and* the person can be seen as just about ready to be fully excited — scared, hesitant, apprehensive, but blocking "in the presence of excitement." In the latter, positive view of anxiety, the person is on the verge of discovering his or her needs, of creatively adjusting in the world by aggressively approaching objects, and of doing so with a mixture of confidence and diffidence. Again from Perls:

> "And when it comes to the moment of performance, and you're not sure whether your performance will be well received, then you get stage fright. This stage fright has been given by psychiatry the name 'anxiety.' "[6]

Along the line I am following, practitioners of the Japanese psychotherapy called Morita therapy also construe anxiety in a positive mode, as F. Ishu Ishiyama[7] has written. Rather than help nervous clients who resent and fight the anxious part of themselves to eliminate or control their anxiety, a Morita therapist encourages them to view their anxiety as in indication of strong desires — for social success, for example, or for a productive pattern of living. A Morita therapist is inclined to tell clients who are unusually anxious that this is because their desire for life is unusually strong. Ishiyama sees anxiety as positive in that it is a cue for action aimed at satisfying this desire, rather than something to be fought or fled from. In my framework anxiety can be interpreted similarly: if the negative side of anxiety is being caught off guard and overwhelmed or confused by social reactions to one's desires — as the playful child experiences in the case of molestation, for instance — the positive side is the recovery of familiarity with one's desires and the urge to try to satisfy them directly in social encounter, even to the point of asserting them anxiously and angrily risking controversial actions in their service. And of course, since the other person or persons in a relation also have needs, there is always some threat that one's desires will not be met no matter what one does; hence more anxious feeling.

Ishiyama presents also an important factor to be remembered by social-change activists when anxiety makes its appearance in the awareness of individuals who are moving toward their own goals. The aim of the positive interpretation of anxious feeling is to help the client stop rejecting self and stop being preoccupied with control of the anxiety. Like any emotion, anxiety is something that happens to one and should be accepted, lived with, and allowed to run its course as part of the person's experience. It is inappropriate for clients to view their anxiety as something they should control as soon and as much as possible. Better that they should be with their anxiety, acknowledging its presence, utilizing its alerting function, living through its tension.

When persons no longer control their anxiety, but instead experience it and attend to it, they are likely to come upon products of earlier identifications. This is more likely, and done more easily, when they have discovered their ways of introjecting and are no longer so blatantly doing so. As Perls et al. argue:

> ". . . anxiety is roused when the voice one hears is not, after all, one's own voice, but the other speakers one has introjected: it is mother or father complaining, shouting, or being fair. This is again . . . the situation of self-conquest; and one is anxious because one again throttles, at the present moment, one's true identity, appetite and voice."[8]

In the context of social action, the voices one hears within may be the voices not only of mother or father but also the voices of other authorities. If at this point one is ready to challenge these authorities in moving to accomplish one's goals, the self-conquest is short-lived. Further, if a person then manages the anxiety well, he or she is likely to discover more precisely the desires that are active within. In general, these desires are what the voices are opposing. One's excitement has caused the voices to say, "You mustn't," even before one sees clearly what is desired. If one accepts the anxious feeling the voices bring and is able to explore and hold on to it as long as it lasts, one will be likely also to find the side of this feeling that is desire. A person can then ask what he or she needs at this moment and what must be done to get it. Perls et al. provide elaboration of this theme:

> "The cure of anxiety is necessarily indirect. One must find out *what* excitements one cannot at present accept as one's own. Since they arise spontaneously, they must be related to genuine needs of the organism. . . . the cure of anxiety is roundabout, involving awareness of what the excitement would express and overcoming the resistances to accepting this as one's own. . . ."[9]

Staying with anxiety over time, rather than avoiding it, enables the person to define more closely both the blocking forces — "Oh, this is the voice of my father from long ago. I can choose whether what it is saying is appropriate now" — and the desires that he or she has been ready to block. Since the anxiety contains both sides of the competing internal forces, prolonged experience of the anxiety fosters awareness of both sides, and with awareness comes the ability to choose which side will be dominant now.

I have been referring here to anxiety that is useful to the individual and that is on the border of simple spontaneous excitement. It is the anxious feeling experienced by persons who see themselves as agents of their lives, not as driven by desires difficult to contain or live out appropriately or controlled by social forces too strong to master. To come to this kind of anxious condition, however, a person must already have faced up to, and won out over, whatever tendencies he or she has to fuse with others, to introject and to project when threatened, and to muffle anger that is arising within; and coming to such a victory itself involves anxiety. Thus the person may already have had many occasions to experience and stay with anxious feelings.

Consider, for example, the reowning of a projection, the learning that something one has experienced as outside oneself is actually related intimately to something within oneself. Sometime in the past one projected, say, a desire or other affect associated with a desire because it was too distressing to manage; and taking it back again was anxious-making. Suppose a woman saw all men as rapists. A woman who does this is doing some projecting in her exaggeration. While all men do indeed have the capacity to commit what is commonly thought of as rape, relatively few do. Whether the woman was projecting around her aggressiveness, her sexual impulses, her image of what it would be like to be a man herself, or whatever, when she recognized that she had been projecting, she again experienced feelings that were dangerous and too threatening to own. She became anxious. And the reowning of the projection depended upon her being able to hold on to the anxiety while taking responsibility for her own feelings.

Now suppose this woman's dominant difficult feeling was desire to be sexually aggressive herself. Having gone through the anxious experience of getting over her projection will be a support whenever that desire later comes to the fore in her life, bringing a new upsurge of anxiety and needing to be dealt with.

There can be a comparable kind of reinforcement in social-action groups. Because the undoing of fusion, introjections, and projections and the reorganizing of anger involves the successful support of anxiety, when the anxiety that is close to spontaneity is focal, social-action groups that work to help their members achieve these changes have ways of helping them manage this anxiety too. For any group to enable its members to attend to their projections, for instance, the group must have found ways to contain the anxious feelings that surface around projections and to permit them to be felt individually and shared socially — healthy ways rather than the pathologically divided sharing practices under which one or a few members come to carry most or all of the anxiety in the group.

In the world of psychotherapy, whether we refer to psychoanalysts, Gestalt therapists, Morita therapists, behavior modification therapists, or other therapists, the basis for the productive management of anxious and fearful feelings is support in the presence of anxiety itself and whatever provokes it. Psychotherapy is built upon the interplay of challenge, which evokes anxiety, and support, which enables the individual to bear the anxiety directly. Behavior therapists, for example, treat phobias by having clients combine relaxation procedures with confrontations, either imagined or real, with those animals, situations, or people that are frightening to them. The relaxation procedures and the assistance of the therapist contribute the support while the connection with the source is evoking the fearful feeling. In psychoanalysis, patients free-associate in a manner such that they inevitably come upon ideas and memories that are scary for them and that have led to repressions. Again, the analyst, by his or her demeanor and presence and by interpretations, provides support in the management of anxiety. In Gestalt therapy the client is helped toward "safe emergencies," either through direct here and now experiences with the therapist or through so-called "experiments," in which the client is encouraged to try to approach a lurking unfinished situation that is anxious-making. The therapist might, for instance, ask a new client who was speaking abstractly to, instead, simply say "what you are experiencing here now with me in this room," sensing that this would arouse some anxiety in this person; or a client with unfinished business with his or her mother might be asked to "put your mother in that empty chair" and first whisper and then shout at her about their relationship, to experience it more richly.

Also, establishment of what is called a "therapeutic alliance" between therapist and client is a critical ingredient of all psychological therapy services. In this alliance the psychotherapist is supportive by being nonjudgmental, trustworthy, willing to accept thoughts and behaviors outside the social norms, and confidential. These relationship factors are additional grounds of support for the client entering anxious areas in search of therapeutic gain.

Those qualities of the psychotherapeutic relationship that facilitate therapeutic progress can be adopted in groups concerned with transformative social change. For instance, a nonjudgmental atmosphere can be created, a climate in which individual members can feel accepted even in their eccentricities and inadequacies, when they are anxious, when they are foolish, when they are doubting and afraid as well as when they are effective and productive. Similarly, members can be provided with graded challenges in which they are pushed to act beyond what is very easy — for instance, asked to themselves challenge authority figures they fear — but are not pushed to levels where their anxiety will become too intense to bear. Groups following this practice would have to differentiate among members in respect to how much they could carry — which is, of course, a vital part of individualizing persons, of finding out just who everyone is, for collective endeavor. Also, persons with different temperaments have different ways of handling anxiety, and this must be taken into account in differentiating among them. But it is important that differences not be used to build power hierarchies. In Chapter 3 I noted how stronger persons manipulate the anxiety of weaker ones in the early stages of projection upon a primed vulnerable other. Groups need to be alert to this propensity and actively protect themselves against it.

On a simpler scale, groups can set out to make it acceptable and indeed easy for members to acknowledge feeling anxiety so that the group can give support to anxious persons. Many political groups are unconscious of the emotional currents running through them, especially those which are uncomfortable, and the norm is more often to disguise and hide one's fears, anxieties, and sadnesses than to stay with them and accept them while they run their course.

Groups can provide symbols of support for a person to hold on to during times of anxious stress. One therapist I know collects pebbles from ocean beaches, shines them, and then offers them to clients who are facing an anxious-making event. It is a sign of his concern and support, he says, and the clients can remember his caring and in stressful moments can ground themselves by holding the stones, feeling their contours, turning them over in their hands. In some cultures worry beads are used to similar purpose. In this country the making of the huge quilt dedicated to people who have died of AIDS has been giving emotional support to their bereaved ones. Not only objects, but songs and rallying cries can be used to acknowledge anxiety and support individuals in managing the emotional storm.

Important also is *self*-support in the handling of anxiety — taking care of oneself in ways that allow one to experience anxiety while still engaging in the tasks and activities that foster the fearful concern. Sometimes self-support is created by withdrawal. For instance, a woman goes into her own world to comfort herself. She may have a favorite place or situation that she can remember with calmness and pleasure, and withdraw into imagining it. Or she may meditate, do Yoga, or play a favorite game in preparation for staying with the anxiety in the task at hand. Or she may simply pay attention to how grounded she is when she is actively engaged — sense the stability of her body, her legs holding her up, the strength of her back, the clarity of her vision, the acuteness of her hearing. She may ask others around for their support directly. (We sometimes forget that we can be self-supportive by asking for what we need from others.) She may actively welcome anxiety and look for desires hidden there. She may breathe deeply and well, remembering to exhale fully as well as inhale fully, to create a rhythm to her breathing that feels good, to sense her intake of fresh air and that air's supportive properties.

A simple, useful, and popular approach to self-support is Herbert Benson's[10] "relaxation response." He suggests that a person choose a favorite word or phrase that carries his basic belief system, whether religious or nonreligious, like "The Lord is my shepherd" or "Peace." In a comfortable position, with eyes closed, the person is to relax his muscles, starting from the feet and proceeding upwards. When he gets to his neck and head, he rolls them slightly to loosen and relax the muscles there. Also, as he relaxes muscles upwards, he attends to his breathing, breathes quietly and slowly, and begins to repeat silently the word or phrase from his belief system. He then says this word or phrase when breathing out, thus ensuring full exhaling. Most people have a bias toward inhaling more fully than they exhale, and so they accumulate more carbon dioxide than is healthy. This is a key factor in the relaxation response: more relaxation comes when one breathes out fully and keeps in less carbon dioxide. Also, it is crucial to the relaxation response to keep a basically passive attitude when ideas and concerns intrude upon experience, dealing with them, if at all, in a casual and unhurried way. Otherwise one starts thinking about them and stress enters in.

Persons who practice the relaxation response will be able to use it as a means of self-support during periods when they are engaged in stressful encounters. Practiced in moments of respite from these, it will enable them to stay in contact with themselves and see more clearly what others are doing. They will then be less likely to introject elements of encounters or otherwise distort their own experience. They will also have more of the support that healthy breathing, our primary active contact with the outside, gives us.

Laughter depends upon abrupt exhalation and is a release that is commonly used, sometimes with awareness though more often not, to overcome anxiety. Freud's theory of jokes[11] can be interpreted as essentially saying that humor itself, partly through the breathing patterns it evokes, releases us from the blocking of excitement. Crying, especially full wailing and sobbing, quickens breathing and forces exhalation. Humor and laughing and crying belong in the repertoire of the individual as well as in the norms of the group if anxiety is to be nurtured into spontaneous living. Social change depends upon living intensely during struggle, and part of the intensity lies in the fun and the sadness that are inevitably encountered. Particularly, too many socially oriented groups are too serious too much of the time. A fine lesson from psychotherapy is that being able to deal with profound and scary issues in life depends on also having happy times in the work that is done.

When individuals and groups are able to anxiously act assertively, they are in the realm of spontaneity and unwilling to accede to the constraints and bargains that constitute the clinch of oppression. They are living out their own lives, agents of their being, more masters of their existence than before. They are on their way. They are vulnerable as well as strong, influenced as well as influential, full of initiative as well as reactivity, joyful and sad, uncertain and committed.

And now, I must begin to bring this essay to its culmination by turning to the question of who takes charge of social transformation — the oppressed, the oppressors, or both in combination?

Chapter 16

Who Wants Social Change, Who Starts It, Who Supports It?

A common view holds that change in an oppressive social relationship or social system is desired by the oppressed, the underside, the underclasses, the weak; and correlatively, change is resisted by the oppressors, those who are on top, who are privileged, who are the strong. The argument is often made, also, that it is the weak, never the strong, who start revolutions and who support them. Obviously, say many who hold this view, those on the upper side of the relationship gain the benefits of the system as it exists more than do those on the underside and all follows from this evident reality.

But in fact, as I noted in Chapter 5, both the oppressors and the oppressed are reluctant to change the social structures that exist. They create the social structures and relationships that are oppressive together, are fused in them, and depend on them to contain a good deal of destructiveness and even violence that their very creation builds up. Thus the common view presented above may be called into question. At the very least, matters aren't as simple as that, and never have been, so that some radical thinkers from Marx onwards who accepted this view have been confounded by the "false consciousness" of the oppressed that keeps them from readily becoming revolutionary.

Let me pose some related considerations about the situation and reactions of the well-off which come from the line of thought I have been developing. To begin with, if the rich are doing so well, why aren't they happy? Why is there so much alcoholism among the power elite, so much drivenness, so much attachment to nonessentials, like "pinstripes on one's Mercedes," as a Philadelphia lawyer once put it? The answer, in my view, is that in an oppressive system in which the strong and the weak are fused, there is systematic oppression of those at the top too, not only those at the bottom, and as a group those at the top also are miserable, to which they react by still trying to get all the satisfactions the system seems to offer them.

Most well-off people look all right until one is privileged to hear how they experience their lives. Most society matrons' marriages seem reasonably good until one hears details. Most high bosses and executives look as if they prospered from the system that has elevated them until one closely scrutinizes their everyday lives and sees their conformism. Most men in sexist relationships seem pleased with their dominance until one looks at the sadness in their eyes and the way they carry their bodies around. These are all people with whom matters are not what they seem on superficial observation, indeed are often the very opposite of what appears on the surface.

By why is a close look needed? If being the strong in an exploitative relation is not wonderful, why don't we all see that easily? The projections of those who are not on top are operative in the illusion that an oppressive system can work well for the strong: "If I were in that position, I'd be fine!" Another factor is the force behind the projections of the strong. After all, they achieve strength dramatically through their projections — of their rage, their anxiety, their unacceptable desires, whatever difficult emotional experiences they have — which are introjected by the weak. In projecting, they are indicating that they are intolerant of dealing internally with, and of taking responsibility for, their social-emotional processes. The maintenance of their projections depends upon their keeping others from facing them with the need to own these processes that are so difficult for them. They become successful at keeping any diagnostic assessment of their functioning quite at a distance. Not diagnosed, they are available for being idealized, and beliefs in their happiness reside in the idealizations.

So far there are no clear signs here of those on top wanting social change. But certainly some and possibly many powerful persons, overwhelmed by failures of the system that they presumably control, passively or directly reveal either an unwillingness to carry on business as usual or helplessness, weakness, and inability to run things. Either kind of withdrawal from responsibility and dominance may be a significant factor in encouraging the weak to organize and assert their desires and demands. It may very well be that revolutions do not arise except when those in power somehow communicate their unwillingness or inability to carry on the way they have done in the past. Barbara Ehrenreich[1] has written a book presenting the thesis that the feminist movement arose *after* men in great numbers had begun to tire of the demands to be responsible and dominant that were placed upon them in a sexist society and had begun to withdraw from fulfilling these demands, which were oppressing them as persons. In the Great Depression of the 1930s, the rise of social legislation may have been correlated with the demoralization of the powerful men in industry. A hint of such a process is contained in the story of John L. Lewis and the Chrysler Corporation negotiations. The Gorbachev era in the Soviet Union may importantly represent withdrawal from a position of power of a top faction of national leaders unwilling to continue supervising exploitative political and social relations — a historic event that might lead thinkers to consider more seriously the possibility that many on top are not happy to stick with things the way they are as long as they themselves remain where they are.

At any rate, withdrawal of the powerful in an oppressive system from the processes of domination is a step that destroys the fusion between the strong and the weak. It is a beginning to claim oneself as an agent rather than as a functionary in the system, even if a highly placed and seemingly favored functionary. But it is not enough of a step to enable the strong to participate fully in undoing the clinch of oppression. For this they need to withdraw from being oppressors and to undo their projections. By reowning and resolving their guilt and their self-hatred, their rage and anxiety, their mistrust and prejudice, the powerful may become more real and more realistic and break apart the chains of their old distorted human relations. Then they will be free, if they wish, to leave the particular oppressive scene they have been in or to stay in the scene and help make it free, probably taking part in it more quietly now, since they will be more involved with their own responsibilities and less with others'. (Incidentally, I would urge historians, political theorists, and social activists to make sure they know what the undoing of projections looks like and to spotlight its happening, as it surely will, whenever strong movements to change social systems are under way, because people don't often have a chance to observe someone undergoing it and learn what is happening.)

For those on top to make the fullest possible movement toward a democratic and equalitarian social order, then, they must acknowledge their discontent, withdraw from the processes of domination, and undo their projections. For those who occupy the weak positions in such social relations to make the same kind of movement, there are complementary tasks that are at least as formidable — a fact that in itself suggests that the numbers of oppressed and oppressors who are ready for social change to end oppression may not be so very different. And indeed one of these tasks of the weak is to discover the ways in which they derive satisfactions from the status quo and so take part in the maintenance of what is. Even the most oppressed hold on to the way things are not only because of the danger of change but also because they have found methods for getting some of their needs met. And they need to become aware of this to become able to withdraw from the fusion that holds the oppression in place.

Another task of the weak is to become aware of their power — the power of their intelligence, of the work they do, of all they create in society, of their being *essential* there. The dialectic of power and weakness, in which we see that we are sometimes forceful, sometimes vulnerable, and that in the best of circumstances and in the worst these are intertwined, must be seen by the weak as they come to terms with their own strengths. Only when they acknowledge their own great power and influence can the weak take responsibility for their lives rather than allocate it to others who become strong, sometimes on their behalf, always in their stead. Taking responsibility, the weak can become agents, not superresponsible but not regularly divesting themselves of their power as they manipulate and connive in oppressive relationships.

A third task has the first two parts of undoing introjecting patterns. First, the weak need to stop introjecting in the here and now. Second, they need to extricate themselves from the powerful influence of old introjects that they carry about within them — standards and values they have taken in and regulated their lives by that violate their very nature.

On the surface there seems nothing in these complementary human processes that suggests that the weak are the ones, or even the prime ones, who desire and initiate social change to end oppression. Yet if we look closely, there is something here that must lead many people to believe the weak are in fact the ones who do these things — something more tangible than the idea that those without benefits are the logical ones to do them.

This vital source of the popular conviction, I believe, is the following: In introjecting, a person takes on more than she or he can shoulder; in projecting, a person tries to shed responsibility. The weak internalize social conflict and try to solve it within their psychic economies, while the strong externalize the conflict and try to solve it in social relations. When the weak give up their self-conquest, they reopen the conflict in the social relations; that is, they put it back where it began. When the strong stop divesting themselves of responsibility, they take it back inside and relieve the social relation of its burden. The open conflict out there in the light of day is conspicuous, the responsibility taken back is not.

Of course, in all contacts both the internal psyche and the social relation are involved, but the emphasis shifts when either an introjection or a projection is being undone. Women who have introjected from childhood and made themselves weak give up selfblame and demand more for themselves in social relations when they start to battle sexism. Racial and ethnic minorities who have degraded and diminished themselves by self-conquest stop this when they turn their efforts toward rectifying the social policies and practices that have meant their occupation of the weak roles in society. Conversely, the powerful give up the regulation of social interactions as they undo their projections, and center upon the experience and expression of feelings and purposes they have avoided, such as yeoman work in social service or costly private philanthropy out of direct strong feeling for people, or serious amateur painting or furniture making. And these different emphases give rise to the appearance not only that the weak initiate social change but also that they benefit more than the strong from the overcoming of exploitative relationships.

In the matter of benefit, the underlying reality, I believe, is that the persons on both sides gain equally as human beings. Whether the oppressed are in fact the initiators of social change remains unclear in that they may be reacting to a withdrawal on the part of the powerful. The undoing of the clinch of oppression is transactional, just as the creation of oppression is transactional. But who takes the first step is much less important than both sides' then going on to overcome domination and submission fully.

Who wants social change? Many people on both sides of the fence, I believe. Who initiates it? Sometimes representatives of the weak, sometimes people from the powerful side. Who supports it? Again, many on both sides of the fence. Then why isn't there more social change? Because all these people also support what is. We are all revolutionaries and all reactionaries, acting sometimes more in one role, other times more in the other. We are all spontaneous, because we cannot help having desires and being aroused by attractive qualities in our environments. We are all also ensnared in webs of fusion, having learned early on in life to give up being agents, to project and introject, to quiet our rage and flee our anxiety. The trick for those who want to be agents of social change is to find that change side in many people, from many walks of life and all social classes, and to bind together in common purpose all who want to move toward a new world of equality.

The idea of the class struggle has narrowed our view of what is possible, limited whom we see as allies and enemies, constricted our vision of reality. The struggle, I believe, is less between classes, less between men and women, less between a white majority and racial and ethnic minorities, than between those working back toward their natural spontaneity and human concern and those holding on to the delusion of fusion.

Chapter 17

Is All This Practical?

When psychological issues surface in social relations and become the focus of discussion, people tend to concentrate on the negative, pathological factors in these issues rather than their positive, productive sides, such as healthy possibilities in anger and anxiety. Psychological issues are most often equated with the unusual, the abnormal, and the irrational. And in line with this tendency, their presence in social intercourse is treated as intrusive, as an unwelcome itch. To talk of the psychology of experience while striving to settle a social dispute, for instance, seems to many like ad hominem behavior that is to be avoided at all costs.

A favorite example of this whole attitude comes from a classroom project I have used. Students who work in human service agencies are asked to study their superiors, not to judge their competence, but from a personality point of view. The task for each student is to choose one superior, whose identity is not to be revealed, study this person, and write a paper on the results, answering questions such as these: What are this person's psychological characteristics? What personal strengths and limitations does one see in observing this person carefully in the work setting? For instance, how does she show anger in staff meetings, or how does he react to having a mistake he's made revealed? And finally, what use might the student make of the observations made and insights gained?

From the discomfort that the students display over this assignment, an outside observer might think they had been asked to peek and watch their parents having sexual intercourse. A majority of the class say they don't want to do the assignment. I hear it is "inappropriate," that they will be "violating" their superiors and "belittling" them, that the papers will amount to "gossiping." I have to insist mildly to get the students started. Then a few do a straightforward, clear job, and none write anything belittling or gossipy. But most don't write much, or they say superficial things, or they write unclearly, or some combination of these. Then, when finished, many report they didn't like doing this chore.

This does not seem a case of respecting or fearing authority fig-ures. The exercise is set up so that the analyzed superior never has to know about it, and many of the students in the class have said they would not want to explore a friend's psychology this way ei-ther, for the same reasons.

Given this kind of propensity for feeling that to explore others' psychology is essentially to spy on them and devalue them, is there any place for talking about our shared psychological trends in nor-mal social endeavors, or does that kind of talk belong only in the psychotherapist's office and in small groups that are organized pre-cisely to talk about such matters?

The fact is that we already bring up psychology in daily discourse about social and political life a great deal, as when someone says, "He's crazy to believe he can lie to us over a long period of time," or "That's a paranoid thing for the chairman to do." Similarly, how often have we heard statements like "She's out of her mind to think we can get rid of war," or "That's emotional when we need a ratio-nal perspective." This common way of talking, however, con-tributes little to serious social endeavor. It doesn't help to resolve differences, build unity, or facilitate democratic practices. Rather, it does in fact devalue others. It does this by expressing disagree-ment strongly but without serious intent to reach toward and con-nect with the other about whom we are speaking. I believe that such application of psychological considerations often derives from a feeling of inferiority or helplessness, and that the person in-dulging it is likely to be diminishing the other in an effort to appear superior or to stand firm with the community against the perceived weakness of the criticized other. In contrast, it seems to me that only if the psychological is brought up in the service of loving, caring resolution of the social issue being engaged is it likely to be useful.

The value of a caring use of psychological insights can be seen in the context of counseling battered women. A victim of battering often feels guilty, as if she had done something wrong, and different helpers have different strategies for dealing with the guilt. Some insist that we say firmly to the woman that she is a victim, purely and simply, and has absolutely no reason to feel guilty. The woman may accept this view overtly but continue to feel guilty and act as if she did not believe in her innocence. A prime way of doing this involves anger. A helper of a battered woman usually is angry at what has happened to her and may still be happening, and wants her to become at least as angry. Rarely does she do so, and meanwhile she cannot control her feeling of guilt, and it bewilders her. It also bewilders her helper. The helper does not know why she should feel guilty for being a victim. But just using common sense and telling such a person her feeling is unnecessary seldom succeeds in freeing her of it.

Alternatively, a helper may explore with the woman what goes on psychologically that may underlie such guilt. Now it emerges that the woman believes that in some way she may have participated in her battering, by tolerating it, by feeling she deserved it, by baiting her batterer, or by some other action that brought her into collusion with the one who has hurt her. For a helper merely to entertain that such participation by the woman is possible often rouses in others the charge that the helper is "blaming the victim." But the helper who tries to work through the guilt typically is trying to blame no one, but rather to get to the bottom of what is causing the guilty feeling so that it can be alleviated. And this kind of helper, who works with the woman's role as maker of her own life — for instance, with how staying with her batterer may be provocative — is, in my experience, more likely to succeed with the battered woman.

To say that any group of oppressed people participate in their own oppression is to risk the same charge of blaming the victim. In fact, I believe, if the speaker is an astute psychological observer, to speak this way usually reflects care for the oppressed. No matter: for many, what he or she has said is easily disposed of by this criticism. And the use of the accusation of blaming others, and thus demeaning and hurting them, extends further, to many contexts where psychology and social existence may be considered together.

Why is this so? What is it about an observer's noticing such psychological happenings as people's fusing with those who hurt them or those they hurt that merits attribution of a blaming and demeaning purpose? Why is it common for people to believe that taking into consideration how another individual functions psychologically, especially when the functioning is not what is conventionally deemed to be rational, is unkind and hurtful? Why is invoking in social effort the understanding that leads to psychiatric diagnosis considered to belittle people rather than show concernful interest? Professionals in the human services as well as lay persons treat the use of psychological insights in this negative fashion, which suggests that doing it must have some deeper base than mere ignorance. And anyone who wants to make psychological understanding useful in a social context needs to sort out what is behind this readiness to see paying attention to the psychological as blaming and diminishing. He or she also needs to understand the intense feelings, especially wrath, that are sometimes aroused in discussions that bring the psychological to bear upon social struggle.

To begin an approach to an explanation, blaming, as we have seen, is a prime action in the arena of projection, and acting aggressively against blaming, as in attacking others for blaming the victim, is itself blaming and is projection. To assert that I am blaming the victim when I am seeing the participation of the victim in his or her own oppression, if the accusation against me is hurled like a thunderbolt rather than shared like a concernful insight, is to blame me as a blamer. Projected material can sometimes be quite true of the person projected on, and if I do in fact blame the victim — have the attitude that the victim's troubles are the victim's fault — I have no cause to complain. If my reference to the victim is not a blaming but a caring one, however, I will be rightly pained by the charge levied upon me that can clearly be construed as disguised projection. I know it is not I who think poorly of a person who is trapped in a weak-strong power relationship and contributes to its continuance. I feel wrongly heard, and sorely mistreated to be angrily accused of cruel insensitivity. My feeling is a reflection of my resistance to this projection that is being foisted upon me, my unwillingness to introject the accusation.

The projection in cries of "You're blaming the victim" seeks to keep psychological issues from being material pertinent to the attacker. As in all projecting that is unawares, the individual is imposing on the object of his or her concern something that is active within. The one who doesn't want the helper of a battered woman to get into dealing with her guilty feelings is not necessarily projecting a criticism of the battered woman, but something is aroused in the objector that is not being fully owned and dealt with. Anyone who has been attacked as blaming the victim when this has been untrue will be able to testify about how fruitless it is to defend oneself rationally — a sure sign of the projecting process.

Some highly loaded words I have been using in discussing blaming the victim — "attack," "accuse," "charge," "hurl like a thunderbolt" — are just as appropriate for the reactions I have sometimes gotten when I have presented the ideas contained in this essay to others for comment. From human service clinicians — persons who work with abused and battered women, for example — I have received understanding and recognition, while from social activists I have elicited a very mixed response. Some respond with interest and ready acceptance or thoughtfully critical remarks. Others think that in even suggesting applying psychological considerations to social struggle as I do, I am being unrealistic or foolish, as if this couldn't be done well or wouldn't work, or diverting focus wrongly from the struggle itself. And they become quite angry with me.

Their anger rouses my suspicion that I am in the presence of a very profound internal state, that the angry person is trying to ward off something by naysaying or challenging me. I think I know what is being avoided by such intense reactions; it is the debilitating feeling of hopelessness. Aaron Bender, metaphorically discussing "transference, countertransference and resistance in the psychoanalytic treatment of war," has made remarks that bear on my hypothesis here:

> "The countertransference feeling . . . in doing such therapy is one of hopelessness . . . . A therapist who would try to work with the illness of war must be prepared to deal with lots of feelings of working with a hopelessly destructive patient and he must also be prepared to field many castrating remarks from the intellectual community which would deny that war is at least partly connected with irrational childhood conflict."[1]

I myself have experienced such hopelessness in preparing the material in this text. Besides having learned anew how resistant many people are to the use of psychological considerations in social action, I have felt anew the despair of knowing that each effort to do so is difficult and each individual gain miniscule. I too wish for big changes which should occur quickly, rather than small, incremental growth while individuals are in the process of becoming agents in the making of their lives in society.

Those who oppose my kind of use of psychological understanding in social action seem to me to operate under the banner of keeping the community whole and unified and moving forward by the sacrifice of individuality. To them, I believe, my approach threatens a hopeless stop of that moving forward. One of the things they often say is "We haven't got time for that approach; we'd get nothing done." My response is that their alternative has proven to be impractical. The attempt to avoid the psychological leads to denial, via projection, of our human nature, which is all we have to work with, and possibly to the misuse of psychology I described early in this chapter.

But hopelessness *is* debilitating, so a first principle for the successful use of psychological considerations in social struggle is that they should be brought up not only in the service of loving, caring resolution of social issues, as I said earlier, but also within a framework of hopefulness.

Where will the hopefulness come from?

The strongest ground for hopefulness we who want to move in this direction have, I believe, is the presence of our allies. As long as there are those who are willing, for instance, to push through the resistance of colleagues and others to help an abused woman work through her feelings of guilt, there is cause for hope that we can have success in the enterprise this essay is about.

My answer, then, to the question of whether using psychological considerations in efforts to undo the clinch of oppression is practical is a qualified yes. To be practical, the psychological considerations must be applied for everyone involved, those who lead and those who follow or stand to the side. They must be part of the ongoing concern with process in social struggle, sometimes figural or central, more often a subsidiary concern. They must be used in a supportive, not denigrating, way. And they must be embedded in an atmosphere of hope, realistic hope, a sense that the struggle is long and difficult but that it is possible to be successful in the long run if we are active, with our allies, in the short run.

Is this program likely to be practical soon? Only rarely, I believe. Two opposite forces — those of putting the community before the individual and those of emphasizing the personal to the point of excluding community endeavors — are entrenched in our customary ways of thinking and acting. We have believed for too long that social welfare and individual welfare are competitive, not congruent, to easily believe that they can be mixed together well. Furthermore, both collective struggle and expansion of individual awareness are scary endeavors, and we are resourceful in our human weakness at avoiding that which is frightening. But even as I put forward this view here, I wonder if this too is a countertransference response of hopelessness. These ideas are practical in the context of hope. This I believe from my clinical experience and assessment of the social movements of the past. This I affirm again.

Notes

Chapter 1: A Beginning

1. Alice Miller, *For Your Own Good: Hidden Cruelty in Child-Rearing and the Roots of Violence*. New York: Farrar, Straus & Giroux, 1983.

2. Lloyd deMause, *Reagan's America*. New York: Creative Roots, Inc., 1984. See also his "The Making of a Fearful Leader: 'Where's the Rest of Me,' " *The Journal of Psychohistory*, 1984, 12(1), 5-21; "The Real Target Wasn't Terrorism," *The Journal of Psychohistory*, 1986, 13(4), 413-426; and "Why Did Reagan Do it?" *The Journal of Psychohistory*, 1986, 14(2), 107-118.

3. Andras Angyal, *Neurosis and Treatment: A Holistic Theory*. Eugenia Hanfmann and Richard M. Jones, Editors. New York: John Wiley & Sons, 1965.

4. John Macmurray, *The Self as Agent*. London: Faber and Faber Limited, 1957.

Chapter 2: Identification with the Aggressor: A Clinical Formulation

1. Allan R. Buss, *A Dialectical Psychology*. New York: Irvington, 1979. Page 56.

2. Frantz Fanon, *The Wretched of the Earth*. New York: Grove Press, 1963. Page 115.

3. Harold D. Lasswell, "Propaganda and Mass Insecurity." In: *Personality and Political Crisis.* A H. Stanton and S. E. Perry, Editors. Glencoe, IL: Free Press, 1951. Pages 19-22.

4. Albert Memmi, *The Colonizer and the Colonized.* New York: Orion, 1965. Page 53.

5. Sandor Ferenczi, "Confusion of Tongues between Adults and the Child." Paper read at the Twelfth International Psycho-Analytical Congress, Wiesbaden, September 1932. In: *Final Contributions to the Problems and Methods of Psycho-Analysis.* New York: Basic Books, 1955. Pages 161-162.

6. Patricia Perri Rieker and Elaine [Hilberman] Carmen, "The Victim to Patient Process: The Disconfirmation and Transformation of Abuse." *American Journal of Orthopsychiatry,* 1986, 56(3), 360-370.

7. Sigmund Freud, *The Ego and the Id.* In: *The Standard Edition of the Complete Psychological Works of Sigmund Freud, Volume XIX.* James Strachey, Editor. London: Hogarth Press, 1961. Page 54.

8. Sigmund Freud, *Civilization and Its Discontents.* In: *The Standard Edition of the Complete Psychological Works of Sigmund Freud, Volume XXI.* James Strachey, Editor. London: The Hogarth Press, 1961. Page 129.

9. Hellmuth Kaiser, *Effective Psychotherapy: The Contribution of Hellmuth Kaiser.* Louis B. Fierman, Editor. New York: Free Press, 1965. Page 113.

10. Cynthia A. Solin, "Displacement of Affect in Families following Incest Disclosure." *American Journal of Orthopsychiatry,* 1986, 56(4), 570-576.

11. Frederick Perls, Ralph F. Hefferline, and Paul Goodman, *Gestalt Therapy: Excitement and Growth in the Human Personality.* New York: Julian Press, 1951. Page 363.

Chapter 3: Projection Upon a Primed Vulnerable Other: A Clinical Formulation

1. Carl G. Jung, *Two Essays on Analytical Psychology.* New York: Meridian Books, 1956. Page 160.

2. Hellmuth Kaiser, *Effective Psychotherapy: The Contribution of Hellmuth Kaiser.* Louis B. Fierman, Editor. New York: Free Press, 1965. Page 115.

3. Peter Marris, "The Social Impact of Stress." In: *Mental Health and the Economy.* Louis A. Ferman and Jeanne P. Gordus, Editors. Kalamazoo, MI: W. E. Upjohn Institute for Employment Research, 1979. Page 311.

Chapter 4: Empowering and Disempowering Reciprocally

1. I refer to the senses of powerlessness and of powerfulness to indicate that a distorted, excessive belief about how weak or strong one is underlies identification and projection processes. I also seek to account adequately to real power differentials characterizing the weak and the strong.

2. Hellmuth Kaiser, *Effective Psychotherapy: The Contribution of Hellmuth Kaiser.* Louis B. Fierman, Editor. New York: Free Press, 1965. Page 115. Norman F. Dixon also describes this well in his *On the Psychology of Military Incompetence.* New York: Basic Books, 1976.

3. Harriet Goldhor Lerner, *The Dance of Anger.* New York: Harper & Row, 1985. Page 33.

4. Erving Polster and Miriam Polster, *Gestalt Therapy Integrated.* New York: Brunner/Mazel, 1973. Pages 93-94.

5. Erich Fromm, *Man for Himself.* New York: Rinehart and Company, 1947. Page 155.

6. Philip Lichtenberg, "On Responsibility." In: *Getting Even: The Equalizing Law of Relationship.* Lanham, MD: University Press of America, 1988. Pages 59-76.

7. Heinz Kohut, *The Analysis of the Self.* New York: International Universities Press, 1971. Page 91.

8. Elizabeth Janeway, *Powers of the Weak.* New York: Alfred A. Knopf, 1980. Especially Chapter 8.

9. T. W. Adorno, Else Frenkel-Brunswik, Daniel J. Levinson, and R. Nevitt Sanford, *The Authoritarian Personality.* New York: Harper & Brothers, 1950. Chapter VI.

10. Vamik D. Volkan, *Cyprus — War and Adaptation.* Charlottesville, VA: University Press of Virginia, 1979. Pages 70-74.

Chapter 5: Some Qualities When People Fuse

1. Erich Fromm, *Man for Himself.* New York: Rinehart and Company, 1947.

2. Abraham Maslow, "The Authoritarian Character Structure." *The Journal of Social Psychology,* 1943, 18, 401-411.

3. T. W. Adorno, Else Frenkel-Brunswik, Daniel J. Levinson, and R. Nevitt Sanford, *The Authoritarian Personality.* New York: Harper & Brothers, 1950.

4. James Mark Baldwin, *Social and Ethical Interpretations in Mental Development*. New York: The Macmillan Company, 1902. Pages 24-25.

5. Albert Memmi, *The Colonizer and the Colonized*. New York: Orion, 1965.

6. Frantz Fanon, *The Wretched of the Earth*. New York: Grove Press, 1963.

7. William H. Grier and Price M. Cobbs, *Black Rage*. New York: Basic Books, 1980.

8. T. W. Adorno et al., op. cit. Page 463.

9. T. W. Adorno et al., op. cit. Page 463.

Chapter 6: Self as Agent, Self as Agency: A General Statement

1. Philip Lichtenberg, *Psychoanalysis: Radical and Conservative*. New York: Springer Publishing Company, 1969, and *Getting Even: The Equalizing Law of Relationship*. Lanham, MD: University Press of America, 1988.

Chapter 7: Cautions on Taking Psychological Ideas Into a Social-Action Arena

1. Heinz L. Ansbacher and Rowena R. Ansbacher, *The Individual Psychology of Alfred Adler*. New York: Basic Books, 1956. Especially Chapters 17, 18, and 19.

2. Wilhelm Reich, *The Mass Psychology of Fascism*. New York: Farrar, Straus & Giroux, 1970.

3. Bertha Capen Reynolds, *Social Work and Social Living*. New York: Citadel, 1951.

4. William R. Beardslee, *The Way Out Must Lead In: Life Histories in the Civil Rights Movement.* Atlanta, GA: Emory University Center for Research in Social Change, 1977.

Chapter 8: The Angry Weak and the Angry Powerful

1. Holly Near and Ronnie Gilbert, quoted in pamphlet with the record *Lifeline.* Oakland, CA: Redwood Records, 1983. Number RR404.

2. Alan R. Buss, *A Dialectical Psychology.* New York: Irvington Publishers, 1979. Page 56.

3. Kay Lehman Schlozman and Sidney Verba, *Injury to Insult: Unemployment, Class and Political Response.* Cambridge, MA.: Harvard University Press, 1979. Page 194.

4. John H. Garraty, *Unemployment in History.* New York: Harper & Row, 1978. Page 185.

5. Frantz Fanon, *The Wretched of the Earth.* New York: Grove Press, 1963. Pages 73-74.

6. Sigmund Freud, *Group Psychology and the Analysis of the Ego.* In: *The Standard Edition of the Complete Psychological Works of Sigmund Freud, Volume XVIII*, James Strachey, Editor. London: Hogarth Press, 1955. Page 105 ff.

7. Ellen Meiksins Wood, *Mind and Politics.* Berkeley, CA: University of California Press, 1972. Page 126ff.

8. Wilhelm Reich, *Sex-Pol: Essays 1929-1934.* New York: Vintage, 1972.

9. Thorstein Veblen, *The Theory of the Leisure Class.* New York: Viking Penguin, 1987. Page 246ff.

Chapter 9: Intense Social Emotions Are Key

1. Frederick Perls, Ralph F. Hefferline, and Paul Goodman, *Gestalt Therapy: Excitement and Growth in the Human Personality.* New York: Julian Press, 1951. Page 203.

2. Marshall H. Klaus, Treville Leger, and Mary Anne Trause, Editors, *Maternal Attachment and Mothering Disorders.* Piscataway, NJ: Johnson & Johnson Baby Products Company, 1975. Page 23.

3. Jack Belden, *China Shakes the World.* New York: Monthly Review Press, 1970. Page 275ff.

4. Gayle Graham Yates, *What Women Want: The Ideas of the Movement.* Cambridge, MA: Harvard University Press, 1975. Page 99.

5. Wilfred R. Bion, *Attention and Interpretation: A Scientific Approach to Insight in Psycho-Analysis and Groups.* New York: Basic Books, 1970.

6. William R. Beardslee, *The Way Out Must Lead In: Life Histories in the Civil Rights Movement.* Atlanta, GA: Emory University Center for Research in Social Change, 1977. Page 59.

7. Ibid. Page 153.

8. Andras Angyal, *Neurosis and Treatment: A Holistic Theory.* Eugenia Hanfman and Richard M. Jones, Editors. New York: Viking, 1973. Page 234.

9. Elizabeth Janeway, *Powers of the Weak.* New York: Alfred A. Knopf, 1980. Page 167.

10. Philip Lichtenberg and Jeanne C. Pollock, "Responsibility as a Personality Characteristic." *A.M.A. Archives of General Psychiatry.* 1967, 17, 169-175.

11. Philip Hallie, *Cruelty.* Middletown, CT: Wesleyan University Press, 1982. Page 83.

12. Ana Julia Cienfuegos and Christina Monelli, "The Testimony of Political Repression as a Therapeutic Instrument." *The American Journal of Orthopsychiatry,* 1983, 53, 43-51.

Chapter 11: Working with the Full Delusion of Fusion

1. Frederick Perls, Ralph F. Hefferline, and Paul Goodman, *Gestalt Therapy: Excitement and Growth in the Human Personality.* New York: Julian Press, 1951. Pages 121-122.

2. D. W. Winnicott, *The Maturational Processes and the Facilitating Environment.* New York: International Universities Press, 1965. Pages 43-46.

3. Cheryl Hyde, "Experiences of Women Activists: Implications for Community Organizing Theory and Practice." *Journal of Sociology and Social Welfare,* 1986, XIII(3), 545-562. Quotation on page 554.

4. Donna Warnock, "Mobilizing Emotions: Organizing the Women's Pentagon Action." Interview by Annie Popkin and Gary Delgado. *Socialist Review,* 1982, 12(3/4), 37-47.

5. Donald R. Catherall, "The Support System and Amelioration of PTSD in Vietnam Veterans." *Psychotherapy: Theory/Research/Practice/Training,* 1986, 23(3), 472-482.

6. Irving D. Yalom, *The Theory and Practice of Group Psychotherapy,* 3rd Edition. New York: Basic Books, 1985. Pages 143 and 145.

7. Hellmuth Kaiser, *Effective Psychotherapy: The Contribution of Hellmuth Kaiser*, Louis B. Fierman, Editor. New York: Free Press, 1965. Pages 133-134.

8. Erving Polster and Miriam Polster, *Gestalt Therapy Integrated*. New York: Brunner/Mazel Publishers, 1973. Pages 95-97.

9. Hellmuth Kaiser, op. cit. Page 154.

Chapter 12: Noticing and Changing Faulty Identifications

1. Thorstein Veblen, *The Theory of the Leisure Class*. New York: Viking Penguin, 1987.

2. Sigmund Freud, *Group Psychology and the Analysis of the Ego*. In: *The Standard Edition of the Complete Psychological Works of Sigmund Freud, Volume XVIII*. James Strachey, Editor. London: Hogarth Press, 1955.

3. Ibid. Page 105ff.

4. E. Y. Harburg, *Rhymes for the Irreverent*. New York: Grossman Publishers, 1965. Page 43.

5. Anton Makarenko, *The Road to Life: An Epic in Education*. New York: Oriole Editions, 1973.

6. Steve Burghardt, *The Other Side of Organizing*. Cambridge, MA: Schenkman Publishing Company, 1982. Page 180.

Chapter 13: Discovering and Undoing Projections

1. Erving Polster and Miriam Polster, lecture notes, March 8, 1982.

2. Marshall H. Klaus, Treville Leger, and Mary Anne Trause, Editors, *Maternal Attachment and Mothering Disorders*. Piscataway, NJ: Johnson and Johnson Baby Products Company, 1975. Page 23.

3. Harriet Goldhor Lerner, *The Dance of Anger*. New York: Harper & Row, 1985. Page 22.

4. Frederick Perls, Ralph F. Hefferline, and Paul Goodman, *Gestalt Therapy: Excitement and Growth in the Human Personality*. New York: Julian Press, 1951. Page 215.

5. Ibid. Page 216.

6. William Ryan, *Blaming the Victim*. New York: Vintage Books, 1976.

7. Zolaka Adams-Sawyer, Martha Adams-Sullivan, Robyn Brown-Manning, Andaye C. DeLaCruz, and Carmen Gaines, "Women of Color and Feminist Practice." In: *Not for Women Only*. Mary Bricker-Jenkins and Nancy Hooyman, Editors. Silver Spring, MD: National Association of Social Workers, 1986. Page 82.

Chapter 14: Recovering and Reorganizing Anger

1. Frederick Perls, Ralph F. Hefferline, and Paul Goodman, *Gestalt Therapy: Excitement and Growth in the Human Personality*. New York: Julian Press, 1951. Pages 342 and 344.

2. Alice Miller, *For Your Own Good: Hidden Cruelty in Child-Rearing and the Roots of Violence*. New York: Farrar, Straus & Giroux, 1983.

3. James R. Averill, *Anger and Aggression: An Essay on Emotion*. New York: Springer-Verlag, 1982. Page 321.

4. Saul D. Alinsky, *John L. Lewis: An Unauthorized Biography.* New York: Vintage Books, 1970. Pages 149-152.

5. J. Raymond Walsh, *C.I.O.: Industrial Unionism in Action.* New York: W. W. Norton, 1937. Page 129.

6. Hyman Spotnitz, *Modern Psychoanalysis of the Schizophrenic Patient.* New York: Grune & Stratton, 1969. Page 39.

7. Barbara Bender, "Scapegoating Behavior Sequential to Battering." *Child Welfare*, 1976, 55, 417-422.

8. Pennie Cohen, "Violence in the Family . . . An Act of Loyalty?" *Psychotherapy: Theory/Research/Practice*, 1984, 21, 249-253.

9. Klaus D. Hoppe, "Chronic Reactive Aggression in Survivors of Severe Persecution." *Comprehensive Psychiatry*, 1971, 12, 230-237.

10. David M. Berger, "The Survivor Syndrome: A Problem of Nosology and Treatment." *The American Journal of Psychotherapy*, 1977, 31, 238-251.

11. Carol Roman, private communication.

12. William R. Beardslee, *The Way Out Must Lead In: Life Histories in the Civil Rights Movement.* Atlanta, GA: Emory University Center for Research in Social Change, 1977. Page 153.

13. Chester M. Pierce and Louis Jolyon West, "Six Years of Sit-Ins: Psychodynamic Causes and Effects." *International Journal of Social Psychiatry*, 1966, 12, 29-34.

14. Sheldon B. Cohen, "Desegregation: A Southern Psychiatrist's View." *Psychiatric Opinion*, 1966, 3(6), 25-28.

15. Elizabeth Janeway, *Powers of the Weak*. New York: Alfred A. Knopf, 1980. Page 61.

16. Gayle Graham Yates, *What Women Want: The Ideas of the Movement*. Cambridge, MA: Harvard University Press, 1975. Page 95.

17. Philip Hallie, *Cruelty*. Middleton, CT: Wesleyan University Press, 1982. Page 83.

18. Joanna Rogers Macy, *Despair and Personal Power in the Nuclear Age*. Philadelphia, PA: New Society Publishers, 1983.

19. Harriet Goldhor Lerner, *The Dance of Anger*. New York: Harper & Row, 1985. Page 33.

20. Ibid. Page 9.

21. Georg Christoph Lichtenberg, *The Lichtenberg Reader*. Franz Mautner and Henry Hatfield, Editors. Boston: Beacon Press, 1959. Page 98.

22. Harriet Goldhor Lerner, op. cit. Page 1.

23. Carol Tavris, *Anger: The Misunderstood Emotion*. New York: Simon and Schuster, 1982.

24. George R. Bach and Peter Wyden, *The Intimate Enemy*. New York: Morrow, 1967. Page 6.

25. Abraham Maslow, *Toward a Psychology of Being*, 2nd Edition. New York: Van Nostrand Reinhold, 1968. Page 162.

26. Hendrie Weisinger. *Dr. Weisinger's Anger Work Out Book*. New York: Quill, 1985. Page 81.

27. Ibid. Pages 81-82.

28. Philip Lichtenberg, *Getting Even: The Equalizing Law of Relationship*. Lanham, MD: University Press of America, 1988. Pages 15-29.

Chapter 15: On Anxiously Acting Assertively

1. Elizabeth Rosenberg [Zetzel], "Anxiety and the Capacity to Bear It." *The International Journal of Psychoanalysis*, 1949, XXX, 1-12.

2. Otto Fenichel, *The Psychoanalytic Theory of Neurosis*. New York: W. W. Norton & Company, 1945. Page 133.

3. Daniel P. Brown and Erika Fromm, *Hypnotherapy and Hypnoanalysis*. Hillsdale, NJ: Lawrence Erlbaum Associates, 1986. Pages 225-226.

4. Elizabeth Rosenberg [Zetzell], op. cit. Page 8.

5. Kenneth Burke, *The Grammar of Motives*. Cleveland, OH: The World Publishing Co., 1962. Pages 33-34.

6. Frederick Perls, "Four Lectures." In: *Gestalt Therapy Now*. Joen Fagan and Irma Lee Shepherd, Editors. New York: Harper Colophon, 1971. Page 16.

7. F. Ishu Ishiyama, "Morita Therapy: Its Basic Features and Cognitive Intervention for Anxiety Treatment." *Psychotherapy: Theory/Research/Practice/Training*, 1986, 23, 375-381.

8. Frederick Perls, Ralph F. Hefferline, and Paul Goodman, *Gestalt Therapy: Excitement and Growth in the Human Personality*. New York: Julian Press, 1951. Pages 426-427.

9. Ibid. Page 131.

10. Herbert Benson, *The Relaxation Response.* New York: William Morrow, 1975, and *Beyond the Relaxation Response.* New York: Times Books, 1984.

11. Sigmund Freud, *Jokes and Their Relation to the Unconscious.* In: *The Standard Edition of the Complete Psychological Works of Sigmund Freud, Volume VIII.* James Strachey, Editor. London: Hogarth Press, 1960.

Chapter 16: Who Wants Social Change, Who Starts It, Who Supports It?

1. Barbara Ehrenreich, *The Hearts of Men: American Dreams and the Flight from Commitment.* New York: Anchor Books, 1983.

Chapter 17: Is All This Practical?

1. Aaron Bender, "Psychohistorians Discuss Psychohistory: Transference, Countertransference and Resistance in the Psychoanalytic Treatment of War." *The Journal of Psychohistory*, 1987, 14, 179-185.

Index

Abused and the abuser 3
Abused parents abusing children 142-143
Abuser, the, see also Aggressor, Oppressor 19
Ad hominem behavior 199
Adams-Sawyer, Zolaka, Martha Adams-Sullivan, et al. 216
Adaptation to the environment 137
Adler, Alfred 6, 66
Adorno, Theodore 52, 55-56, 210
Adult molesters 19, 22, 26
Adult-child relation 27
Aggressor, the; aggression 16-26, 33, 51, 53, 55-56, 71, 122-123, 160, 164; fantasies of aggression 38
AIDS quilt, the 188
Alcoholics Anonymous 7
Alcoholism 191
Algeria 70
Alienation 63
Alinsky, Saul 161-162, 217
Allende, Salvatore 105
Ambiguity 6, 96, 123-124
Ambiguity, intolerance of 55-57
Ambivalence 55, 96
American Indians and alcoholism 155
Anger 38-41, 43, 53-54, 58-59, 68, 72, 74-77, 79, 85, 88, 90, 92-94, 98, 101-104, 109-112, 120, 134, 137, 139, 144, 148, 155, 157-179, 199, 201, 203; productive/ political uses 171-179, 186
Anger and political endeavor 169
Anger as focused on rule setting 167
Anger management 40, 43
Anger, contactfulness of 170
Angyal, Andras 4, 207, 213

Angyal, Andras, theory of universal ambiguity 4
Ansbacher, Heinz L. and Rowena R. Ansbacher 211
Antiabortion groups 152
Anticommunism, hysterical 90
Antinuclear groups 99, 170-171
Antiwar and peace movements 68, 144.
Antiwelfare individuals 152
Anxiety 12-13, 34, 36, 41, 58-59, 79, 84, 88, 90, 94, 96-97, 101-102, 105, 109-112, 120, 134, 139, 143, 148, 155, 179-190, 193, 199
Anxiety disorder 181
Anxiety of anticipation and excitement 35
Anxiety of dread and fear 35
Anxiety, manageable and unmanageable 182
Anxiety, productive management of 35-37, 142, 187
Anxiety, traumatic 13
Apathy, political and social 69
Assembly line workers 12
Association for Psychohistory, Inc. 6-7
Authentic intimacy 123
Authoritarian groups, persons and systems 36, 45, 52, 55-56, 100, 133
Authority figures 187, 200
Authority, (oppressive) 17, 151, 176
Authority, irrational 42, 156
Authority, legitimate 97, 160
Automation behavior 13
Averill, James R. 160, 216

Bach, George R. and Peter Wyden 176, 218

Balance of desire and self-regulation 24

Baldwin, James Mark 52, 211

Battered, abused women and wives 71, 84, 201, 203, 205

Beardslee, William 66, 86-88, 167, 212-213, 217

Behavior modification therapy 186

Belden, Jack 81, 84, 213

Bender, Aaron 203, 220

Bender, Barbara 164, 217

Benson, Herbert 189, 220

Berger, David 165, 217

Bion, Wilfred R. 213

Black rage 54

Blaming the victim 152, 201-202

Blocked excitement 182-183

Body politic, the 4

Bonding 104

Bourgeois ideology 69

Bourgeois versus socialist individualism 73

Breaking the will of the child 1

Bricker-Jenkins, Mary and Nancy Hooyman 216

Brown, Daniel P. and Erika Fromm 182, 219

Brownmiller, Susan 85

Bureaucratic military persons 39

Burghardt, Steve 133, 215

Burke, Kenneth 6, 219; dramatistic method of dialectical analysis 182

Buss, Allan R. 9, 69, 207, 212

C.I.O./Chrysler Corporation Labor negotiations, 1937 161-163, 193

Caldwell, Reverend 86

Capitalist system 74

Catherall, Donald R. 116, 214

Change-oriented groups 126

Character armor 75

Child abuse as cultural phenomenon 166

Child abuse, abused children 2-3, 8, 22, 46, 51, 54, 139, 145, 164, 167

Child abuse, sexual; molested children 9-10, 12, 14-16, 20, 25-27, 41, 46, 63, 139, 183

Child molesters 63

Child's environmental conditions 5

Chinese revolutionary movement 81, 84, 171

Chrysler, Walter 161

Cienfuegos, Ana Julia and Christina Monelli 104, 214

Civil rights movement 68, 70, 86-87, 99, 101, 156, 167-168; psychodynamic factors 168

Class struggle and what is possible 196

Clinch of oppression, the 190, 193, 196, 205

Cohen, Pennie 164, 217

Cohen, Sheldon 168, 217

Collective action 86, 88-89, 170, 188

Collective behavior 131

Colonizer and colonized 54

Committed passivity 71

Community caring 148

Community control 145

Community mental health movement 65

Compassion and love for one's tormentors 84

Compelled dependence 22

Concentration camps, campguards 9, 19, 22, 54

Confidence 5

Confluence 40-41, 45, 58, 79, 100-101, 106, 110-111, 113-115, 118, 120, 178

Confrontations 186

Confusing guilt and self-hatred phase 16, 18, 29, 31

Confusion 13

Conscience 128

Contact, differentiation and articulation as antidotes 118

Contemporary society 1

Control-dependence bonding 28

Conversion reactions 181

Cult of personality 73, 131
Cut-off 178

Deadness 45
Defense mechanisms 55
Defiance 13
Defusing 178
Delusion of fusion 22-23, 53, 58, 62, 70, 72-73, 79, 85, 87, 89, 100-101, 106, 109-110, 112, 114, 116-120, 156, 197
Delusional ideology 118
Delusions 181
Demanding other 38
DeMause, Lloyd 3, 207
Democratic and equalitarian social order 194
Democratic practices, democracy 1, 8, 114-115, 119, 126, 131-133
Dependence 5
Depression 4, 45, 105
Desires, insatiability of 63
Desperate insistence of the powerful 20
Dewey, John 6
Diagnostic assessments 192
Dialectic of union and diversity 115
Dialectical movement 52
Dichotomizing, see also Splitting 55-56
Diminished individuals 1
Disempowerment 27, 32, 37, 40-45, 51, 137
Disgust 125, 139, 142; as a natural barrier 80
Divorce proceedings 173
Domination 2-4, 8, 11, 17, 20, 31, 72, 82, 84, 88, 91, 93-95, 97, 100-101, 123, 145, 147, 160, 167, 179, 192-194
Drug-addicted mothers and their children 166
Drug-addicted, the 4, 167

Ego 17

Ego-ideal 15
Ehrenreich, Barbara 193, 220
Empathy 141, 159
Empowerment, self-empowerment 28, 32, 35-37, 40-41, 45, 137, 161, 170-171
Established habits 2
Ethical persons 129
Ethics, authoritarian 42
Ethnic group antagonism 90
Ethnocentrism 71, 86
Existential guilt 95
Existential therapy 89
Experience and expression of feelings avoided 196
Experienced anger phase 14, 18, 28-31
Exploitation: exploiters and exploited 4, 51, 70-71, 73, 89, 99, 101, 145, 147, 192-193, 196
Eye contact 154

False consciousness 191
Family and marital therapy 89
Fanon, Frantz 6, 9, 54, 70, 207, 211-212
Fear, fears 139, 149, 188
Feminist movement 68, 144, 167-169, 173, 175
Feminist perspective 175
Feminist therapy 154
Fenichel, Otto 6, 219
Ferenczi, Sandor 9, 11-16, 19-20, 25, 41, 46-47, 208
Figural social-emotional characteristic 34, 40
Forgiveness 120
Fraiberg, Selma 81, 142-143
Free association technique 187
Frenkel-Brunswik, Else 55, 210
Frequency of interruption 128
Freud, Sigmund 15, 73, 131, 208, 212, 215, 220; social theory 121; theory of jokes 190
From, Isadore 134
Fromm, Erich 42, 52, 210

Fused power-dependence relationship 45
Fused, reciprocal empowering-disempowering transactions 43
Fusion, see also Confluence 40-41, 45-48, 51-56, 62, 71, 77, 148, 150, 178, 185-186, 191-192, 194, 196, 202
Fusion of own and aggressor's desires phase 14, 16, 18, 30-31, 33
Fusion of part-persons 8

Gambits and counters 178
Garraty, John 70, 212
Gestalt therapy and theory 40, 134, 182-183, 186-187
Gestalts of health and neurosis 5
Goal-directedness 130
Gold Flower's story 81-84, 90
Goodman, Paul 6, 113, 157, 209, 213-214, 216
Gorbachev era in Soviet Union 193
Great Depression, the (1930s) 193
Greeks and Turks on Cyprus 48-49
Green party 72
Grier, William H. and Price M. Cobbs 54, 211
Group criticism 127
Group dynamics 130
Guided meditation 171
Guilt 15, 34, 40-45, 53, 58-59, 71, 79, 85, 88, 90-91, 93-95, 101-104, 109-112, 120, 143, 152, 157, 193, 201, 205
Guilt of the abused 20, 41, 43, 45

Hallie, Philip 99, 170, 214, 218
Harburg, E. Y. 131, 215
Health care activists 123
Hedging 177
Hefferline, Ralph F. 113, 157, 209, 213-214, 216
Helplessness 137, 193, 200
Here and now, the 2
Hierarchies authoritarian 44; military 39; power-oriented 49, 188

Hitler, Adolph 9, 90, 93
Holding environments 115-118, 122
Homosexuals 49
Hopefulness 204
Hoppe, Klaus D. 165, 217
Human service clinicians 203
Human species 3
Humanization/dehumanization 74, 92, 132
Humiliation 136
Humility 150
Hyde, Cheryl 116, 214
Hypercriticism 127
Hypertension as psychosomatic illness 168
Hypnosis and anxiety 182

I and it statements 151-152, 159, 177
Idealization 131-133, 192
Identification with the aggressor 8-11, 13-14, 16, 18-24, 26, 28, 32-33, 42-43, 48, 52-54, 57, 59, 63, 71-73, 79-81, 84, 90-94, 102, 110, 120, 122-126, 130, 134, 142, 144-45, 164
Identification with the projector 149
Identifications and identifiers 31, 33, 42, 52, 54, 58-59, 63, 72-74, 76, 80, 84, 91, 94, 96, 100, 121, 123-127, 129-131, 168, 173, 184
Incest disclosure 17
Incestuous seductions 10, 54
Independence 160
Individual life 1
Individual, the 6
Individuals as agents and agencies 34
Industrial organizational development consultants 117
Inferiority 200
Ingroups and outgroups 47-49, 56-57, 85, 101, 143
Institutional leaders 3
Internal danger situation 181
Internal regulating devices 29

International Society of Political Psychology 6
Introjecting, right now 134-135
Introjection 63, 72, 80, 91, 101, 106, 111, 114, 126-129, 134-140, 148, 157, 164, 173-174, 178, 184, 186, 190, 192, 195, 203; of guilt 13, 15, 41, 63; of the aggressor 10
Introjections, living now the influence of past 135
Irrational childhood conflict 204
Ishiyama, F. Ishu 183-184, 219
Isolation 5, 113, 150

Janeway, Elizabeth 47, 97, 168, 210, 213, 218
Jealousy of imagined sex lives 155
Joy 157, 179
Jung, C.G.; Jungians 21, 30, 209

Kaiser, Hellmuth 16, 22-23, 25, 31, 118-119, 208-209, 215
Keller, K.T. 161-162
Kelley, Nicholas 161, 163
Kinesthetic sense 154
King, Martin Luther, Jr. 156
Klaus, Marshall H., Treville Leger and Mary Anne Trause 213, 216
Kohut, Heinz 46, 210

Labor unionists, union organizing 66, 75-76, 99-101, 123, 135, 148, 169-170
Labor, organized; unions 162, 178-179
Lasswell, Harold 6, 9, 208
Laughter 190
Lazarsfeld 70
Leadership choices and styles 36, 39
Left-wing political groups 66, 73
Lerner, Harriet 40, 145, 175-176, 209, 216, 218
Levinson, Daniel J. 55, 210
Lewis, John L. 161-163, 193
Lichtenberg, G. C. 176, 218

Lichtenberg, Philip 210-211, 214, 219
Love 157-158, 166
Loyalty 164

Macmurray, John 6, 207
Macy, Joanna 170-171, 218
Makarenko, Anton 132-133, 215
Management, corporate 123-125, 135
Mao Zedong 73
Marcuse, Herbert 6
Marris, Peter 24, 209
Marx, Karl 191
Marxists and marxism 69-70
Maslow, Abraham 52, 176, 210, 218
Masochistic personality 43
McCarthy, Senator Joseph 90
Meditation and yoga 189
Memmi, Albert 9, 54, 208, 211
Memory 2
Middle-class people 152
Military system, military life and values 38, 67, 133
Miller, Alice 2, 5, 159-160, 207, 216
Modern world, the 2
Molested children 25, 27, 139
Morita therapy 183, 186
Mutual destruction process 157

Narcissistic personality-disordered individuals 46
Natural biological rhythms 57
Natural spontaneity 12-13, 18, 27, 31, 57-58, 111, 197
Nazi persecution, survivors of 165, 167
Nazis and Nazism 9, 39
Near, Holly and Ronnie Gilbert 68, 212
Negative phenomena 153
Negativism 127
Negotiation process 122, 127, 133
Neurosis 181

Neurosis, vicious circle foundation of 119
Nixon, President Richard 29
Nonjudgmental atmosphere 187
Nonviolent resistance 174
Norms, adherence to 44
Norms, bureaucratic 86
Norms, group, social norms 130, 132, 187

Obedience 3, 38, 43
Obsession 181
Occupational safety 123
Open negative valuation 152-153
Opening pathways through movement 171
Oppressed ethnic and racial minorities 71, 195-196
Oppressed, wisdom of the 147
Oppression 2-3, 5-6, 8, 31, 142, 145; sexual component 3
Oppressor/oppressed relation 8, 20, 43, 45-46, 51, 53, 55, 73, 75-76, 79, 81, 88-91, 93-101, 103-105, 111-114, 117, 129, 146-147, 156, 157, 168, 173, 190-195, 201-202

Pain 3, 182
Panic disorder 181
Paranoia 45, 53
Parental teaching 1
Parents abusive 81, 143; overprotective 45
Peer groups 99-102, 104, 117; character structure of members 100
Perls, Frederick, et al. 17, 79-80, 113, 150-151, 157-158, 183-185, 209, 213-214, 216, 219
Permission-giving probes 164
Personality 4
Personality development 52
Personas 4
Phobia treatment 186
Physicians 44
Pierce, Chester M. and Louis Jolyon West 168, 217

Political demobilization 67
Political organizing, see also Social activists 67-69, 71, 73
Political prisoners 105
Political prisoners, tortured 66
Politicians 1
Pollock, Jeanne C. 214
Polster, Erving and Miriam 40, 118, 142, 210, 215
Post-traumatic stress disorders 116
Power elite 191
Power relationships 141, 148
Power-dependence relationships 40
Powerfulness 34
Powerlessness 24, 34
Powers of the weak 168
Prejudiced behaviors 143-144, 149, 155, 193
Pressman, Lee 162
Prestige 21
Priests 44
Prioritizing grievances 174
Process and process focus 117, 137, 177
Profound, experienced anxiety phase 12, 18, 27, 31
Progressive education movement 65, 68
Projected guilt 30
Projected self-hatred 30
Projection and projectors 31, 33, 42, 52, 54, 58-59, 72-74, 76, 84-85, 91-92, 94-96, 100-101, 106, 111-112, 114, 124-125, 141-157, 159, 170-174, 178, 192-196, 202-203; as signal of family cohesion 143; reowning of a projection 185-186
Projection upon a primed vulnerable other 26, 28-34, 37-39, 42, 45, 51-54, 57, 59, 63, 71-73, 79, 90, 95, 97, 102, 110, 120, 125, 141-144, 152, 188
Proletariat, working class 69
Psyches 4, 6, 120, 127
Psychic economies 195

Psychic resolution 76
Psychoanalysis 19, 89, 181, 186-187; analyst and analysand 46; countertransference 203-205; transference 89, 203
Psychoanalytic concepts 9, 89
Psychoanalytic treatment of war 204
Psychological functioning 124, 130
Psychological insights 148-149, 199, 201-202
Psychological issues in social action 125
Psychological re: social/political activity, the 7
Psychology of experience 199
Psychotherapeutic instruments 105
Psychotherapeutic lexicon 9
Psychotherapy, general principle of 125
Psychotherapy, psychotherapists 1, 5, 7, 44-45, 66, 79, 81, 96, 105, 118-119, 134, 143, 146-147, 154, 163-165, 167, 180, 186-187, 190; holistically-oriented 5, 7
Public health movement 65

Quaker-style individual participation 131
Quick-circuiting 51, 58-59, 102, 110-111

Racists, racism 53, 57, 70-72, 86, 97, 143, 149, 154-156
Rage 38-39, 41-42, 51, 53, 56, 70, 72, 76-77, 79, 84-85, 88, 92, 96, 110, 120, 122, 138, 141, 144-45, 157, 167-170, 174, 193; productive uses 77
Rage, helpless 97-98, 103, 148, 156
Rage, repressed 56
Rage, retroflexed 168
Rape, rapists 10, 19, 23, 44, 54
Raw force 55
Reagan, President Ronald 90, 93
Reason, rationality 4-5
Reich, Wilhelm 6, 66, 74, 211, 212

Relationships of unequal power 3
Relaxation procedures 186
Relaxation response 189
Religion, fundamentalist, punitive 86
Rendering the other's rage helpless 29
Repression 160, 187
Repression and exploitation, overt 69
Repression, political 104
Resignation 137
Resistance 203, 205
Resolution of social issues 204
Responsibility 193, 195
Retroflection 106, 109, 143
Reynolds, Bertha Capen 66, 211
Rieker, Patricia Perri and Elaine Carmen 14, 208
Right-wing politics, forces of reaction 69, 75, 169
Risk-taking aptitude 45
Roman, Carol 167, 217
Russian October Revolution 132
Ryan, William 152, 216

Safe emergency technique 187
Sanford, R. Nevitt 55, 210
Schizophrenic patients 163-164
Schlozman, Kay Lehman and Sidney Verba 70, 212
Schools 1
Self as agent/self as agency 59, 62-63, 73-74, 77, 90, 95, 175-176, 179, 193, 195-196, 204
Self, the 17
Self, the incomplete 5
Self-abasement, self-degradation 44
Self-actualization 49, 122
Self-actualizing 16
Self-affirmation 147-148, 176
Self-assertion 61
Self-censorship 46
Self-control 29, 38, 40, 42, 47, 54, 95, 150
Self-criticism 153

Self-definition 179
Self-domination, self-conquest 47, 122, 138, 150, 184, 195
Self-esteem 99
Self-evaluative standards 21
Self-examination and grieving process 116
Self-expression, individual 131
Self-forgiveness 109
Self-hatred 42-45, 53, 58-59, 79, 85, 90-91, 93, 96, 100-103, 109-112, 120, 142, 157, 193
Self-help groups 7
Self-regulating activities 61, 92, 122, 182
Self-righteousness 152
Self-subordination 13
Self-support 188-189
Self-victimization 96
Sexism 57, 71, 86, 144, 155, 193, 195
Sexual activity 11
Sexual aggressiveness 186
Sexual arousal 166
Sexual curiosity 129
Sexual desires and social relationships coordinated 57
Sexual fantasies of children 10
Sexual play of children 26
Sexual pleasure 63
Sexual relations 44
Sexual trauma 9
Sexuality 53
Signal function 182
Significant others 73
SNCC 72
Social accommodation 61-62
Social action and struggle 7, 65, 72, 86, 92, 103, 106, 171, 178, 202-205
Social controls 49, 55
Social conventions and the powerful 49
Social emotions management 90
Social emotions, Social-emotional phases 110-11, 120, 142, 156

Social legislation 193
Social life 1
Social movements and change 4, 55, 67, 85, 87, 140, 178-179, 187, 190, 193-195
Social reformers and revolutionaries 6, 54, 191
Social relations, relationships 23, 67, 77, 102, 113-114, 122, 130, 150, 156, 158, 169, 199
Social relationships, distorted, confluent 62, 110
Social relationships healthy 61-62
Social service agencies 1, 133
Social structures, existing 55
Social system, the 1, 55, 76-77, 161, 169
Social vs. individual welfare 205
Social workers 166
Social-emotional complex 34, 37, 75, 120, 141
Social-emotional executive powers 36
Social/political activists 9, 72-73, 184
Socially committed mental health activists 65
Society for the Psychological Study of Social Issues 6
Solidarity 103-104, 148, 178
Solin, Cynthia 17, 208
Southern blacks and violent intraracial aggression 168
Speak bitterness sessions 81, 171
Splitting 55
Spontaneity of behavior 6, 179, 190, 196
Spontaneous excitement 185
Spotnitz, Hyman 163-164, 217
Spouse abuse, see also Wife Batterers 54
Stalin, Josef 73, 90
Status quo, the 40, 55, 72, 110, 126, 194
Stereotyping 154
Striving actions 163

Strong and the weak, the 142, 145-148, 153, 159, 168-169, 188, 191-196
Structural social change 65
Subjects of the realm 1, 4, 6
Submission 2, 39, 63, 72, 88, 97, 101, 113
Submissive mode 16, 22
Subordinate 39-40, 44, 52, 63
Suicide 53, 133
Super-ego 15-17, 42
Superior 52, 63, 72
Suppression of dissent and resistance 75
Symbols of support 188
Symptoms, hysterical 181
Symptoms, psychosomatic 181

Tasks of ordinary life 4
Tavris, Carol 176, 218
Temper tantrums 40
Terror 143
Therapeutic alliance 187
Therapeutic change 89
Therapeutic communities 65
Toilet training 2
Transformation of individuals and society 4
Transformative encounters 98, 147, 156
Transformative relationships 94, 98-99, 103
Trauma management 107, 116
Tyranny, tyrants 2, 22-23, 31, 38, 50, 52, 72, 74-76, 88, 95, 113, 147-148

U.A.W. 161-163
U.S.A. 48
Unconscious, the 53
Underclasses, the 98

Unemployed workers 70-71
Unfinished business 187
Unorganized workers, exploited 162

Verblen, Thorstein 6, 77, 121, 212, 215
Victims and victimizing relationships 2-4, 17, 51, 53, 71, 93, 97, 154-155, 201
Vietnam War, Vietnam vets 40, 116
Violence, violent force 10, 75, 191
Volkan, Vamik 48, 210
Vulnerability 25, 39, 44, 47, 93, 95, 103, 190, 194

Walsh, J. Raymond 163, 217
War neuroses 67, 106
Warnock, Donna 116, 214
Watergate 29
Weisinger, Hendrie 177, 218
Welfare system 75
Westmoreland, General William 40
Wife batterers, battered wives 19, 22, 45
Winnicott, D.W. 115, 214
Woman activists 116
Women's consciousness-raising groups 86, 173
Womens Pentagon Action 116
Wood, Ellen M. 73, 212
World War II 39

Yalom, Irving D. 117, 214
Yates, Gayle Graham 85, 168, 213, 218

Zetzel, Elizabeth 181-182, 219

Errata from the First Edition

p. 6, line 5: for "purists. While" read "purists, while"

p. 34, line 7 from bottom: for "entirety" read "entirely"

p. 41, line 3: for "tn" read "to"

p. 49, line 4: for "to" read "too"

p. 55, line 5: for "hope," read "hope."

p. 72, line 10: for "use, I believe" read "use. I believe"

p. 86, line 6: for "inward" read "toward"

p. 87, line 2 from bottom: for "acceptance," read "acceptance"

p. 129, line 8 from bottom: for "inner-desires' " read "inner-desires"

p. 139, line 5 from bottom: for "a" read "at"

p. 163, line 6 from bottom: for "new" read "now"

p. 183, line 19: for "in" read "an"

p. 193, line 14 from bottom: for "a historic" read "an historic"

p. 221, line 5 from bottom: for "automation" read "automaton"

p. 229: for "Verblen" read "Veblen"
   for "Womens" read "Women's"

Donald W. Hudson Jr.

ASSERTI-CARE
ASSERTION TRAINING FOR THE ELDERLY
CLIENT

American University Studies: Series VIII (Psychology). Vol. 1
ISBN 0-8204-0039-4   169 pages   paperback US $ 17.35*

*Recommended price - alterations reserved

Reports of successful treatment, utilizing assertiveness training, have been established mainly through research efforts coordinated with youthful populations. Lengthy literature reviews reveal only five attempts with the elderly population; only three interventions were empirically based and results have been inconclusive. This book discusses negative stereotypes of the aged and prevailing attitudes found within our profession which influence the psychological diagnosis and treatment of the elderly (i.e. «Why bother with them when there's no need to effect a change so late in life?»). The author reports a study which examines the effect of an assertiveness training program on assertion, self-esteem, locus of control, and health for an elderly population.

Contents: Assertion training provides a re-vitalization process. The elderly can acquire social skills enabling to defend their dignity.

GESTALT INSTITUTE
OF CLEVELAND

Gestalt Institute of Cleveland Press
1588 Hazel Drive   Cleveland OH 44106